Founders,
Classics,
Canons

Founders, Classics, Canons

Modern Disputes over the Origins and Appraisal of Sociology's Heritage

Peter Baehr

Transaction Publishers

New Brunswick (U.S.A.) and London (U.K.)

Learning Resources
Centre

12425850

Library of Congress Catalog Number: 2002072141
ISBN: 0-7658-0129-9
Printed in Canada

Library of Congress Cataloging-in-Publication Data

Baehr, P. (Peter)
    Founders, classics, canons : modern disputes over the origins and the appraisal of sociology's heritage / Peter Baehr.
        p. cm.
    Includes bibliographical references (p.) and index.
    ISBN 0-7658-0129-9 (alk. paper)
        1. Sociology—History. 2. Sociology—Philosophy—History. I. Title.

HM445 .B33 2002
301' .09—dc21   2002072141

Hedda

Contents

Acknowledgements

This book is a corrected, updated, and expanded version of a text that first appeared under the auspices of the International Sociological Association (ISA) journal *Current Sociology* 42:1, Spring 1994, entitled "Founders, Classics and the Concept of a Canon." I am very grateful to the ISA for enabling its republication, and to Irving Louis Horowitz for inviting me to submit it in elaborated form as a book. A version of the appendix appeared in *History and Theory* 40 (May 2001), pp. 153-169 (copyright 2001 Wesleyan University). Part of chapter 3 draws on work previously published in the *Canadian Journal of Sociology Online* (May 1999). The material appears with the kind permission of the journals' editors and publishers.

My partner in the original *Current Sociology* endeavor was Mike O'Brien, then a graduate student in history, who worked as my research associate for a semester under the auspices of a grant provided by the Memorial University of Newfoundland. Busy with other initiatives, he decided not to participate in the revised edition. Mike O'Brien's important contribution is warmly acknowledged, though he obviously cannot be held responsible for many subsequent additions, deletions, or revisions I alone have made to the text.

Current Sociology was until a few years ago a journal devoted exclusively to Trend Reports aiming, as the ISA blurb put it, "to review new developments, to discuss controversies, and to provide extensive bibliographies." I have retained this format in the revised version believing that a change in style would trigger an entirely different project. At the same time, the synoptic emphasis is framed by a particular argument, or, rather, set of related arguments, about the sociological tradition.

Over the years that I have been thinking about classical sociology, I have benefited greatly from the friendship, guidance, and intellectual engagement of Judith Adler, Volker Meja, and Stuart Pierson.

In addition, Terrell Carver, Anne Furlong, David Gallop, Daniel Gordon, Robert Alun Jones, David Kettler, Neil McLaughlin, Stein Haugom Olsen, and John Seery were kind enough to read parts of the manuscript. I benefited greatly from their observations, as I did from the rigor and attentiveness of Transaction's Senior Editor, Larry Mintz.

Hong Kong,
February 6th, 2002

1

Introduction

This book is a work of synthesis and argument. It arranges and critically evaluates a series of debates about the origins, meaning and value of the sociological tradition. Unlike many other studies of classical sociology devoted to the ideas of, say, Marx, Durkheim, and Weber, the present enquiry contains very little exegesis. Its concern is not to rehearse what "the classics" said, but to delineate what classics *are*: how they are best comprehended and how they gained their textual prominence. Nor does this book purport to offer a history of sociology. Instead, it is an investigation into some of the organizing and authoritative categories through which sociology's history continues to be understood. Two categories—founders and classics—have been particularly important in helping to frame sociology's precarious identity. They have recently been joined by a third: "canon." Today this identity is being challenged as never before. Within the academy, a number of positions—feminist, postmodernist, post-structuralist, post-colonial—converge in questioning the status of "the tradition." These currents in turn partly reflect wider social questioning about the meaning and uses of knowledge in technologically advanced societies.

The key aim of this study is to review and assess a considerable body of literature that deals with the interpretation and reception of sociology's "classic" texts. The concept of classics is a complex one, but essentially it draws our attention to a scale of judgment according to which a particular work is deemed to be especially worthy. A classic, in other words, belongs to a pantheon of texts by virtue of its peculiar eminence and exemplary character. But what is the nature of this eminence? Chapters 4 and 5 examine various responses to this question, notably those that focus on the functions classics perform for the scholarly community that employs them;

the rhetorical or suasive force classics are said to possess; the conflicting or complementary ways in which they are best to be understood by modern interpreters; and the processes of reception through which they have been elevated to their current standing. Although these chapters are largely documentary in tone, they also suggest why attempts to establish abstract criteria of classicality are likely to fail. More positively, chapter 5 provides an analytical framework by means of which, I contend, classic formation is usefully charted.

The concept of classic is often equated with two other notions: founders and canon. The former has a well-established pedigree within the discipline, while widespread usage of the latter in sociology is much more recent. Chapters 2 and 3—on Founders—and 6—on Canons—present arguments against the use of these notions in interpreting, defending and attacking sociology's great texts and authors. Those chapters show why, in logical and historical terms, discourses and traditions cannot actually be founded, and why the term founder has limited explanatory value. Equally, they demonstrate that the analogy between a theological canon and sociological classic texts, though seductive, will not bear close scrutiny. Even so, the job of the sociologist is not exhausted, indeed is it only just beginning, with the demonstration that some idea is erroneous or problematic. Far more interesting to discern is why people subscribe to it. "Founders" is part of sociology's collective memory (to use Maurice Halbwachs's felicitous term), a tenacious simplification of complex events and processes that reduces the real history of sociology to a basic archetype. The sources of this archetype, I conjecture, derive from myth, religion[1] (or at least theology) and notions of paternity all of which have migrated to the sociological domain. Canon, a concept with theological overtones, is also problematic. Part of a broader struggle for control of the academic curricula, it has become embroiled in a polemic from which there is little hope of rescuing it. My opposition to these concepts (founders, canons) is certainly not an objection to myth or to religion or even to collective memory per se. It is an objection to arguments that mistake the metaphorical for the literal, and that caricature an ambiguous and complex sociological legacy.

How then are we to understand "classic" texts in sociology or, indeed, classics more generally? There is no simple answer. Bernard Knox (1993: 21) remarks that the "primacy of the Greeks" in Western literature "is neither an accident nor the result of a decision imposed by higher authority; it is simply a reflection of the intrinsic worth of the material, its sheer originality and brilliance." Harold Bloom (1994: 3), thinking paradigmatically of Shakespeare, contends that the principal quality of a great work of literature is "a mode of originality that either cannot be assimilated, or that so assimilates us that we cease to see it as strange." These sentiments, which some might be tempted to echo when defending the classics of sociology, are admirable in their forthrightness. They are also, of course, highly question-begging, even for those of us who are in sympathy with them. While an aesthetic defence of the classics of literature is possible, even plausible, aesthetic profundity of itself is no guarantee of a text's ascent to classical stature. The text must not only be great but be recognized as such and that is a culturally mediated process. To survive, to be transmitted, it must secure agents of enthusiasm whose success is, like everything human, contingent not guaranteed.

The great works of Marx, Weber, Durkheim, and Simmel, among others, also have a powerful aesthetic quality and pathos. They, too, have, in their manner, assimilated and shaped us. Though each of these authors claimed, with justice, to address particular social, political, and economic constellations, many of their ideas speak to the very nature of being human and of living in the modern world. But will their works survive for the same time, and in the same ways, that the works of Shakespeare, Milton, and Hobbes have endured in literature and political theory? The sociological classics are just too recent for us to be confident of their longevity.[2] Perhaps they will survive, vouchsafing a protean ability to make sense of radically different social conditions (for the society of subsequent centuries is unlikely to bear many characteristics of its nineteenth- and twentieth-century predecessors).[3] Still, because appeals to "originality" and "intrinsic worth" can all too easily become circular and will, in any case, convince no one who is temperamentally hostile to them, I avoid such claims in this book. Instead, I argue that the achievements of the classical tradition are best appreciated through comprehending the arduous road that any text must travel to become, and remain, classic; and through a related understanding of the contribution that classics make to the conversation about the nature of human knowledge and existence.

A classical legacy can both be a source of inspiration for an epoch or a crushing and stagnating burden on it (Collins 1992: 75-77).

It can both exclude potentially valuable ideas and prove capable of embracing them. It can both be a source of mindless regurgitation and of bracing intellectual challenge. Anyone who reads this study will quickly discern how much value its author accords sociology's classical legacy and the liberal university tradition that nourishes it. It is my expectation nonetheless that, in the spirit of a report and an argument, rather than a polemic, those who disagree will find here ample material with which to do so.

Notes

1.   The relationship between myth (in the anthropological sense) and religion is not a matter I pursue here. Both encompass frameworks dealing with the most important questions of Being: of our origins, nature, and redemptive possibilities. As such, the secularist who identifies religion with myth can still accept the moral seriousness of both. The religious believer, committed to the reality of God, will go still further, convinced that while one can subscribe to a myth, one cannot worship it and that the secularist's

> Blind unbelief is sure to err,
>   And scan his work in vain;
> God is his own interpreter,
>   And he will make it plain

(William Cowper [1731-1800], *Light Shining out of Darkness*).

2.   An International Sociological Association opinion survey, conducted in 1997, asked ISA members to rank five twentieth century books that had been most influential to them as sociologists. With a response rate of 16 percent (455 out of 2,785 members replied), the top ten books of the century were Max Weber, *Economy and Society* (20.9 percent); C. Wright Mills, *The Sociological Imagination* (13.0 percent); Robert K. Merton, *Social Theory and Social Structure* (11.4 percent); Max Weber, *The Protestant Ethic and the Spirit of Capitalism* (10.3 percent); Peter Berger amd Thomas Luckmann, *The Social Construction of Reality* (9.9 percent); Pierre Bourdieu, *Distinction: A Social Critique of Judgment and Taste* (9.5 percent); Norbert Elias, *The Civilizing Process: Power and Civility* (6.6 percent); Jürgen Habermas, *The Theory of Communicative Action* (6.4 percent); Talcott Parsons, *The Structure of Social Action* (6.2 percent); and Erving Goffman, *The Presentation of Self in Everyday Life* (5.5 percent).
      "Which five books do you believe constitute the sociological classics?" may well have produced a different ranking since, as I will argue later, one can accord a book classic standing but not find it personally persuasive or important for one's own work. Still, it is interesting that not one of the texts of Marx, Durkheim, and Simmel appears in the ISA's top ten.

3.   To be sure, a classic's survival in sociology depends not only on its being pertinent to changed conditions, but also on its being read, especially by competent readers (i.e., those who can understand and apply its concepts, and who are motivated to understand and apply them). One can readily imagine a situation where the former condition holds, but where the latter does not because of the atrophy of the sociological tradition.

2

Founders of Discourse

Introduction

Few terms are more commonplace in descriptions of sociology's past than those of "founders" or "founding fathers." That sociology has founders is a disciplinary platitude, evidence of a metaphor that has died "off into literalness," and become one of those "skeletons which remain after the capacity to arouse the senses...has been rubbed off by familiarity and long usage" (Rorty 1989:16, 152). Yet that description is only partly accurate: the "founder" idea is also the source of various bones of contention. What, then, makes a person a "founder," and in what, more generally, might the "act" of founding be said to consist?

In this chapter and the next, I probe some of the key assumptions behind the notions of founders and founding as they have come to be employed in sociological literature, current and otherwise. The main purpose of the present chapter is to examine critically two major attempts—those of Michel Foucault and Sheldon Wolin—to identify the formative "moments" during which, supposedly, discourses and disciplinary traditions are established. The next chapter, in contrast, deals with the question of institutional innovation. The distinction between the founding of discourses, and the founding of institutions will, in these truncated remarks, appear rather obscure. So let me now offer some conceptual discriminations that will both clarify these comments and also make intelligible the narrative organization of this chapter and the one that follows it.

Founders: Discursive and Institutional, Deliberative and Appropriated

Though the terms "founder" and "founding fathers" circulate as common currency in sociological discussion, a survey of actual usage reveals that not one but four rather different ideas are being canvassed under these labels. The first is of a Founder with a magisterial capital F. Founders in this sense include the so-called Founding Fathers of sociology—minimally, the trinity of Marx (1818-1883), Durkheim (1858-1917), and Max Weber (1864-1920), but also often including Comte (1798-1857), Simmel (1858-1918), and Pareto (1848-1923) among others. These Founders are primarily invoked as heroes of a discipline that would be unrecognizable without their presence. Their iconic status is based, ostensibly, on a twofold contribution. First and foremost, they are believed to be responsible for founding a specific *discourse*, that is, a stock of presuppositional ideas formative of one of sociology's traditions (e.g., Comte and positivist sociology; Weber and interpretive sociology). Second, these figures provide important symbolic markers for sociology by conferring on it a lineage and by circumscribing its professional domain in relation to other disciplines; in short, Founders (I shall henceforth drop the upper case) are an aspect of sociology's professional legitimation. It was this second feature of founders that prompted Alvin Gouldner (1959: ix) to write that

> A "founding father" is a professional symbol which can be treated as a trivial detail by no one who wishes to understand the profession as a social organization. Where there are conflicts, by later generations, concerning who their "founding father" was, we suspect that this may be a serious question essentially reflecting a dispute over the character of the profession.

"Discursive" founders, it transpires, are often imagined to lay the "tracks" of traditions. Their importance is held to derive more from the stock of ideas they have provided for sociology than from any organizational contribution to it they have made. This distinguishes them from "institutional" founders—our second category—which refers to people whose significance lies in the fact that they established some artefact or institution demonstrably related to the sociological enterprise: for instance, a sociology journal, an academic society or association, a university department. In this sense it comes naturally for us to talk of, for instance, Albion Small (1854-1926) as the founder of the first Department of Sociology in the U.S.A. at the University of Chicago in 1892, and of the *American Journal of Sociology* in 1895 (Maus, 1962 [1956]: 97);[1] or of René Worms (1867-1926) as the founder in 1893 of the Institut International de Sociologie and (in the same year) the *Revue internationale de sociologie*; or of Durkheim as the founder of the *Année sociologique* in 1896—though in all these cases, the actual "founding" presupposed a number of conducive social conditions, and was the product of a collaborative endeavor. Contrasted especially to Small and Durkheim,

> Max Weber's activity as a sociologist was much less institutionalized. He was not a professor of the subject; he supervised for a limited period several research projects for the *Verein für Sozialpolitik* [Association for Social Policy]; he tried—and failed—to institutionalize two research projects on the press and on voluntary associations through the *Deutsche Gesellschaft für Soziologie* [German Sociological Society]; he wrote *Wirtschaft und Gesellschaft* [Economy and Society] as one section of a comprehensive series of handbooks on economics, organized by the publisher Siebeck; he edited a great journal of social science and social policy, very little of which was devoted to sociology. The connections of his sociological activities with institutions were peripheral, fragmentary, and transient (Shils 1982 [1970]: 309).

Table 2.1
Founders

	Discursive	Institutional
Worms	-	+
Small	-/+	+
Durkheim	+	+
Weber	+	-/+
Marx	+	-

The above analysis yields at least the possibilities laid out in table 2.1. Two features of it call for immediate comment. To begin with, the relationship between the discursive and the institutional domains is, in reality, immensely porous. Small was not only instrumental in setting up the Department of Sociology at Chicago. He was by virtue of that position a constitutive member of that ethnographic, politically liberal, and socially reformist tradition known as the Chicago School. Furthermore, to the degree that the work of so-called discursive founders is taken up by academics as material for research programs, in curricula, etc., it becomes institutionalized. With these provisos, the division between discursive and institutional is still a useful one. For one thing, it highlights different *sources* of influence on sociology; for another, it points to the *relative autonomy* of discourse and of academic institutions. This enables us, in turn, to recognize that in sociology it is discourse, general theory, above all, which appears to make a founder iconic. Albion Small was a founder of a university department, a journal, and a school—but few would accord him the founding stature of Marx and Weber, even though the direct institutional contribution of Marx to sociology was zero, and, as we have already noted, of Weber was minimal. And while Durkheim is the exemplar of both institutional and discursive founding, it is not the former that sociologists usually recall when they describe him as a founding father. Georges Davy, one of Durkheim's collaborators on the *Année sociologique*, anticipated that judgment (and simultaneously helped to promote it) when he observed, in 1919, that "if Durkheim was...the chief of a school, it is because he instituted a new doctrine. It is he, in point of fact, who was, despite illustrious predecessors such as Montesquieu and Auguste Comte, the veritable founder of French sociology" (quoted in Clark 1968b: 88, n. 36). Small (and Park, Thomas et al.) may be considered as founders of one of sociology's many branches; Marx, Durkheim, and Weber are considered as founders of the enduring traditions and conceptual apparatus, in short, the theoretical continent, that constitute the discipline of sociology itself.[2]

We should also note, second, that discursive and institutional founding raise very different problems of validation. In the case of institutional founding, the criteria of validation are *empirical* and, in principle, straightforward. The achievement of the founder in question appears to be a palpable fact that can be readily checked and verified using a variety of conventional, commonly accepted indices: for instance, in the case of the founding of a journal, one can establish the date marking its legal registration, or identify the members who formed its original committee, drafted its editorial position ("line"), put up the original finance, etc. Moreover, while the success or failure of such artefacts and institutions will normally depend on whether they can garner a readership or attract a constituency of some kind, their treatment by posterity cannot alter the reality of the founding act; it can only vindicate it or make it redundant.

On the other hand, the origins, coordinates and authority of a discourse are a matter of insoluble controversy; there are no accepted criteria of validation that can definitively settle the issues they raise. Or to put it in more technical terms, the criteria of validation for discourse are aporitic,[3] which is to say, intrinsically open-ended, endlessly hypothetical and contestable (cf. Gallie1955-6). As I will show, this inherently equivocal and uncertain property of discourse reveals itself in at least four sociological or sociologically relevant debates. These concern the dissensus that surrounds: which concept or theme in the founder's discourse is the central one; which intellectual tradition the founder's work is closest to; who the first "real" sociologist was; and what kind of break with the past founding entails. It is important to stress that the aporitic quality of discourse is not supposed to reflect an ontological difference between discourses and institutions such that the former are deemed to be less real, material, substantial than the latter. Rather, the aporia of discourse rests on the fact that discourse can only be known through, and has no animation without, the categories and interests of interpretive communities: and these are constantly in flux.

Cutting across the distinction between discursive founders and institutional founders is another contrast, implicit in the literature but which will bear explicit clarification: whether the figures who concern us actually did, or did not, consider sociology to be their *métier*—their prime intellectual vocation, their "master status." This second contrast, hinging as it does on a motivational criterion, also suggests the distinction between those individuals ("deliberative" founders let us call them) who intentionally and strategically sought to build, and were in some part successful in building, the institutional matrices of sociology—for instance, establishing a sociology curriculum, journal, or department—and those people for whom sociology was not part of their own identifying self-concept but who have been adopted retrospectively by sociology as founders nonetheless. Marx is a clear example of the latter; Durkheim "whose paramount mission in life was to make the academic community heed this new discipline as a rigorous scientific" subject, of the former (Tiryakian 1981: 115). Edward Tiryakian (1988: 373) adds that "Unlike Marx and Weber who have over the years *become* sociologists,...Durkheim from the very beginning of his academic career to this day has always been thought of as a primary figure of the discipline" (emphasis in the original). This suggests yet another distinction: between those who have consistently—that is, at least from their deaths onwards—been considered as fundamental to "the discipline," and those whose reputation as exemplary sociologists has been much more episodic and discontinuous: as is the case with Simmel who when Donald Levine began his researches on him in the mid-1950s "was widely regarded as an archaic amateur" (Levine: 1981: 61). Still, one must be cautious here. Sociology consists of many national traditions that have never been synchronized, and we cannot assume that an exemplary figure in one country, at one time, can be generalized to other countries and other periods.

Figure 2.1

FOUNDERS	DISCURSIVE (criteria of validation: aporitic)	INSTITUTIONAL (criteria of validation: empirical)
Appropriated	**A.** Marx (Weber)	**B.** ——
Deliberative	**C.** Durkheim (Weber)	**D.** Durkheim Small, Worms, etc. (Weber)

We can now employ the grid of figure 2.1 to bring together, and illustrate, the two major sets of distinctions employed thus far. Of course, like all models, this grid is simplistic; its utility lies in being able to identify clear cases and distinctions manifest or latent in the literature on founders, but, just as important, in locating cases that do not fit comfortably in any of the cells. Consider, for instance, cells A, C, and D where Weber has been put into parentheses. I have done this to signal, first, that there are degrees of appropriation (Weber, unlike Marx, did write specifically on sociology, even if sociology was not his master status) and degrees of deliberation. Hence, Weber, like Durkheim, was involved in the construction of recognizably sociological institutions—for instance, and as he himself put it, "his active part in the founding" of the German Sociological Society in January 1909.[4] Unlike Durkheim, however, Weber's intervention in institutional sociology was episodic, and largely unsuccessful. As early as January 1911 he resigned from the executive of the Society, and thereafter lost interest in it to the degree it strayed from doctrinal positions compatible with his own. Much the same situation applies to Weber's friend, Georg Simmel. Here again we have someone who is often considered a founder but whose commitment to sociology was, certainly when contrasted with Durkheim, as equivocal as it was erratic. On the one hand, Simmel made an early contribution to sociological discussion and institutions. He delivered his first lecture programme specifically on the subject in 1894; published a programmatic statement on "The problem of sociology" in the same year (it became the first chapter of his *Soziologie* [1908]); while in the mid-1890s Simmel was also seeking to advance sociology's cause with the Prussian minister of education, Althoff—all of this some years before Max Weber's own sociological interventions began (Frisby 1981: 33-34; 55). On the other hand, Simmel's enthusiasm for sociology, in contrast to Durkheim's, was very ambivalent. By 1899, in what has become a notorious statement in the Simmel literature, he was informing Célestin Bouglé:

> You should not forget that the *sciences sociales* are not my subject. My sociology is a wholly specialized subject of which I am the sole practitioner in Germany....In general it somewhat saddens me that abroad I count only as a sociologist—whereas I am a philosopher, see in philosophy my life's task and practice sociology really only as a sideline. Once I have done my duty by it by publishing a comprehensive sociology...I shall never probably return to it. (Quoted in Lepenies 1988 [1985]: 243)

With that attitude, it is not surprising that he refused the offer in 1910 to become the first president of the German Sociological Society. To be sure, Simmel taught sociology in some form every year between1900-1909, and thereafter taught a course in sociology in 1909-10, 1911-12, 1914-15, and 1917-18. However, after 1908 he became ever more engrossed in aesthetics and philosophy, and where he "did continue to write upon sociological themes, he did so increasingly within the context of a philosophy of culture."[5] It is this intellectual profile, together with the anti-Semitism that shadowed and disabled his career, that lends credence to Käsler's (1988 [1979]: 209) portrayal of Simmel as a sociological "outsider." Even so, while

Simmel himself wanted to be remembered above all as a philosopher, it is as a sociological founder, ironically, rather than as a great
philosopher, that he is today most often celebrated.

With this definitional task now completed, let us move to a critical
discussion of the literature on founding.

Foucault's Founders

Of all the attempts to make the idea of discursive founding plausible, none are more systematic than those of Michel Foucault and
Sheldon S. Wolin. It is true that neither author can be considered a
sociologist. Foucault's hybrid writings defy disciplinary classification,
but are closest to the interface of philosophy and history. Wolin's texts
fall squarely into the field of political theory. Yet their work has a
special pertinence to our subject. To begin with, both authors explicitly raise an issue—the nature of founding—that sociologists have for
the most part treated only casually and ritualistically. While references
to founders and founding pervade sociological discussion, surprisingly little attempt has been made by sociologists themselves to scrutinize these concepts directly or in any detail—even where, as in the
essays collected in Timothy Raison's *The Founding Fathers of Social
Science* (1979 [1969]), or in Philippe Besnard's *The Sociological
Domain: The Durkheimians and the Founding of French Sociology*
(Besnard 1983a), the term would appear to cry out for explicit analysis. The virtue of Foucault's and Wolin's work, in contrast, is the rigor
with which they enable sociologists to think through the founding
project. Furthermore, both writers examine figures—notably Marx and
Weber—who have been embraced by sociology as "founding fathers."

Common to Foucault and Wolin is a concern to identify and tackle
the same basic problem: the relationship among authors, texts, and
the discursive consequences that flow from authorial-textual achievement. More specifically, they are interested in a particular kind of
authorial-textual achievement: one considered seminal for, and formative of, a discourse (Foucault) or/and of a social science (Wolin).
In "What is an author?" Foucault (1984a [1969]), notes that modern
Western culture equates authorship with distinctive kinds of writing.
The private letter, a deed of contract, wall-graffiti, a shopping-list,
for instance, may all bear the traces or signatures of particular agents,
yet they are not normally thought of as acts of an "author." Evidently, then, authorship is not simply an attribute of an agent who

writes; rather, it is in virtue of specific discursive structures (conventions, idioms) and organizational arrangements (legal, economic) that authorship as such is constituted, and becomes recognizable as a determinate kind of activity. Hence in modern times the author's status is inseparable from property relations determining who owns the text (consider copyright laws). In addition, the author is expected to be a person with a name, (anonymity seems incongruous to us), and to occupy a position in a classification of writing genres (an author composes as a novelist, a philosopher, etc.). None of this means, however, that an author writes as, or is treated by others as being, an autonomous, unitary self. On the contrary, authors are typically expected to comply with certain discriminating protocols and conventions governing composition: a loving dedication is fine in the acknowledgments of a book, but would appear inappropriate and embarrassingly eccentric if inserted in the course of describing a scientific experiment.

Moreover, there is another sense in which authorship is not monolithic. We tend to think of authors as identifiable individual people who produce, for instance, books. Yet there are also types of authors, Foucault tells us, who are responsible for something much more robust and remarkable than a text. The first type he calls "transdiscursive" (1984a: 113 = 1969: 89). These authors are as old as Western civilization itself and inaugurated not just a book but "a theory, tradition or discipline in which other books and authors" have, in turn, found "a place"; examples are "Homer, Aristotle, and the Church Fathers, as well as the first mathematicians and the originators of the Hippocratic tradition."

In partial contrast to these "transdiscursive" authors are others who are distinctively modern: writers whom Foucault calls "founders of discursivity."[6] Arising first in the nineteenth century in Europe, they are figures "whom one should confuse with neither the 'great' literary authors, nor the authors of religious texts, nor the founders of science." These founders of discursivity "are unique in that they are not just the authors of their own works. They have produced something else: the possibilities and the rules for the formation of other texts" (1984a: 114 = 1969: 89). But what sort of possibilities and rules are these?

When I speak of Marx or Freud as founders [*instaurateurs*] of discursivity, I mean that they made possible not only a certain number of analogies, but also (and equally

important) a certain number of differences. They have created a possibility for something other than their discourse, yet something belonging to what they founded. To say
that Freud founded psychoanalysis does not (simply) mean that we find the concept of
the libido or the technique of dream analysis in the work of Karl Abraham or Melanie
Klein; it means that Freud made possible a certain number of divergences—with respect to his own texts, concepts, and hypotheses—that all arise from the psychoanalytic
discourse itself.' (1984a: 114-5 = 1969: 90)

Founders of discursivity, then, are notable for initiating a discourse
that encourages emulation *and* transformation, orthodoxy *and* heterodoxy. In this way their work is different, Foucault maintains, from
other authors who, though influential, establish a genre incapable
of, or at least inherently resistant to, radical metamorphosis. The
motifs of the Gothic horror romance, for instance, have not substantively changed since they were established by Ann Radcliffe in the
late eighteenth century; such change as has occurred has been restricted to recycling and recombining a standardized repertoire of
basic themes regarding the heroine's predicament, a mysterious
castle, the battle between good and evil, and so on. In contrast,
founders of discursivity establish "an endless possibility of discourse"
(1984a: 114 = 1969: 89); their work prompts creative disagreement,
unexpected applications, and new departures.

"Founders of discursivity," we have seen, are a modern phenomenon; in this at least they are different from their "transdiscursive"
counterparts. They should also not be confused with another type of
author Foucault mentions: "founders of *science*"—though his comments on this distinction are hedged-in with qualifications and are
rather opaque. Like the founder of discursivity, the founder of a
science—the examples offered include Cuvier (biology) and Saussure
(linguistics/semiotics)—furnishes the conditions for creative divergence. But in the case of a science, "the act that founds it is on an
equal footing with its future transformations; this act becomes in
some respects part of the set of modifications that it makes possible"
(Foucault, 1984a: 115 = 1969: 90-91). Foucault goes on to suggest
that while subsequent developments in a given science always preserve, however modified, some aspects of the founding act, that act
itself is effectively levelled and displaced by the consequences of
the founder's own achievement. In other words, the founder's
contributions enjoy no privileged status or priority in regard to subsequent scientific innovations or developments. Instead the propositions of scientific founders are assessed in terms of, and subordi-

nated to, the sciences –for instance, biology, semiotics—they created. However in the case of a founder of discursivity, where "the
initiation of a discursive practice is heterogeneous to its subsequent
transformations," the founding act is repeatedly returned to by later
practitioners of the discourse in order to determine the "primary coordinates" (1984a: 116 = 1969: 91) of the discourse itself. It would
appear, then, that in regard to the founding figure there is a recursive
durability, a reflexivity, to "discourses" that is typically absent in
"sciences." This explains why exponents of a discourse are constantly and explicitly revising the founder's statements; "one defines
a proposition's theoretical validity in relation to the work of the
founders [instaurateurs]" (1984a: 116 = 1969: 91), as distinct from
its truth-value. And in the case of founders of discursivity, the
recursiveness of the discourse ("the return" to the founding figures)
is no mere embellishment; "on the contrary, it constitutes an effective and necessary task of transforming the discursive practice itself.
Re-examination of Galileo's text may well change our knowledge
of the history of mechanics, but it will never be able to change mechanics itself. On the other hand, re-examining Freud's texts modi-
fies psychoanalysis itself, just as a re-examination of Marx's would
modify Marxism" (1984a: 116 = 1969: 93). Foucault ends the discussion of founders or initiators by acknowledging that his analysis
is "schematic," that the line between founders of discursivity and
science is not cut and dried, and that, accordingly, they are not "mu-
tually exclusive" phenomena (1984a: 117 = 1969: 93-4).

Foucault's account is a thought-provoking attempt to identify what
discursive founding putatively entails but what he says remains puzzling nonetheless. For instance, the difference between "transdiscursive" authors and "founders of discursivity" seems to hang on
little more than the modernity of the latter, but that is an historical
rather than an analytical distinction. Nor is it clear whether Foucault
intends us to distinguish between discourse and "discursivity" or
whether instead he is using the terms synonymously. And, as if this
were not enough to confuse us, Foucault's concept of discourse itself suffers from inconsistent application (as does the concept more
generally: see Meinhof 1993). He admitted as much, remarking,

instead of making the rather hazy meaning of the word "discourse" more distinct, I
think that I have multiplied its meanings: sometimes using it to mean the general domain
of all statements (énoncés), sometimes as an individualizable group of statements, and

sometimes as an ordered practice which takes account of a certain number of statements. (Foucault, quoted by Frank, 1992: 110)

One supposes that in speaking of founders of discursivity, Foucault is employing the last of these three usages, but the nature of the "statements" that compose the discourses established by the founders, and the rules of their formation, are left unspecified. And there are other, related, problems with his analysis.

We have seen that for Foucault the recursiveness of discourse—the perennial return to the founder's work—is integral to the economy and dynamic of the discourse itself. This continual return takes the founder's work as the "primary coordinates" of the pertinent discourse; its consequence is to expand the discourse through innovative disagreement. But how are these primary coordinates to be conceived in any one case? And how divergent can an interpretation be and yet still remain part of the founded discourse it claims to embrace? On the latter question Foucault is silent, on the former mysterious. For what he tells us is that a discourse like psychoanalysis is identified by trying "to isolate in the founding act an eventually restricted number of propositions or statements to which, alone, one grants a founding value, and in relation to which certain concepts or theories accepted by Freud might be considered as derived, secondary, and accessory" (1984a: 116 = 1969: 91). "In addition ... when trying to seize the act of founding, one sets aside those statements that are not pertinent, either because they are deemed inessential, or because they are considered 'prehistoric,' and derived from another type of discursivity" (1984a: 116 = 1969: 91). Now not only is this explanation quite vague; it also entails a discernible slippage from what we give a founding value to and what Freud himself accepted as foundational.

Similarly, Foucault's reluctance to specify the meaning of the expression "primary coordinates," or to expand on the limits of the divergence it enables, is actually very revealing in its own way because it highlights a significant problem: namely, that there are no unequivocal means of deciding, of validating, what the essential components of *a work or a discourse* are, or of adjudicating among rival claims of what they are. In short, we have an aporia. There are various reasons for this chronic uncertainty. To begin with, it is by no means obvious what a founding author established or considered essential—as the debate in current sociology about Max Weber's "central" theme or *Fragestellung* so strikingly testifies. Nominated to stand as Weber's "central" concept or problematic include: "the heterogony of purposes understood in a negative sense" (Stark 1967: 261); rationalization (Tenbruck 1980: 343-4), "the polar opposites" of capitalism and socialism (Mueller1982: 165); "modern *Menschentum*" (Hennis 1983: 157); *Arbeitsverfassung* (Scaff 1984: 200). From these accounts Weber is so centripetal he is implosive. But in that case why does his work continue to evade a consensus on what it is fundamentally about? It is because a textual corpus of any depth or range is an unstable entity, as Foucault himself was keen to point out elsewhere (e.g., Foucault 1972; [1969a]); it contains fractures, tensions, contradictions, discontinuities, second thoughts, revisions indicating a variety of objectives at work. These, in turn, reflect a complex mixture of biographical factors, unintended consequences of argument, intellectual developments, and the author's location in the changing events of his or her time. Furthermore, an author's work often straddles a number of discrete idioms—scientific, political, journalistic, and so on—informed by differing projects, so that the very notion of "centrality" or "primary coordinates" imposes a coherence and unity on a person's work (and life) that is usually quite artificial (Skinner 1969: 16-22).

Equally complex and shifting are the multiple viewpoints brought to the text by the reader. The meanings imputed to a great author's work will vary according to the horizon and preoccupations of interpreters and the traditions of which they are part. Locating the elements in the work that function as "primary coordinates" is thus always something that is mediated and negotiated, rather than being transparent in the founding "act"; it must be reconstructed, and this reconstruction is ongoing for so long as the author is deemed to be interesting.

How, then, might we improve on Foucault's analysis? And, if it can be improved, what might the implications be for sociology?

1. Improving the Analysis.

In the first place, we need to be clearer than Foucault himself was on the distinction between an author's *work* and the *discourse* around that work. Notwithstanding the problems of interpretation mentioned in the previous paragraph, one thing is clear: the author's texts constitute a finite and determinate body of work to interpret. That work contains various terms, propositions, concepts and theories, all of which can be reconstructed and assessed. The work of sociologists represents the theoretical practice in which they have been engaged. Though what this work means in its essentials is impossible to determine with finality, since we can only grasp it from particular perspectives, it is possible nonetheless to make statements about particular propositions or emphases without succumbing to interpretive nihilism. Thus no one is seriously going to argue that, according to Marx, the "superstructure" has consistent causal primacy in a mode of production over the "base" or that Napoleon III was a political genius; that Durkheim's *Rules of Sociological Method* is a manifesto of methodological individualism; that Simmel ignores the issues of social dualism and exchange-relationships; that, for Weber, religious beliefs ("psychological premiums") play an epiphenomenal role in social change.

But a discourse is a very different phenomenon from an author's work, as complex as the latter is in its own right. Accordingly, and in the absence of a compelling concept of discourse in Foucault's own work, it is worth returning to the term's roots for guidance. As Manfred Frank (1992: 99) reminds us,

> Discourse is taken from the Latin *discursus*, which in turn comes from the verb *discurrere*, meaning "to run hither and thither." A discourse is an utterance, or a talk of some length (not determined), whose unfolding or spontaneous development is not held back by any over-rigid intentions. Holding a "discourse" is not the same as holding a conference.

Nor is it the same, one might add, as enunciating a religious canon, declaiming a political dogma, reciting a poem, reading a script, delivering an academic lecture or homily. In the context of authorship, we can say that a discourse arises when the author's work is considered significant enough to be the subject of sustained discussion; and discussion, by definition, involves two or more parties in a "conversation" about the author's achievement. One does not found a discourse; one is subject to it (exclusively so, if one is dead), or one takes part in it. In either case, one's intervention contributes some of the theoretical and material conditions under which the discourse can take place. But no one's work can define or legislate the terms of the discourse itself. This is particularly true once we consider the nature of the written word. For once a set of ideas has become fixed in writing "textual meaning and psychological meaning have different destinies" (Ricoeur 1981a: 139). Cut loose from the immediate context which defines the spoken word, the text as work becomes a common property resource, constantly de- and re-contextualized by "an audience which extends in principle to anyone who can read" (ibid.).

That being the case, it is entirely unclear what it might mean to say that a discourse like Marxism "belongs," in some respect or other, to what the founder founded (Foucault, 1984a: 114 = 1969: 90). And, as it happens, Foucault himself seems in part to concur with these points. After all, his emphasis on the divergence from the founder's work that accompanies the interpretation of it is precisely aimed at showing that "the initiation of a discursive practice does not participate in its later transformations" (1984a: 116 = 1969: 91). But his way of putting matters is still confusing in failing to distinguish rigorously enough a body of work from a discourse about it. The former *can* be "founded" in the loose sense of being an accomplishment accrued over the lifetime of the author; the work is thus contemporaneous with the author who produced it. Discourse, on the other hand, cannot be founded because its substance and direction is dependent upon the interpretive strategies of other people; discourse is an engagement (typically retrospective) with the work the so-called founder produced. Moreover the relationship between the two—work and discourse—is highly indeterminate, so that to speak of founders producing "the rules for the formation of other texts" (1984a: 114 = 1969: 89) is an obfuscation. On the contrary, it is the very *absence* of clear rules that permits, and helps to explain, the perennial debate around a founder's work and that is the key testament to its significance.

For this reason, it has been possible to link what, for instance, Marx wrote to an astonishing battery of intellectual traditions including, those associated with Hegel (Lukács, Marcuse), Kierkegaard (Sartre), Kant and Rousseau (Colletti), Spinoza (Althusser), Pascal (Goldmann), Machiavelli (Gramsci), and so on. (from Anderson 1976: 61-74). Which of these interpretations bear on the primary coordinates of Marx's work? Both Althusser and Lukács, for example, saw radically different coordinates. Who was right? There is no way of knowing for sure, and the question itself seems absurd. Everything hangs on which of Marx's statements, and which "stage" of his thought, is assigned interpretative priority: in other words, it hangs on the transition from Marx's *works* (what he actually wrote: the terms he used, the concepts he elaborated, the theories he proposed) to the *discourse* (or, rather, discourses) about them—and over the latter it is not Marx who is the guide but those who seek to appropriate his work for their own purposes. "There have always been multiple Marxes," Terrell Carver observes, "and each one is a product of a reading strategy." Today we witness shifts in what texts of Marx are read, in how Marx is read, and why he is read (Carver 1998: 234, 2). To give another illustration, the works of Comte prompted two antithetical discourses in nineteenth- and early twentieth-century France. A republican version, advanced by people such as Leon Gambetta and Jules Ferry, settled on Comte's earlier writings. An authoritarian one, enunciated by members of the proto-fascist Action Française (like Henri Vaugeois and Charles Maurras), concentrated on Comte's later theory of positivism.[7] Both groups could lionize and claim Comte, but which group had discovered his primary coordinates? Or consider Simmel who, as Donald Levine (1997: 189-196) observes, has been read as a utilitarian action theorist (by Raymond Boudon and Jonathan Turner); as a (functionalist) conflict theorist (by Lewis Coser and Randall Collins); and as a theorist of alienation with Marxian resonances (by Andrew Arato).

In sum, "founders of discursivity" is a misnomer. Discursivity cannot be founded since it is inherently an interaction, not a deed of the founding figure. One can produce a body of work that becomes the focus for a discourse but one cannot found a discourse (work + interpretation) itself since discourses entail what happens to a work when it is identified as significant.

2. Implications for Sociology

We have seen that Foucault's analysis of founders of discursivity might be improved by making a distinction between a work and a discourse about that work. In effect, this attempt at improvement suggests some major problems with the idea of founding. What, more specifically, does this imply in the case of sociology? The question is clearly germane because of the pervasiveness of the founding motif in sociology and by the fact that some support for Foucault's general approach to founding has come from an unlikely source: Jeffrey Alexander, in his major work on the presuppositional logic of sociology.[8] Alexander himself is no Foucaultian, and shows no sign of being influenced by Foucault on this question. The language and framework he employs differ significantly from Foucault's own. While the latter is happy to speak of "discourse" and "coordinates," Alexander prefers the vocabulary of "tradition" and theoretical "dilemmas." However, Alexander shares Foucault's belief that creative divergence from, as distinct from imitation of, the founder's work is an integral aspect of its dynamic. On the other hand, he is much more specific about how this occurs, and much more radical in his interpretation of what happens to the founder's legacy in the process. For what Alexander suggests is that the most talented and imaginative of the founder's followers move in a direction that actually threatens to break with, but rarely goes the whole way in breaking with, the master's own one-sided theoretical commitments. And this is so because these followers are engaged in an attempt, as they see it, to compensate precisely for what the pioneering figure appeared to have either omitted or underemphasized, that is, deemed *inessential*. On this account, the development of Western Marxism, for instance, can be seen as a series of attempts to redress the imbalance of Marx's economistic bias by attending to the symbolic, cultural, and political aspects of social relations and the voluntaristic (choice laden) dimension of social action. To be sure, revision "is made under the cover of loyal exegesis, but it is structured—often unconsciously—by the strains in the original work, and in the greatest students it involves the attempt to overcome them" (Alexander 1982b: 7). Suspended between homage and critique, exponents of the tradition wrestle with the dilemmas, inconsistencies, and inadequacies that become evident in and among the master's theories.

It will be obvious from the above that Alexander believes that sociology has something akin to discursive founders. In his interpretation, founders establish the tracks along which key sociological traditions develop. The idea of creative divergence, cryptic in Foucault, is given a rigorous sociological application. Much of Alexander's analysis is persuasive; it also helps clarify some aspects of the relationship between an author's work and its reception. What is unnecessary and misleading is its use of the "founder" concept. The "theoretical logics" (Alexander) that Marx, Durkheim and Weber embraced consisted of philosophical positions and traditions— idealism and materialism, Hegelianism and neo-Kantianism for instance—which they both brilliantly exemplified and dynamically transformed for their own unique purposes. Later figures appropriating the work of Marx et al. were thus also appropriating, and responding to the strategic biases in these wider and earlier traditions, now duly sedimented in the work of sociology's great figures. Alexander would doubtless agree. But in that case the "founder" metaphor is inappropriate because one could just as well say that the real founders of sociology's underlying "logic" are, for instance, Hegel and Kant—or perhaps Plato and Aristotle. More generally, the concept of founder, as applied to academic disciplines, is misleading for at least three reasons. Each of them indicates that "founders" are retrospectively sought out by a discipline, rather than being its presuppositional condition of existence.

In the first place, sociology typically counts among its founders individuals who never aspired to this status; these are the *appropriated* founders mentioned above. Marx is the most obvious case—he seems to have equated sociology with the "trashy positivism" of Comte (Marx 1955: 169; Bottomore and Rubel 1956: 28-9). Weber is another prominent, though more complex, example. It is true that Weber wrote a number of works that both set out the framework for sociological understanding and that sought to apply it to a range of issues. Nonetheless, Anthony Giddens (1987: 182) is quite right to say that, during his lifetime, "Weber was not regarded either by himself or by others as primarily 'a sociologist,' but saw himself, and was seen, as a historian, economist and theorist of jurisprudence" (also Tribe 1989: 1). Not only was Weber "firmly against the creation of chairs of sociology" (Lepenies 1988 [1985]: 247), he also, from 1910 onwards, adopted the term "sociology" to depict his own social scientific approach largely for reasons of convenience—thus distancing himself from the political sympathies (bureaucratic, monarchical) associated with the older members of the Verein für Sozialpolitik (Roth, in Bendix and Roth 1971: 39). As late as 1917, Weber was still describing himself as an "economist" (Weber 1948a [1917]: 129). The more general point to be recognized here is that "sociologists in the 'classical period' themselves did not believe the origin story" and that "as late as the 1920s…there was no sense that certain texts [in sociology] were discipline defining 'classics' demanding special study. Rather, there was a sense of a broad, almost impersonal, advance of scientific knowledge with the notables being simply leading members of the pioneering crew" (Connell 1997:1513-14). It is what Connell calls an "encyclopaedic, rather than a canonical, view of the new science by its practitioners" that the founding story, and, more importantly, disciplinary consolidation, effectively eliminates.

A second reason to believe that disciplinary founding is a retrospective process can be gleaned from the fact that the list of founding fathers is prone to become steadily longer, or more inconclusive, the more aware we become of sociology's own complex history, its association with the other social sciences and humanities, and its relationship to modernity. Instructive in this respect is the 1979 edition of Raison's *The Founding Fathers of Social Science*, a volume mostly concerned with sociology rather than with the social sciences as a whole. In that edition, six founders are added to the book's original twenty-five: they are Montesquieu, Gramsci, Freud, G.H. Mead, Mauss, and Adorno. Precisely why these new figures were chosen is not entirely clear, but the writer of the preface speaks of the need to "emphasize the European, rather than the American, tradition in social science," remarks that Montesquieu is "an important precursor," and observes that Gramsci is a "controversial" and "contemporary" figure (Barker 1979: 8)—even though the author of the entry on Gramsci flatly declares that "Gramsci was no more a founding father of social science than he was of Eurocommunism;" on the contrary "the historical Gramsci was essentially a marginal figure, as man and Marxist" (Williams 1979: 259-60). Still, it is editorial decisions like these that are crucial in deciding who founders are, or—and this is the third reason for a retrospective emphasis—who they are not.

For omission, like inclusion, will be determined by one's interpretation of the past and this in turn will hinge, fundamentally, on one's current project and one's view of what sociology is. Few people today would consider Condorcet or Leibniz as "founders of sociology." But Victor Branford once specifically did: Condorcet because of his role as a theorist of, and activist in relation to, the "practical organization of society," Leibniz because of his contribution to "the idea of social evolution" (Branford, 1904: 110, 119). That view is by no means absurd if one makes a distinction between the "predisciplinary" and "disciplinary" stages of social science (Heilbron 1995 [1990]: 3 and passim). Or consider Marx in this context. Since, for Giddens (1971), the development of sociology is in good part a response to the consequences of modern, bourgeois capitalism, to exclude Marx from the pantheon of sociological founding figures would be nonsensical. Tom Bottomore and Maximilien Rubel (1961 [1956]: 30) said something similar, adding, in a revealing phrase, that Marx's own "science of society" is "closer to the present concerns of sociology than is the theory which gave its name to the discipline." Bottomore, concerned in the 1950s and 1960s to establish the credibility of Marxist sociology, cited three names as the "founders of sociology"—Comte, Spencer and Marx. Weber and Durkheim are missing. Why? Apparently because the "most interesting [intellectual legacy of the founders] is the endeavour to describe and interpret the economic and social revolutions which produced modern industrial societies" (1960: 33), and Bottomore was of the opinion that Weber and Durkheim made inferior contributions to this problem. This was a view, which at least in relation to Durkheim, he still held some twenty years later.[9] In contrast, an approach like Therborn's (1976), heavily influenced by Althusser's account of Marx's "epistemological break" with ideology and his "founding" of an utterly new science of history (historical materialism), keenly underscores Marx's remoteness from the sociological "problematic." Similarly, the insistence that the "sociological contribution has essentially consisted in the discovery and study of the ideological community —i.e. community of values and norms,"[10] determined Therborn's conceptual gradations of "proto-sociology" (the work of Scottish Enlightenment figures such Ferguson and Millar), "pioneer" sociology (Saint-Simon, Comte, Spencer), sociology's "forerunners" (for example, Condorcet), and the "classical" sociology of, notably, Durkheim and Weber, which constitutes sociology's "mature" phase.[11] Ironically, such an account echoes that of Parsons, who had also sought, though for a different combination of logical, methodological, and theoretical reasons, to distance Marx from modern sociology. While Durkheim and Weber "seem to me to be the *main* founders of *modern* sociological theory," both being "in explicit revolt against the traditions of both economic individualism and socialism," Tocqueville and Marx "provided the wing positions relative to this central core." For Parsons, neither Marx nor Tocqueville attained, when contrasted with Durkheim and Weber, "a comparable level of *technical* theoretical analysis" (1968 [1937]) xiii-xiv, emphasis in the original). Moreover, while for all these writers Simmel is a relatively marginal figure, he becomes a pivotal one for theorists of postmodernity: hence Bauman's (1991: 46) tribute to Simmel "who started it all."

It is this fact—that discursive founders are created by later generations under the guise of "discovering" them—that helps explain the puzzle identified by Giddens but left unsolved by him: how it is that "Weber and Durkheim are regarded as among the principal founders of modern sociology" yet seem to have so little sociologically in common? To explain the anomaly that "sociology counts among its classics two scholars whose work manifests an almost complete divergence of method and substance,"[12] Giddens (1987: 188) argues in paradoxical vein that it is "contextual association through dissociation" that links the authors together. From his perspective, it is the legacy of the Franco-Prussian War of 1870-1, and the crisis provoked by the First World War that form the context in question. These episodes provided the agenda of problems (e.g., regarding political leadership, bureaucracy, moral solidarity, liberalism) that Durkheim and Weber addressed in their own idiosyncratic and contrasting manner. But Giddens's account does not actually explain the original puzzle: why *modern* sociology should consider authors with such divergent positions as "founders." The explanation, I have been suggesting, lies not in their context, but in those of later generations.

To sum up: The previous analysis has suggested that the idea of founding a discourse is mistaken. Discourses are the product not of an action but an interaction, and they must be distinguished from the "work" of the putative founding figure. If a discourse is a product of sustained interlocution, so too is the notion of a founder of that discourse. In such wise, so-called discursive founders are the result of the interface between an author's work and its peculiar reception. I shall be saying more about the processes of reception in chapter 5, but for the meantime let us turn to the second major account of founding that concerns us here.

Wolin and "Epic Theory"

Foucault, we saw, employed the term "founders of discursivity" to examine a kind of authorship arising in the modern period. Wolin's founders, in contrast, stretch back to Greek antiquity. Moreover, there is a specific equivocation in Wolin's approach that is lacking in

Foucault's. In "What is an author?," Foucault evidently subscribes to the founding idea. That essay, written in the late 1960s, formed part of his attempt to advance an "archaeological" method.[13] Wolin writes more cautiously. His work attempts to describe both how founding was understood by the aspirant founding figures themselves—how they envisaged their own practice—and how such ostensible founding has been received by disciplines and discourses that acknowledge the founder's claims (the great tradition of political theory), or seek to displace or marginalize them (modern empiricism). Such an analysis does not commit Wolin to a defence of the founding notion. But nor does it exactly distance him from it either. Indeed, founding would appear to have real attractions for a thinker such as Wolin who has consistently championed the "epic" tradition of political and social theory against its scientistic, and post-modernist, detractors (see 1960, 1990). Still, the reader should be aware of this ambiguity in the description that follows.

Wolin advances our discussion beyond Foucault by arguing that the founding of a social science, and theoretical founding more generally, "has both a *political* dimension and a *politics*."[14] Founding is "political" in that it is

> the constitutive activity of laying down basic and general principles which, when legitimated, become the presuppositions of practice, the ethos of practitioners. This definition is modelled upon the Aristotelian conception of "the political" (*he politike*) as the "master science" that legislates for the good of the whole that is, for the purpose of shaping the whole to the concept of the good relevant to it. Founding is thus *political* theorizing. (Wolin1981: 402)

In addition, founding entails a "politics," that is, a project of defeating and destroying "rival theoretical claims. It is Socrates against Thrasymachus. This politics is conducted by means of strategies (e.g. 'the Socratic method,' Locke's 'clearing Ground a little, and removing some of the Rubbish') and intellectual weapons (various logics, conceptions of 'facts')" (ibid.).

In its turn, theoretical politics—the battle to prevail in the intellectual sphere—can be either "profane," that is to say, limited in its goals, or "ontological," a form of global theoretical activity "preoccupied with gaining access to the highest kind of truth, which is about the nature of ultimate being" and considered as a "solution to the fundamental political riddle, how to combine vast power with perfect right" (Wolin 1981: 403). Still, whether profane or ontological,

The point of engaging in the politics of theory is to demonstrate the superiority of one set of constitutive principles over another so that in the future these will be recognized as the basis of theoretical inquiry. Thus the founder's *action* prepares the *way* for *inquiry*, that is, for activity which can proceed uninterruptedly because its presuppositions are not in dispute. Inquiry is both a tribute to the triumph of a particular theory and its routinization. Or, to say the same thing differently, inquiry signals that the legitimation struggle is over; it is depoliticized theory. This explains why inquirers are usually quick to deplore as "political" (or "ideological") those who challenge the dominant presuppositions and who seek to refound the activity. (Wolin 1981: 403-4, emphasis in the original)

"Political" activity in the theoretical mode is, then, the attempt to constitute some discursive domain; to establish a framework of concepts, methodological procedures and protocols that subsequent inquiry will respect through emulation. As a mode of activity it is successful and influential to the degree to which its ground-rules are accepted as unproblematic by later practitioners and exponents: that is, to the degree to which its "politics" triumphs. And this "politics" will normally be most evident in the early stages of the constituting process, when theoretical rivals have to be obliterated or at least marginalized. Once established, the politics of theory in regard to a specific discourse will be muted because naturalized. The politics of theory will only become conspicuous again when challenges emerge to contest the founder's colonization of theoretical space.

Theoretical founding, for Wolin, is thus imbued with a special kind of power and ambition. It parallels, and models itself on, two other notions of founding: the creation myths of religion, and the secularization of such myths in the idea of state constitutions (though of course, such secularization itself contains an intense metaphysical charge). Consider the former, and as perhaps the most striking example of the phenomenon, the case of Yahweh, the God of the Hebrew Bible:

He performs the supreme political act: he doesn't merely create the world; he constitutes it, that is, he orders it, differentiates levels of power and being, assigns jurisdictions and issues rules for their regulation. What is constituted by these actions is nothing less than "the political," that is, the basic terms on which politics can then take place. For in ordering the world and defining relationships among mankind, between mankind and God, between man and woman, mankind and animals, and mankind and nature, Yahweh has set the conditions and reference points against which the politics of rivalry, or comparative advantage, the quest for power, the exercise of cunning or strategy, and the testing of limits all take place. (Wolin1985: 228)

However, as Genesis shows, this political act is itself destabilized by the unruly and rebellious actions of Man, that is, by politics—

notably the revolt of Adam and Eve, and the rivalry of Cain and Abel. Following the Flood, God establishes a new covenant with Man through Noah, but this too is subject to Man's perversity and hubris in the attempt to build the Tower of Babel. The result is the dissolution of Man's combined power and possibility of coordination through the dissolution of its basis, a unitary language, and its replacement by a multiplicity of tongues.

This myth of the origins of the world finds its counterpart in the myth of the origins of political constitutions. "In antiquity the myth was identified with the labors of a political hero, a Moses, Solon, or Lycurgus" (Wolin 1985: 230). In more modern times, the myth could be just as potent. The *novus ordo saeclorum* invoked by the makers of the American Revolution expressed the idea "that the 'fundamental law' of the Constitution was a real embodiment of the laws of nature, the eternal decrees by which the Creator had defined the everlasting nature of all things" (Wolin 1985: 231).

So far we have ascertained that, on Wolin's account, theoretical founding entails both a political, constitutive dimension and a corresponding politics, that is, a strategy and tactics by which the constitutive dimension is secured. But who have been the chief actors in and enunciators of this process? In two essays published in 1969 and 1970, Wolin coined the term "epic tradition" to describe a series of thinkers with founding ambitions. Significantly, these essays themselves involved a strategic theoretical manoeuvre, that is, a politics. Reacting against behaviorist political science, Wolin sought to reaffirm the distinctive skills, idiom and emphases of the theorist's vocation. Enter the "epic theorist" who illustrates these characteristics most vividly. By introducing this figure, Wolin sought to capture something of the excitement that motivated the great political theorists. He wanted us to consider the history of political theory, not only analytically, but also from the standpoint of the impulse, the "structure of intentions" (Wolin 1969: 1078), of those "epic theorists" who drove it. In a lecture on Hobbes he suggests that

> from Plato to modern times an epic tradition in political theory has existed and ... Hobbes is one of its ornaments. The phrase "epic tradition" refers to a type of political theory which is inspired mainly by the hope of achieving a great and memorable deed through the medium of thought. Other aims that it may have, such as contributing to the existing state of knowledge, formulating a system of logically consistent propositions, or establishing a set of hypotheses for scientific investigation, are distinctly secondary. (Wolin 1970: 4)

This "thought deed" (Wolin 1970: 7) has as its objective the fundamental reshaping of the political continent: "Let us proceed to found the state by word," Plato has the Athenian Stranger say in *The Laws*. "By an act of thought, the theorist seeks to reassemble the whole political world...(S)uch efforts involve a new way of looking at the familiar world, a new way with its own cognitive and normative standards" (Wolin 1969: 1078). Responding to the political crises of his time, rather than simply to the prevailing concepts, the epic theorist insists that the current polity is "systematically deranged" (Wolin 1969: 1080); hence the need for it to be radically refashioned. A condition of this restructuring is a type of theory that establishes a novel symbolic universe generating its own notion of the empirically significant "facts."

Wolin develops this idea of the epic theorist most forcefully in his essay on Hobbes. But later it is Max Weber to whom he turns as an exemplar of the modern theoretical founder. According to Wolin, the reception of Weber's writings has been characterized by an artificial separation of the political and methodological works. The separation is artificial because Weber's writings on method were themselves profoundly "political" in orientation. The political intention is most evident, Wolin claims, in Weber's definition of social science as a cultural science. So conceived, Weber could prise it away from positivistic notions of reality that de-politicized the social realm. They did so by making it seem mechanical, predictable, and by suggesting that science was separate from values. In contrast, the cultural sciences as delineated by Weber were dependent on shifting frameworks of meaning and significance; and in turn these frameworks rested on subjective presuppositions and the choices of agents. For evidence of Weber's political purpose, consider chapter 1 of *Economy and Society* (1922) where Weber sets out the basic lexicon of sociology. Wolin (1981: 408) understands this to be "a constitutive act that brings order to a distinct realm," a realm subject to great polemical disturbance in Weber's day as it is in ours.

Weber's political sensibilities are not, then, just evident in his directly political essays on, for instance Bismarck, the Russian Revolutions, parliament, nor in the striking "prominence of 'power-words' in his vocabulary; struggle, competition, violence, domination, *Machtstaat*, imperialism" (Wolin 1981: 408). They can be discerned even where Weber is at his most abstract. More than this, he was compelled to express his political ambitions in a specifically methodological, rather than merely theoretical-scientific or party political form. The quandary Weber faced was as follows. On the one side he had come to believe by the turn of the last century that honest scientific practice precluded open political partisanship. He thus abandoned his earlier view, formulated with brutal clarity in the Freiburg Inaugural lecture of 1895, that the science of political economy was to be the handmaiden of the geo-political requirements of the German Reich. From around 1903-4 onwards, Weber accepted that the gods and demons governing science were the disciplined search for uncomfortable facts, the pursuit of rational inquiry, and distanced impartiality. However he also recognized that commitments such as these were themselves normative, that is, involved judgments of what is worthwhile and valuable, which a supposedly value-neutral science could not logically vindicate. On the other side of the quandary lay Weber's own passionate political ideals and ambitions that could not be satisfied or fulfilled within the political system of the Second Empire. As a result of this situation, Wolin argues, Weber sublimated his political aspirations into the methodological sphere:

> He never created a political theory even though the manifest breakdown of German politics and society cried out for one. His political-theoretical impulse was turned inward upon social science where he replicated the problems, dilemmas, and demands which he perceived in the "real" political world. For that impulse to be released, Weber had to find a way of modifying the scientific prohibition against the injection of politics into scientific inquiry and locate a domain within science where he could theorize both the profane politics of theory and the ontology of theory. (Wolin 1981: 408)

That domain was methodology, and in particular the ideal-type construct with its deliberately one-sided "utopian," fictive emphasis. Methodology, to Weber, is not a handbook of techniques or an attempt to legislate actual practice in regard to specific and substantive problem areas of research. It is, rather, the attempt to show that facts do not speak for themselves, that they only assume meaning within given presuppositional frameworks; in addition, methodology seeks to lay down the foundations of vocational standards according to which research practice can be assessed and adjudicated. This takes on particular importance when research traditions are in crisis and have lost, or are palpably losing, their vitality, legitimacy, and social relevance. In that conjuncture, the founding methodologist may delineate a new conceptual space consonant with new "evaluative ideas," may point to new standards of significance. If that occurs, the political (constitutive) thrust of methodology will be joined by a politics: an attempt to rout other, competing attempts to establish the rationale for social scientific investigation.

Wolin's article on Weber is a *tour de force* of interpretation. It represents the antithesis of the view that Weber's methodological writings "always remained in large part reflections upon established practices of social and historical research, rather than constituting a methodological manifesto in their own right" (Giddens 1987: 184). Weber scholars will make up their own minds on this issue. My primary concern in this chapter, however, is less with the accuracy of Wolin's account of Weber, than with what it suggests more generally about the idea of theoretical (discursive) founding.

Constitutions, Discourses, Founders

The earlier critical discussion of Foucault offered a number of reasons to suggest why, strictly speaking, a discourse (or tradition, for that matter), cannot actually be founded. To speak of a discourse being founded is actually to mistake a "work" with the discourse around that work. It also fails to acknowledge that so-called founders are recovered by later generations under the pretext of "discovering" them, a process that in turn reflects contending views on what sociology is about. If one agrees with that argument, it will be impossible to accept that Hobbes, Weber, or any other person could actually found a discourse, though this is not to deny the possibility that such people may have nursed the ambition to do so. What, then, can we extract from Wolin's analysis to help us make sense of the founder question? Of particular value is its recognition that founding is linked to a quest for legitimation, a project that is manifested in discourse as much as it is in religion or the state. Or, more precisely, that founding is itself part of a discourse that theory, the state, and religion recurrently employ when they seek to justify themselves. Presently, I shall develop this idea so as to illuminate some of the connections between the rhetoric of social science and of politics. However, in order to avoid misleading analogies, it is first necessary to remind our selves about the distinctiveness of sociological practice.

Attempts to legislate sociological practice through the creation of a "political"- methodological manifesto are not hard to find.

Durkheim's *Rules of Sociological Method* (1895) is a salient example of the genre. So, too, is Talcott Parson's *The Structure of Social Action* (1937). Indeed, Charles Camic has argued that the conceptual matrix, terminology and programmatic argument of *Structure* offered nothing less than a "charter" or, even a "Magna Carta," for sociology, as Parsons sought, in the embattled intellectual climate of the 1930s, to constitute the discipline as an autonomous science and defend it from the imperialist claims of bio-psychological behaviorism and neoclassical economic theory. In this sense, Camic maintains, the *Structure of Social Action*

> resembles what Anglo-American law terms a "charter of incorporation": a public document designed to constitute a formal association or corporate group by delineating its distinct purposes, intended operating procedures, available resources, historical background, and future objectives and so claiming for it a fixed identity and the various rights and privileges attendant on separate corporate status. (Camic 1989: 48)[15]

At the same time, we need to be aware of the limits of the comparison between political and legal formations, on the one hand, and social science disciplines on the other. In particular, Wolin's claim that the thought-deed of the epic theorist produces something (or has the ambition of producing something) analogous to a constitution in the political sphere requires qualification. To begin with the obvious: constitutions, once established, are normally protected by state apparatuses that are, in the last instance, coercive. Sociology is in an entirely different position. All of the social sciences today are professionalized to some degree; in consequence, they are affected by bureaucratic rules and conventions that lend them a modicum of order and organization. Nonetheless, social science practice itself is inherently pluralistic. Professional bodies have been unable to insist on, or enforce, the exclusivity of one discourse or one curriculum— or the use of one set of basic terms or standardized concepts.[16] Equally, *theoretical* pluralism is "integral to the socially patterned cognitive processes operating" in the social and natural sciences. Indeed, with "the institutionalization of science, the behaviour of scientists oriented toward norms of organized scepticism and mutual criticism works to bring about such theoretical pluralism" (Merton 1981: v).

One might, of course, say much the same thing about a pluralistic state. After all, it too allows various interests to compete with one another. But there is a decisive difference. Liberal democratic states, while allowing competitive pluralism in civil society, are assiduous in resisting it within the state itself. A modern state, even a federal one, cannot permit two separate standing armies, or two equal assemblies, to exist within its borders; it must insist on sovereignty. Social science disciplines, on the other hand, have far weaker means of social control, unless they have become an arm of the state, in which case they discharge an essentially propagandist, apologetic function—as Marxism did in state-socialist societies. Under liberal democratic conditions, conversely, the professional bodies that regulate and inform a discipline such as sociology have no unequivocal means of securing the writ of one discourse: hence the proliferation of traditions, sub-traditions, schools, schisms, and the never-ending hackneyed talk of "crisis." Helmut Koester once remarked that "the test of orthodoxy is whether it is able to build a *church* rather than a club or school or a sect."[17] By that measure, no orthodoxy has ever reigned in Western sociology—even if some sects (organizations where membership if typically voluntary, and is achieved rather than ascribed)[18] have periodically been more influential than others.

We should also note the absence in social science disciplines of any substantial equivalent to constitutional "super-legality." In jurisprudence, the concept of super-legality refers to a constitutional provision that explicitly prohibits the formulation of any law, or the initiation of any action, whose purpose is the undoing of the constitution. Super-legality, therefore, "means strengthened validity of certain norms;" its aim "is to hinder any rapid changes of government with small, unstable majorities and coalitions," and "with respect to revisions, ... not to allow a procedure to set aside the system of order established by the constitution" (Schmitt 1987: 75-76). An example of super-legality is the stipulation in Article 21:2 of the German Federal Republic's Basic Law that declares unconstitutional "Parties which, by reason of their aims or behaviour of their adherents, seek to impair or abolish the free democratic basic order" (Finer 1979: 205-6). There is no counterpart to super-legality in the human sciences—even if some of its major figures have wished it were otherwise. Thus Freud (1986 [1914]) could neither prevent Adler and Jung from developing versions of psychoanalysis divergent to his own, nor prevent the break-up of the psychoanalytic movement these disagreements heralded. Significantly, the language Freud employed to describe his rivals' challenge to his authority borrowed from political-constitutional imagery: theirs was "a cool act of usurpation," a "secession" (Freud, 1986: 63, 108, 118, 128) from the fundamental principles of psychoanalysis. Adler and Jung indicated their own distance from Freudian psychoanalysis by coining, respectively, the labels "Individual Psychology" and "Analytical Psychology" to denote distinctively heterodox positions.

"Super-legality" also has limited compulsive force. The ultimate factor that protects a state from dissolution is physical force, not a clause in a constitutional document. But the main point here is that the *provision* of super-legality is intelligible in the context of a state constitution in a way that would be absurd in a social science. For while a state can legitimately identify and designate what factors are likely to contribute to its undoing, and can then provide the force to forestall such a possibility, a social science discourse is constantly being re-constituted in the very process of its activity. Because of this, a stipulation that formulated in advance what would count as an illicit topic of "conversation," would not be a means of preserving the disciplinary discourse but would be a violation of its basic logic. Such a stipulation, to the degree to which it was enforced, would produce dogma, but it would not facilitate discourse.

I conclude, then, that comparisons of social science with political constitutions, legal charters and the like need to be handled with care lest what is applicable in one sphere be inappropriately stretched to another. Even so, Wolin's discussion of the "politics" of the founding ambition, and the rhetoric that adorns it, is particularly important in one key respect. It helps us appreciate that wherever founding is invoked, a legitimation claim is never far behind.[19] This claim itself can function in different ways. Its most common mode, almost synonymous with the very idea of legitimation, is the creation of a hierarchy in which moral value or intellectual worth are invidiously graded and contrasted. This is the point Hitler (1939 [1925/26]: 243) sought to convey in *Mein Kampf* when he divided humanity into three categories: "founders of culture, bearers of culture, and destroyers of culture" among which "the Aryan alone can be considered as representing the first category. It was he who laid the groundwork and erected the walls of every great structure in human culture." Hitler adopted the architectonic metaphor to make a claim about cultures that was crude and barbaric. But theorists display their own peculiar will to power when they take hold of the founder idea or when they exhibit the founder mentality. The compulsion is nothing new. "In fact," as Giddens (1979: 241) notes,

> members of each generation of social thinkers since at least the early part of the eighteenth century have been inclined to assert that they were initiating a newly scientific study of man in society, in contrast to what went before. Vico conceived himself to be founding a "new science" of society. Montesquieu and Condorcet made similar claims, and held they were breaking with what went before. Comte said much the same thing in his time, acknowledging the contributions of these forerunners, but largely relegating them to the prehistory of sociology, which was only coming to be placed on a scientific basis through his own efforts. And so it continues: Marx argued much the same in respect of Comte; Durkheim in respect of Marx, and yet another generation later, Parsons of Durkheim and others.

Or consider, once more, the case of Freud, the "embattled founder" as Peter Gay (1988: 153) called him. "Psychoanalysis is my creation," Freud declared in 1914, even though five years' earlier he had given Josef Breuer the credit for bringing "psychoanalysis into existence." To square the circle, Freud settled on the following solution: Breuer's "cathartic procedure" was demoted to "a preliminary stage of psychoanalysis" which really began with Freud's abandonment of the technique of hypnosis and his introduction of free association (Freud 1986: 63-4).

The logic of this kind of argument is as clear as it is delusive. Once the idea of discursive founding, or some variant on it ("my creation") is entertained, intellectual subordination and sleight of hand become almost inevitable. Because founding suggests priority, a first step, an infrastructure upon which *other* contributions rest, it must entail, too, a narrative strategy in which the contributions of historical others and contemporaries become secondary *and separable* from the founding "act." For if they were not secondary and separable, then the act could not be a founding one, but instead would need to be visualized as a transformation of conditions and materials without which it would be unthinkable.

I have said that the founder motif works to assert dominance and subordination through the construction of a conceptual hierarchy. It offers the metaphorical tools for an imperious legitimation strategy. Its dominant mood is hubristic. But we should also note that while the concept of founding can function to separate and segregate categories of agent or effort, it can also be employed defensively to close the gap, to even the odds, to secure recognition for something previously ignored or marginalized. A political example will help underscore the point before we examine its theoretical counterpart.

During much of the 1990s, Canada was in the throes of rewriting its constitution. Demanding a new political status in the constitutional settlement were "aboriginal" peoples. In part, they sought to secure their objectives by insisting on the "inherent rights" of aboriginal peoples to self-government, reminding other Canadians of the existence of Native "self-government" prior to colonial conquest. Their claims were doubly foundational. To being with, theirs was—and is—an argument about origins; they were in Canada first, that is, before the Europeans. Second, by virtue of these origins, individuals who claim to represent native peoples insist that they have certain rights that current political arrangements and practices deny or degrade. When Ovide Mercredi, a past leader of the Assembly of First Nations (the organization that officially represents Canada's "status" Indians) protested against the way that Canadian customs officials handle objects regarded as sacred by natives, he asserted that this raised "an issue of fundamental religious freedom, a question of respecting fundamental human rights" (the quotations come from the *Globe and Mail*, 1 and 11 November 1991).

These and countless other possible examples indicate, *pace* the postmodernists, that what we are witnessing today is not a decline of foundationalist claims but instead their proliferation, not the loss of Enlightenment grand narratives but rather their expansion and loss of exclusivity. Strictly speaking, of course, the self-validation claims of particular native peoples of Canada—now significantly called "First Nations"—to "have been here first" is problematic. In most cases, the linguistic and archaeological record reveals a much more complex pattern of migration, of demographic wave and counter-wave (Flanagan 2000: 11-26). Aboriginality literally means being located in a place from the beginning. But from the beginning of *when*? Very few groups, natives included, have lived continuously in the same place for thousands of years. But the facts are less important than the foundational rhetoric through which some native people seek to derive authority, thereby enabling them to extract financial resources from the state and to bolster land claims.

Founding is, thus, a concept that can be used to assert primacy and power in cases where it has previously been denied. So, to return to our main theme, it is not at all surprising that when modern writers seek to make good the deficit in our recognition of Eastern social thought, they gravitate towards the founder notion—for instance in writing of Ibn Khaldun as a/the founding father of sociology (Dhaouadi 1990; Conyers 1972). Nor is it surprising that some modern feminists, seeking to retrieve women's early contributions to sociology, have also been drawn to the notion of founder, though now suitably re-gendered. "Founding mothers" is today becoming a fairly common expression (e.g., Lengermann and Niebrugge-Brantley 1992; Hess, Markson, and Stein 1988; cf. Spender 1982). But for a real sense of the ideological payload and legitimating intent (as distinct from the explanatory value) of the defensive use of founder, consider these reflections by Mary Deegan (1991: 2-3) on why she was led to formulate her concept of "founding sisters":

> I do not define the most powerful women in sociology as "founding mothers." I do not favor the imagery and meaning of maternity in the context of brilliant women. Many of these women dedicated their lives to the elimination of traditional female roles, particularly the oppressiveness surrounding mothering. The symbol of motherhood, furthermore, often is rooted in emotional rather than intellectual care. In addition, mothers are nurturant but often subservient to men...The founding sisters of sociology are not in this subservient relationship to founding fathers...Founding sisters speak with authority on both public and private worlds, engaging both sexes, and transcending traditional limits of sociology and women.... "Founding sisters" may sound weaker today than the term "founding fathers." I hope that the feminist intention underlying sisterhood and the patriarchal intention underlying both fatherhood and motherhood become clearer over time. "Founding sisters" will then sound not only more harmonious to the ear, but also more powerful in its message.

Feminism is thus just the latest doctrine to take over a very old idea. Worse, it has also subjected that idea to its own idealization. It is one thing to say that sociologists would have a more sophisticated understanding of their own history if they paid more attention to the contribution of women. That is hard to gainsay. We now know, for instance, that many of the ethnographic and quantitative-ecological methods practiced by the Chicago sociologists of the 1920s were pioneered in the previous decade by social workers and reformers, many of whom were women: not only Jane Addams, but individuals such as Maude Royden and Louise de Koven Bowen. (Platt 1996: 263). We also know that women like Addams and her circle were first considered as sociologists before being redefined as social workers or hived off to departments of "home economics" (Deegan, 1988).[20] Equally, it has become evident, thanks to the research of Deegan and Jennifer Platt, that a history of sociology will miss much of what has happened to the discipline if it focuses solely on formally accredited "sociologists." Consider the case of Ethel Sturges Dummer who, if she is remembered at all today, is recalled primarily as a wealthy sponsor of sociological research. But there was much more to Dummer than that.

> In particular, she was responsible not just for commissioning W.I. Thomas to undertake the work for *The Unadjusted Girl* (1923), but also for contributing data and ideas to it. She published an article on the Soviet Five-Year Plan in the *American Journal of Sociology*...and organized several symposia which led to publications quite well known at the time....Her activity in the American Sociological Association included involvement in the foundation of the Section on the Family; she organized, chaired and gave reports at its sessions, and was its secretary in 1925-26. She was a member of the executive committee of the ASA from 1927-30. All this (and much more) was done without her ever holding a paid job, although she was practically and intellectually as important to the discipline as many who held a job title. (Platt 1996: 261)

To learn of the existence of people such as Dummer is salutary. However, it is quite another thing to imagine, as Lynn McDonald (1997: 114)[21] does, that our estimate of the so-called male founders of sociology and politics would be decisively different if we had read their work in the light of "women founders." According to her, "there would be less esteem for Herbert Spencer if Beatrice Webb's devastating critique were heeded; the empirical, practical, and more applied sides of Max Weber would be more prominent if Marianne Weber's interpretation of her husband's work had not been rejected by later scholars; Thomas Hobbes...would have a lower place in the political pantheon if [Catharine] Macaulay's critique were accepted." These claims not only recycle the discursive founders myth, now suitably re-gendered, and make exemplary what never happened. They are also puzzling in their own right. Herbert Spencer has not been held in high esteem by most sociologists for at least sixty years. Marianne Weber's "interpretation of her husband's work"—her biography—has received enthusiastic praise since its publication in 1926, though this has not deterred scholars from noting its anachronistic moments (Scaff 1998: 62). In addition, it is unclear what "empirical, practical and more applied sides" of Weber are being alluded to; he had so many, and Weber scholarship has been steadily unravelling them since his death. Thomas Hobbes is a giant in political theory because of an extraordinary powerful and disturbing account of man as a dangerous animal requiring the Leviathan to keep him in civilized bounds. It is hard to see how any single critique of Hobbes, however brilliant—and there have been several since Locke—will deflate his importance because that importance does not rest on his account's being true but precisely on its being controversial.

Conclusion

This chapter has offered an extended definition of the "founder" concept; critically reviewed Foucault's and Wolin's theories of founding; and, by so doing, concluded that while discourse cannot be founded, the founder idea is nonetheless a fertile resource for arguments and activities seeking legitimation. The next chapter rounds off the discussion of founding by examining the nature of institutional innovation.

Notes

1. In fact, if anyone was the real creator of the AJS, it was William Rainey Harper, the University of Chicago's first President. It was Harper who, with the offer of a reallocated subsidy, challenged Small to convert the ailing *University Extension World* into what became the *American Journal of Sociology*. Small's colleagues in that undertaking were, among others, Charles Henderson and W.I. Thomas. For details, see Abbott 1999: 83-5.
2. Abbott (1999: 85) points out that for Small, sociology meant "neither an academic discipline nor a subject matter. For him 'sociology' denoted a loose claim that formal theories of society were relevant to practical social reform...Sociology was simply the academic avatar of the ramshackle empire of social welfare." Contrast that attitude to the work of Durkheim, Weber and Simmel, each of whom developed systematic sociological frameworks and general sociological theories.
3. From the Greek *aporia*, literally "roadlessness": see Pagels 1979: 144; Norris 1991: 49-50.
4. Marianne Weber1988 [1926]: 424; Roth, in Bendix and Roth1971: 40.
5. Frisby, 1981: 26, 34-35; Frisby 1984: 25; personal communication with the author.
6. Foucault 1969: 89-90 = 1984a: 114. The English translation—an abbreviated version of the French original—tends generally to render both *instaurateur* and *fondateur* as "founder." Foucault himself uses *fondateur* less frequently than its partner term.
7. Lepenies 1988 [1985]: 41-2.
8. Alexander 1983a, 1983b, 1982a, but especially Alexander 1982b: 299-370.
9. See Bottomore, 1981; yet also, Bottomore 1993: 632, where Weber and Durkheim, with Marx, are now described as "the founders of the modern subject" of sociology.
10. Therborn 1976: 224, emphasis omitted.
11. Therborn 1976: 116-7, 137, 150, 156, 275, 280, 297, 317, 399, 417.
12. Bendix, in Bendix and Roth 1971: 297.
13. Foucault 1970 [1966], and 1972 [1969].
14. Wolin 1981: 402, emphasis in the original; cf. Muñoz 1989.
15. Also Camic 1989: 47, 54, 72-3, 74-6, 89, 91.
16. On this issue, see Wallace 1991a, 1991b, and the criticisms of Alexander1991, and Levine 1991.

17.   Quoted in Pagels 1989 [1979]: 147; the emphasis is hers.
18.   Weber 1948b [1906]: 305-6.
19.   A similar observation about founding narratives is made by Palonen 1999: 7, and Butler 1992 [1991]: 7.
20.   More generally, it is important to point out that, in America, "sociology" was, until 1925, a term for an aggregate of people who sought to apply "formalized knowledge to social problems. Sociologists proper were a group of perhaps one hundred to two hundred people who were attempting to precipitate, out of this diverse interest in social life and problems, a specialized academic discourse" (Abbott 1999: 81). Far more numerous, as Abbott observes, were those involved as nascent social workers, and proponents of the social gospel, in the charity organization movement. Still, it was the smaller, more disciplinary oriented, group that was instrumental in establishing a departmental beachhead for sociology in American liberal arts university programs.
21.   See also McDonald 1998.

3

Founders of Institutions

Introduction

In this chapter, I examine the second dimension of founding: the founding of institutions. My case study is the *Année sociologique*, sometimes simply referred to as "the Durkheim school."[1] We shall see that what is routinely called "founding" is actually a series of actions rather than a single one, and is a process dependent upon a range of material and social conditions. My intention is not to deny the reality of human creativity and of pioneering effort, but only to suggest that we learn to think about these qualities in a sociological way. By so doing, we can grasp the many-sided character of innovation. The chapter concludes with an attempt to explain why, aside from its legitimating function, the concept of founding has the enduring attraction it does, why, in other words, the idea of founding—both discursive and institutional—appears to be so rhetorically attractive.

The Social Context of Innovation

The argument that innovation is a collaborative and collective enterprise has been a truism in the sociology of knowledge and science for more than fifty years. Yet such a perspective has had little impact until fairly recently on how sociology's "founders" are perceived. Perhaps this is because any tradition is resistant to historicizing its charismatic figures, for once this occurs their work, or at least its success and prominence, is effectively demythologized by appearing contingent and precarious—that is, human, all too human.

An early contribution was Alvin Gouldner's (1980) attempt to delineate a double context of authorship. The first relates to the "shadow group" in front of whom the author rehearses pertinent ideas, often in informal settings and in a casual way. People within this group consist of friends, lovers, spouses, close students, assistants, comrades, trusted colleagues, disciples, and other intimates or associates in front of whom ideas can be presented and whose feedback helps shape these ideas as they emerge and develop; the Webers' Sunday salon in Heidelberg might figure as an example. In Marx's case, the "shadow group" consisted of many of his correspondents, members of his family, and Helene Demuth—whose description as a housekeeper in some Marx biographies disguises the very intimate relationship, both intellectual and emotional, she had with Marx and, in a somewhat different way, later with Engels.

Engels himself, Gouldner points out, is too salient a figure to be thought of as part of Marx's "shadow group"; his collegial relationship with Marx, though not necessarily his importance to Marx, was well known during his lifetime. Engels offered not just counsel and material help, as fundamental as these were to Marx's ability to write. He was also part of a team effort, with its own division of labor and pattern of intellectual and moral reciprocity. Thus the name "Marx" on a manuscript is really very much an abridgement and a symbol of the Marx-Engels partnership[2]—as well as of all those other sources (e.g., scholarly traditions, rules of composition, etc) on which they jointly drew.[3] The totality of these conditions constitute the "intellectual work group" and sources which the author's name makes concrete. Hence one can say that "all theory work is not simply influenced by but is always the product of some collective" undertaking (Gouldner1980: 277). Still,

> If the "author" is in part the conventional emblem of the creativity of the collectivity, he is, nonetheless, not the inanimate puppet of the work group, and his voice is not simply the group's ventriloquistic projection. The work group is stratified and has leadership. For the author recruits and discharges members from his work group, taking initiatives of his own, and responding actively and selectively to their criticisms and suggestions. While individual authorship is always to some extent fictional and conventional, it may also in part express the real initiatives of an individual theorist whose collaboration with a work group helps produce those theoretical performances traditionally termed authorship (and scholarship). (Gouldner 1980: 279)

In addition, Gouldner observes that this leadership is typically exercised not through force but through hegemony—in other words, members of the work group willingly subordinate themselves to the leading figure because they accept his authority, though this is a form of compliance that does not preclude disagreements and tensions between the leader and collaborators, and among members of the group as a whole.

Gouldner's analysis of the creative process has many applications and resonances. Thus Dennis Brown (1990a: 17) shows how the circle that comprised T.S. Eliot, James Joyce, Wyndham Lewis, and Ezra Pound, effectively "operated as a work group, especially between 1914 and 1924"—initially under the leadership of Pound. From Brown's account a picture emerges of a group whose internal dynamics were a vital stimulus to their quest to "create a new literature for a new age." And Brown (1990a: 17) goes on to make the wider point:

> It does not seem that this is an atypical instance. The more one thinks about it the more important types of groupwork appear in the development of intellectual history. Plato's philosophy, influential for Aristotle as well as for neo-Platonists (and hence triply significant in Western history), was itself developed out of the group-dynamics among Socrates' disciples. St Paul's formulation of "justification by faith" surely developed out of his struggle with neo-Judaism, represented by such "co-workers" as St Peter and St James.[4]

Similarly, the Royal Society and the Manhattan Project provide notable examples of the dramatic impact that social context can have on the process of innovation. Pellicani (1986-7: 122), drawing on Ortega y Gasset, has sought to distinguish "invention"—the result of personal genius—from "innovation," envisaged as "the process through which the former becomes a use, a widespread way of thought". Yet if Gouldner and Brown[5] are right, invention itself is inescapably a collective endeavour, though one in which genius is often an irreducible component.

Creativity, Reputation and Intellectual Networks

"One cannot help wondering why there does not exist today a sociology of philosophy"—Leo Strauss 1952: 7

By far the most sophisticated attempt to explain creativity and innovation from a sociological perspective is Randall Collins's remarkable *The Sociology of Philosophies: A Global Theory of Intellectual Change* (1998). Prodigiously learned and controlled, the book is a formidable achievement, in both size and scope, straddling more than two and a half thousand years of history. No sociologist who is seriously concerned with understanding intellectual life can afford to ignore it. For Collins, "sociological analysis is our x-ray vision, allowing us to see the combinations which make up the specific configurations of history as the arrangement of universal ingredients" (381).[6] What "combination" in intellectual history, then, does Collins see?

The Sociology of Philosophies is a comparative study of "the principles that determine intellectual networks" (xviii) in general, and of philosophy ("the oldest and most central intellectual community": 789) in particular. These principles are universal in scope; Collins examines their manifestation in both Asian and Western civilizations: Ancient Chinese, Indian and Japanese intellectual communities are juxtaposed to those of Ancient Greece, the Islamic and Judaic worlds, medieval Christendom and modern Europe.[7] And it is these intellectual networks, or "coalitions of the mind," that are the collective loci and agents of change. Understand how they work and you have the key to explaining such otherwise mysterious attributes as creativity, reputation, influence, greatness, and even thought itself. In turn, the animating force of intellectual life is conflict: conflicts of positions ("the history of philosophy is the history not so much of problems solved as of the discovery of exploitable lines of opposition": 6), conflicts over intellectual resources, and conflicts for control of the "attention space" within which ideas are articulated and become socially persuasive.

Like the wider society to which they belong, intellectuals depend on interaction rituals to imbue their symbols and codes with sacred status. Equally, intellectual interaction rituals are rooted in the local situation of everyday life. This is where all explanations of social activity must start. For the

> macro-level of society should be conceived not as a vertical layer above the micro, as if it were in a different place, but as the unfurling of the scroll of micro-situations. Micro-situations are embedded in macro-patterns, which are just the ways that situations are linked to one another; causality—agency, if you like—flows inwards as well as outward. What happens here and now depends on what has happened there and then. We can understand macro-patterns, without reifying them as if they were self-subsisting objects, by seeing the macro as the dynamics of networks, the meshing of chains of local encounters that I call *interaction ritual chains*. (21)

The specificity of intellectual interaction chains lies in the peculiar sacred object contested—textually based claims to "truth" (struggled over even by those who scoff at the concept)—and in the cultural capital, emotional energy and opportunity structure that typify these chains. During times of intellectual stasis, cultural capital is monopolized by those museum keepers of the mind who gaze transfixed on the great achievements of the past. In a period of innovation, cultural capital is accumulated to the degree that its owners can stake out a territory fertile of new puzzles and conundrums; the more taxing the problems, the more likely that they will attract interest, and that the person behind their enunciation will become emblematic of a durable school or tradition. Mere solutions, by contrast, will impede long-term recognition for the simple reason that they offer no challenges for contemporaries to chew on and successors to ponder. Great doctrines must have great imperfections it they are to continue to generate excitement (32). And those who are most theoretically creative in developing these doctrines will typically be individuals with exceptional amounts of drive, stamina, and independence of mind. Such attributes of emotional energy (EE) are in part reducible to individual character formation, but they also ebb and flow in intensity in so far as their bearers are at the center of the cultural fray. Those who possess EE are likely to cultivate more of it in a value-added spiral as their careers progress. However, EE may also dissipate when a thinker overreaches himself or when the stakes of the debate in which he has been focally implicated change. Moreover, while cultural capital and EE typically feed off and reinforce each other, they are best thought of as independent variables. Hence someone with a great deal of EE, but without the cultural capital to exploit it, is likely to become frustrated and disappointed; as a result, native ambition and enthusiasm may simply drain away.

Similarly, neither CC nor EE will flourish without an appropriate opportunity structure to nurture them. As with all social structures, the opportunity structure of intellectual networks is internally stratified, but it is so in a distinctive way. The key media of intellectual exchange are lectures, texts, debates and discussions. Intellectual activity is oriented toward the appropriation of past accomplishments, the setting of new agendas, and the projection of "influence" into the future. "It is a deep-seated part of intellectual structures that questions are asked, debates take place; polemics and denunciations also often occur, in a circulating structure that resembles equally the *kula* ring, the potlatch, and the vendetta. Even when intellectuals sit silently in the audience, they are conscious of their own part as members of this ongoing community. Their own ideas have been formed by the chain from the past; the situation before them is merely one more link in that formation" (28). Yet intellectuals, directly or vicariously, face a key constraint: the boundedness of their audience's "attention space." Collins's investigations indicate that the "structure of intellectual life is governed by a principle: the number of active schools of thought which reproduce themselves for more than one or two generations in an argumentative community is in the order of three to six" (81). Conflict dynamics define both the lower and upper limits of this "law of the small numbers." The lower limit is set because arguments by definition require opposition, and the existence of polarized groups typically invites the intervention of a third mediating position (or one that summons a plague on both houses). The upper limit is a function of how much conflict can actually be assimilated within a particular cultural arena; empirically, it is very rare that more than six groups can coexist. Overcrowding of the attention space rarely lasts for long. Creativity is intensified when groups put a premium on their distinctiveness—polemical "fractionalizers" like Heraclitus and Parmenides, Mo Ti and Chuang Tzu, are archetypes of this tendency—or when (as "synthesizers" in the style of Aristotle or Chu Hsi) they absorb their rivals through accommodation or amalgamation (133). (Syncretism, a milder form of synthesis, is also an oft-exercised historical possibility.) In any event, the most creative periods are those when the friction between rival positions is most intense: "Strong positions subdivide, weak positions combine: this is the inner dynamic of intellectual politics" (116).

How are ideas affected by exogenous factors? Collins's "materialist constructivism" (537-8) offers a causal but not, he avers, an economically or politically reductive analysis of intellectual dynamics. Certainly, culture is not autonomous (nothing is), truth "arises in social networks" (877) as distinct from disembodied human minds, and ideas emerge from group activity rather than monadic individuals. For all that, intellectual networks have their own distinctive properties—rivalry for the attention space etc.—that cannot be read off economic and political macro-structures. These structures "do not explain much about abstract ideas, because such ideas exist only where there is a network of intellectuals focused on their own arguments . . . It is the inner structure of these intellectual networks which shapes ideas" (2; also 82). Where external causality is operative, we should think of it proceeding in two steps. "First, political and economic changes bring ascendancy or decline of the material institutions which support intellectuals; religions, monasteries, schools, publishing markets rise and fall with these external forces. [Second], Intellectuals then readjust to fill the space available to them under the law of small numbers. Expanding positions split into rival philosophies because they have more slots in the attention space. On the losing side, weakening schools amalgamate into defensive alliances, even among former enemies" (380).

Collins's sociological criterion of intellectual "greatness" and "creativity" turns on the extent to which a thinker's ideas are carried across generations. Philosophers are ranked "according to how many pages of discussion they receive in various histories of philosophy" (58; 951 n. 5). Employing such composite ratings, it is sobering to note that the number of major philosophers of world history is only around 135; about 500 if we include the minor figures; approximately 2,700 if we add still less elevated persons to the network, and this of a global population between 600 B.C.E. and 1900 C.E. of some 23 billion people (76). For the law of small numbers is unrelenting. "The attention space is limited; once a few arguments have partitioned the crowds, attention is withdrawn from those who would start yet another knot of argument. Much of the pathos of intellectual life is in the timing of when one advances one's own argument" (38).[8] In philosophy, a period of innovation is most evident when abstraction and reflexivity are proceeding apace (787ff), though even the eclipse of a position can produce a last star burst of imaginative endeavor, as the third century C.E. "pagan" doctrine of Plotinus brilliantly attests (125-6). Eras of stagnation, by contrast, are characterized by three kinds of condition: depletion of cultural capital through social amnesia (e.g., the loss of Stoic logic in late antiquity); dominance of the classics, not as a mode of reinterpretation and creative misreading, but as dogmatic oracular pronouncement (e.g., the three hundred year reign of Ch'eng-Chu Neo-Confucianism); technical refinement—as in the late medieval logic-chopping and analytical acrobatics that followed the magisterial achievements of Thomas Aquinas and Duns Scotus (502-4). Stagnation is caused by many factors. Among them are upheavals in, and especially dispersals of, the intellectual community due to war or other crises which, by reducing its critical mass, denude cultural capital and emotional energy; the imposition of a rigid state orthodoxy centered on a single school (507); and the scholasticism that accompanies academic routinization and formalization, slackening the tensile strength of opposing positions (520-1).

Can any thought-form escape the law of the small numbers? From ancient times till the 1500s C.E., the activity of "natural science" had operated on broadly the same lines as philosophy, prone to periods of fractionalizing and synthesizing. "Science" and "Philosophy" were not clearly delineated areas. By the same token, research in anatomy, astronomy, medicine, and so on followed the law of the small numbers. But traditional natural science was transformed by the inauguration around 1600 of Western "rapid-discovery science." While rivalry, controversy and the law of the small numbers continue as before during the ongoing phase of "science-in-the-making," the rapidity of the research front makes it argumentatively and professionally unproductive to remain stymied in old quarrels. Scientists are eager to remain on the cutting edge of research, rather than to remain defenders of antiquated positions. As a result, a consensus coagulates around past achievements, and the real battles are saved for the drive to create reputations in new areas or sub-fields (534-5). Rapid-discovery science arose not because of the discovery of organized empiricism, for traditional science, throughout the world, also produced observational knowledge. Instead it emerged from a transfiguration of the older philosophical networks into ones that put a premium on crossbreeding laboratory technologies (these develop their own machine-to-machine lineages); and on methods that maximize the repeatability and standardization of scientific experiments, and that increasingly rely on mathematical modes of calculation and notation. (Logarithms are a product of the early 1600s; the = sign, used for the first time in Recorde's book on commercial arithmetic, is of the mid-1500s [540, 994, n. 13]).

Such is the basic synchronic logic of Collins's theory of global intellectual networks. The narrative is far harder to summarize because of the wealth of comparative material that Collins draws on, but two important theoretical points are worth emphasizing. The first is Collins's contention that decimal units of time, such as the decade or the century, are of no real historical value in understanding the flow of intellectual networks. Far more appropriate is a span of roughly thirty-three years, a generation, both because this is the natural period of authorial productivity and of the cohort to which it typically belongs. On such a reckoning, we are living only five generations after Hegel and ten after Descartes. Second, Collins explains that it is of the very essence of intellectual networks to be centered on "chains of personal contacts, passing emotional energy and cultural capital from generation to generation" (379; 68-74). These chains are both vertical and horizontal. The vertical ones comprise those of masters and pupils in which the latter emulate the symbol of intellectual heroism while, through "creative departures," challenging "the content of the master's ideas" (36).[9] Horizontal chains are those between contemporaries and peers. Face to face contact with leaders, competitors and opponents charge up emotional energy and stimulate creativity (68-74). And even when actual co-presence is lacking, intellectuals are people who recurrently enact "interaction rituals in their head" (52), conjuring up figures they admire, audiences they wish to impress, opponents they detest and seek to rebut. Equally, the "most notable philosophers are not organizational isolates but members of chains of teachers and students who are themselves known philosophers and/or of circles of significant contemporary intellectuals" (65). Posthumous fame is very rarely awarded to the sequestered thinker. Those who had to wait for two or more generations to achieve greatness were almost invariably part of a major intellectual school during their own life time, were copious publishers, and were capable of being transported by the network of which they were a nodal point. Creativity—the transformation, recombination or negation of ideas—is prompted by rivalry but mediated through various "circles," the number of which turns out to be remarkably small: some fifteen of them dominated European philosophical thought in the eleven generations from 1600 to 1965. Typically, such circles are characterized by an organizational leader who arranges the group's material resources, and an intellectual leader who is the legendary symbol of its doctrine: respectively, for example, Mersenne and Descartes, Fichte and Kant, Bauer and Marx. Occasionally, however, organizational and intellectual roles are combined in one person, as they were in the case of Goethe, and, one might add, in that of Durkheim.

Like all major works in historical sociology, *The Sociology of Philosophies* invites us not only to consider the past but also to reflect on our current predicaments. True, the chronology breaks off at around 1935; Collins insists that the significance of our own generation, and the one directly before it, is something that can only be judged from the perspective of future alignments and appropriations (620). Still, he is painfully aware of the particular "structural crunches" that modern intellectuals face in a period of cultural production that generates annually more than a million publications in the natural sciences, and about a tenth of that in both the social sciences and humanities (521). We moderns are not only drowning in texts; we are also witnessing an explosion of credentials. "As each level of education becomes saturated and deflated in value, superordinate markets of cultural credentials are added beyond them" in a self-reinforcing spiral (522). Worse, modern intellectual culture appears, on Collins's account, to be suffering three kinds of stagnation simultaneously: a loss of nerve and ability to build on past achievements; a growth in curator scholarship "in which *doing* intellectual history becomes superior to *creating* it"; and a consolidation of insider vocabularies and esoterica, impenetrable to all but the cognoscenti. More important than bemoaning this situation is, however, to understand it. And this in turn requires us to consider the exponential expansion of higher education since the early 1950s, the credential inflation that has been its result, and the enormous strain put on the attention space by the proliferation of schools and sub-schools. Chronic disagreement is not the source of our ills; on the contrary, creativity demands it. Our current malaise is rather due to the absence of "a nexus where disagreements are held in tension, the limited attention space which historically has been the generator of creative fame" (522; 782-784). The erosion of "a center of intersecting conflicts," of "the small circle of circles at which our arguments can be focused" explains the prevailing mood of postmodern ironism, "an ideology of cultural producers in a highly pyramided market structure, where nothing in sight seems to touch solid earth" (522).

Despite this, Collins believes that philosophy has a robust future. Its subject matter, after all, is "deep troubles" (878) and these will remain as long as human beings inhabit the earth. What about the future of sociology? Collins says very little about it; his topic is philosophy, not the discipline that provides him with his toolkit. But broadly he understands sociology to occupy an intermediate region between philosophy on the one hand and rapid-discovery science on the other. Sociology shares a concern with "deep troubles" while devoting itself to "investigations of empirical topics . . . on moderate levels of abstraction" (878). Similarly, sociology resembles philosophy in its organization, fractionalized under the law of small numbers, yet, like the natural sciences, capable of some cumulation (876). Collins himself is by temperament a synthesizer rather than a fractionalizer, confident in sociology's ability to advance, irritated by doomsayers, and committed to the symbiotic interplay of theory and empirical research. As he puts it elsewhere, "For all its conflicts and divisions (and often because of them) [sociology] has been a creative community. We are part of that community right now. Theory is our collective memory, the brain center in which we store the basic elements of what we have learned and the strategies we have available to carry us into the future" (Collins 1988: 8).

Moreover, the "collective memory" we possess is not arbitrary. It is sociologically meaningless, Collins argues, to invoke "a reservoir of 'deserving' but unknown thinkers in the shadows throughout history, just as 'creative' as the ones whose names were trumpeted, as if there was some trans-historical realm in which their achievement is measured. Ideas are creative because they hold the interest of other people" (58). Nor can one say that the relative absence of women in philosophy has produced a monolithic male standpoint, for in fact there is no such thing. "The basic structure of intellectual life is division among rival viewpoints. Maleness does not predict who will be an idealist or a materialist, rationalist or mystic, or any of the other lines of demarcation which have existed within philosophy" (77). Conversely, we might add, femaleness does not determine under the more favorable opportunity structure of today who will be a standpoint theorist, a post-structuralist, a critical realist; or, in political terms, who will be a libertarian, a supporter of censorship, an enthusiast of the "therapeutic state" or a vilifier of it. (Equally, being a female philosopher fails automatically to translate into a feminist perspective, as the careers of Hannah Arendt and Judith Shklar indicate.)

For Collins, greatness and reputation are essentially descriptions of the success of a person's ideas in being culturally transmitted across generations, and this is by no means a smooth process (89). Spinoza's elevation to the philosophical pantheon came a hundred years after his death, while Aristotle had to wait until medieval Islam and Christendom to emerge from the shadows of Platonism to become a "master in his own right" (61, 59). All other measures of greatness based upon appeals to "intrinsic worth" are usually circular, betraying only the preferences of the appellants. Are the ideas of a putative "great" still being widely discussed and appropriated two generations after his or her death? That is the acid test and even then it is no guarantee that the person's reputation will survive indefinitely. Consider the case of sociology. Today, most social scientists would accept that the classic sociologists of the first two decades of the twentieth century are Durkheim, Weber, and Simmel but this appraisal was by no means evident until the 1950s (61). Nor is it necessarily secure because intellectual life is characterized by "goal displacement" as questions previously deemed seminal are shunted to the periphery by new alignments of problems, positions and schools. The result is war between conservatives and radicals who condemn each other for myopia or worse. Ironically, neither side ever gets what it wants, for goal-displacement is in principle unending; hence, "subsequent intellectual history is always a matter of rude surprises" (789). It follows that, strictly speaking, there are no real founders of discourse establishing first principles from which subsequent thought emanates (525, 532). On the contrary, thought is always *in media res*: always, that is, in the middle of things like "time, space, discourse, other people" (860). Though canons are subject to change, self-conscious attempts to enlarge them for egalitarian reasons are likely to languish longer term since contemporaries do not decide canonicity.

A sociological interpretation is only as powerful and illuminating as the categories it employs; Collins's derive from a combination of theories of conflict, of interaction ritual, of exchange, and of social networks. This explains both the strengths and the weaknesses of his argument. The strengths—rigor, range, the ability to derive sociological patterns from an enormous and varied literature, absence of polemic—should be apparent in the description I have provided. But the argument becomes somewhat forced when it attempts to explain the social psychology of intellectual life. This is not a trivial point because Collins's explicit concern "is not with 'non-intellectual motives' but to show what intellectual motives are" (7). As he remarks, "there is a social construction of eminence which does justice to the inner processes of intellectual life" (xviii). Perhaps there is, but Collins has failed adequately to provide it.

Intellectuals, in Collins's portrait, are essentially attention seekers faced with the constraints of a finite attention space. Their goal is to prevail in the battle of ideas,[10] and this requires access to and, if possible, domination over intellectual networks. The "feeling of exultation" accompanying bursts of emotional energy arises from the sensation of "ideas that feel successful" (52), and it is "the ideas which have mattered historically" (3) that Collins wishes to explain: "My sociological criterion for creativity is the distance across generations that ideas are transmitted" (58). Furthermore, "creativity comes to those individuals optimally positioned to take advantage" of "market opportunities" (51).

What has happened to the "inner processes of intellectual life" now that creativity has been subsumed under attention seeking, the emulation of heroes, and the brute realities of success and reputation (69)? Surely, no one will sensibly deny that these motives and features are a major part of the intellectual habitus. Yet something vital is missing in Collins's expressed claim "to show what intellectual motives are." Did Boris Pasternak write *Dr. Zhivago* to seek access to the "attention space"? Obviously, there would have been no point in his writing the book without the hope that it would one day be read. But why did Pasternak hope for that eventuality? Because he wanted, in a highly unfavorable and dangerous environment, to defend individuality against those who sought so violently to destroy it.

Or, keeping to a Soviet theme, consider the poetry of Osip Mandelstam. Mandelstam was not simply a poet who wrote "between the lines"[11] but who composed, as it were, "off the lines," hiding or destroying work, and committing it to memory, because it was simply too dangerous to publicize it openly. Vying for the "attention space" was the equivalent of signing his own death warrant. His great Stalin lampoon[12] was recited often to like-minded friends, one of whom betrayed him. As his widow recounted, the Stalin and other critical poems were written not principally to be effective, let alone to prevail in the battle of ideas —a poem was no match for the Cheka (secret police)—but to protest against evil. Mandelstam believed that "poetry must take a civic stance," even in a country of subjects not citizens (Shentalinsky 1995: 170).

Since it might be said that Pasternak's and Mandelstam's work are too recent for us to accord them eminence and greatness in sociological terms, let us take a different case. Did Machiavelli write *The Discourses*, an act of sociological creativity par excellence, to become famous? Perhaps he did, but one could just as well say that he wrote it because of his desperation at the plight of Renaissance Italy, an emotion that is consistent with his wishing his ideas to become known and celebrated. (People have *many simultaneous* motives for writing.) The individuals and works could easily be multiplied. To survive as part of the conversation of humanity, a text must reach the attention space; all writers want recognition and this is one of their chief motives for writing. But the motives of intellectuals are complex, and success, or the expectation of it, is not their only sine qua non. Nor is the source of intellectual "exultation" reducible to "ideas that feel successful." The sense that ideas are apposite or beautiful is also a powerful source of exhilaration.

Consider the reflections of one writer who is well into the second generation of his eminence, and who understood clearly the need of intellectuals to attract attention. In "Why I Write," George Orwell observed,

> Looking back through the last page or two, I see that I have made it appear as though my motives in writing were wholly public-spirited. I don't want to leave that as the final impression. All writers are vain, selfish, and lazy, and at the very bottom of their motives there lies a mystery. Writing a book is a horrible, exhausting struggle, like a long bout of some painful illness. One would never undertake such a thing if one were not driven on by some demon whom one can neither resist nor understand. For all one knows that demon is simply the same instinct that makes a baby squall for attention. And yet it is also true that one can write nothing readable unless one constantly struggles to efface one's own personality. (In *The Decline of the English Murder*, Penguin: 1965, pp. 180-8)

Now contrast this with what Collins has to say about mental processes. Creativity, he says, "is forced by changes in the structure of intellectual communities, like fluid squeezed through the spaces as blocs shift their alignment" (131). "A writing style is the precipitate of a particular kind of emotional energy flow. A crabbed and involuted style, full of false starts and shaky transitions, come form a weak and hesitant EE flow" (948, n. 6). "Camus's split with Sartre came ostensibly on political grounds" but the break "between the two stars of the existentialist movement was fated by the dynamics of creative energy in a necessarily enclosed space" (781-2). The term "ostensibly" here is revealing because Camus's political commitments are simply brushed aside as marginal to his break with

Sartre. "Politics provided the occasion of the break; but the break itself, and its intellectual form, came from the oppositional structure of creativity" (782). But on what grounds can one conclude that the "oppositional structure of creativity" rather than Camus's enormously complicated feelings about Algeria, or his dislike of Sartrean apologias for the Soviet Union, or his anti-Communism, provoked "the break itself"? One might just as well argue that these political passions were more important for Camus than securing his place in the existential boxing ring.

I do not want to caricature the argument of *The Sociology of Philosophies*. Collins is right to be wary of appeals to intrinsic worth; and he is probably correct to reserve judgments of "greatness" to works that stand the test of time. But he cannot have it both ways. Either he really is interested in intellectual motives, in which case their range and complexity must be taken into account as contributory factors to what they help create: the work. Or, motives are to be circumscribed to those consistent with success and fame in which case creativity has simply been elided with reputation.

The Shadow Group Revisited

We can learn more about the creative process if we look outside formal intellectual networks to other kinds of "coalitions of the mind." One area that has attracted increasing interest of late is the domestic and private life of the "founders" —an area more likely to straddle than fit comfortably into the "shadow group" and "intellectual work group" categories to which Gouldner referred above. Here the importance of women—the founders' dependence on them and desire to impress, challenge and reach accommodation with them—is a subject that repays investigation (see Gane, 1993; Appignanesi and Forrester 1992; Overbye,1990). The ability of Durkheim to lead a relatively settled life and concentrate on scholarship was in no small part due to the labour of his wife, Louise Dreyfus, and the managed household her efforts ensured (Lukes 1973: 99). More than this, Mme. Durkheim provided valuable administrative support in helping her husband edit contributions to the *Année sociologique* (Clark 1968b: 85, 87). Scientific innovation could also flow from the ecstasy and torments of erotic passion. Thus Auguste Comte's idolization of Clotilde de Vaux seems to have been a factor in the transition from the rationalistic *Cours de philosophie positive* (last volume,

1842) to the more obviously religious *Système de politique positive* (the first volume was published in 1851), a transition that marked the "rehabilitation of feeling," the "enhancement of the value of literature" (Lepenies 1988 [1985]: 29), and a revaluation of women's position in society. Yet, as Mary Pickering argues, the impact of Vaux on Comte's intellectual development can easily be exaggerated. There were in fact two main women in Comte's adult life, Vaux and Comte's first wife Caroline Massin whom he described as a prostitute in the Secret Addition to his Last Will and Testament. The truth of the accusation is very doubtful. More likely it was an act motivated by Comte's paranoia and a polarized view of women in which the complex, independent-minded, and shrewd Massin simply did not fit. In any event, Massin was a great help to Comte, especially during his bouts of insanity, all the while resisting his attempts to control her. According to Mary Pickering, Vaux's chief significance was to enable Comte "to fill in the details of his image of the ideal woman"; Vaux "helped to confirm the direction toward religion that he was already beginning to take". In contrast,

> Massin, who was not as well educated as Vaux, appeared, nevertheless, more devoted to Comte's scientific doctrine. She was able to persuade Emile Littré to take a large role in eliminating the religious accretions of positivism and making the original scientific strand triumphant. She also induced him to write a biography of Comte, which highlighted his "first" career and denigrated Vaux and the Religion of Humanity. Finally, she helped establish the positivist periodical, the *Revue de la Philosophie positive*. Thus although Clotilde de Vaux is the woman most usually associated with Auguste Comte, her influence was really inadvertent. In the end, it was Massin who did the most to solidify Comte's reputation. Yet positivists neglected her role in the hope of ensuring that the new scientific discourse of positivism remained firmly masculinist. (Pickering, 1997: 40-41)

A notable example of a woman's co-authorship of a classic text is Harriet Taylor's contribution to "On Liberty" (1859)—a contribution whose importance has often been contested (e.g., McCloskey 1971: 11-13), but which John Stuart Mill emphatically affirmed both in his autobiography (Mill 1961 [1873]: 143) and in the dedication to the essay itself (Mill 1961: 254; see also Gane, 1993: 128-140). Usually, though, collaboration has been more "indirect." Marianne Weber is now widely acknowledged to have been a key figure of Max's "work group"—both as intellectual soul mate and as a tireless advocate of Weber's greatness;[13] just as Weber's mother, Helene, was a crucial moral presence for them both. Moreover, in the "shadows" of Weber's private life, other intimates of great intelligence and sensuality—especially Else von Richthofen and Mina Tobler—played a significant role as lovers and confidantes, each offering occasion and stimuli for the provocation, rehearsal, defense, and amendment of ideas that would later become exclusively associated with the texts of one man.[14]

Still, for the paradigm case of the social and collaborative nature of scientific innovation in sociology, we can do no better than return to Durkheim: an archetype of discursive, institutional and deliberative (see pp. 5-12 above) founding whose career, and its context, have been scrupulously documented by historians of the discipline.

Institutional and Deliberative Founding: Durkheim and the *Année Sociologique*

At least three types of condition—conceptual, cultural-political, and organizational—were responsible for the prominence Durkheim's sociology attained in France. The conceptual conditions comprise not just the traditions of thought that Durkheim assimilated and adapted—positivism, social liberalism, French neo-Kantianism, organicism, solidarism, the moral realism of the German *Kathedersozialisten* ("Socialists of the Chair"), among others—but also the historical emergence of ideas that predated, but were pivotal to, his own understanding of sociology. The two most important ideas that Durkheim harvested were "society" and "religion." Simplifying the much more refined discussion of John Bossy (1982) and Raymond Williams (1976: 243-247), we can say that the sense in which Durkheim employed these terms—to denote a real, unitary, essential object or thing from which all particularities can be abstracted—is of fairly recent origin: more precisely, it surfaces in a recognisably modern form during the late seventeenth century. Before that time, in both France and England, "society" and "religion" had typically referred, on the one hand, to an emotion or an active state of mind entertained by two or more individuals (e.g., a "reverent, worshipful or pious attitude to God," a feeling of "companionship" and "fellowship," Bossy [1982: 4, 8]) and, on the other, to an encompassing set of concrete human relationships to which people were symbolically and collectively attached (*a* religion, *the* Christian religion, *French* society, societies). By 1750, a transformed notion of society and religion was in the process of being firmly established, drawing on previous usage, but incorporating a novel element: the idea of society and religion as "a kind of sublimated essence" (Bossy, 1982: 8), transcending or distilling all particular instances of it. It was this sense of society and religion, highly abstract and essentialist, which Durkheim required to define and delineate his sociology of "social facts" and to make intelligible his view of "the elementary forms" of religious experience. Neither concept was his invention; both of them were necessary for his project.

Durkheim's "founding" of sociology also required cultural-political conditions which were met by the social and political dynamics of the Third Republic (1870-1940) itself. No one has ever doubted Durkheim's crusading zeal for the new science of sociology. Steven Lukes, in a session of the American Sociological Association in August 1974, even went so far as to endorse (his thesis supervisor) Evans-Pritchard's view of Durkheim as "quite mad": "He was a monomaniac...[with] a manical concern to relate everything to Society" (Lukes 1979: 131). As "propagandist and researcher in one" (Lepenies 1988 [1985]: 63), Durkheim was as much the indefatigable promoter of his own vision of sociology as he was the supreme practitioner of it. But the crystallization of Durkheimian sociology in France required more than intellectual brilliance and organizational skill. It needed political backing, and this it received from influential French Republican circles during the late 1880s and the 1890s.

Supporters of republicanism were met by a double challenge. First, they faced increasing working-class discontent. A solution to the "social question"—the euphemism for the problem of how to contain proletarian insurgency—gained especial importance during this era. Syndicalism was at its zenith, and accelerated capital accumulation in the last two decades of the century found its counterpoint in increased strike activity: from "an average of around 100 strikes per year in the 1880s, the norm rose to over 1000 per year in the 1900s" (Magraw 1983: 303). Second, the danger of an authoritarian backlash appeared all too possible, dramatized by the Boulanger crisis of 1888-9, and the Dreyfus affair (1894-9). Republicanism needed all the friends it could get, and Durkheim's social philosophy was a valued resource in the state's ideological struggle against its enemies (Weisz 1983: 90-119). "Durkheim's criticism of egoism..., his appeal to the importance of communal values, and his advocacy of a revived form of corporatism" (Bellamy 1992: 63) mirrored the desire of fellow republicans, and the regime itself, to reconcile the market with social justice, individualism with social order, secular attitudes with moral commitment.

And there were other, related, cultural-political conditions on which the foundation of Durkheimian sociology depended. Of capital importance was the trauma of France's defeat in the Franco-Prussian war, and the demoralization that followed the bloody suppression of the Paris Commune. These lacerations to the body politic only stiffened the resolve of France's rulers to modernize the Republic. The educational system was to be one of the engines of this process. Durkheim's nationalism and his firm commitment to the Republic commended him to the Ministry of Public Instruction, one of whose departments was responsible for higher education. So, too, did his celebration of scientific rationalism, and associated antipathy to the traditions and institutions that hampered the quest for free scientific enquiry and secular knowledge. Foremost among these impediments was the legacy of Catholicism, the target of the 1882 Primary Education Law "providing free, obligatory, non-religious education for all children from ages six to thirteen":

> Substitutes had to be found for 50,000 Catholic nuns and brothers; moreover, opening new schools as well as expanding the student body created strong demands for additional new teachers. The debasing of Catholic orthodoxy—the prior foundation for moral and civic training in the schools—created a void that educational administrators actively sought to fill during the 1880s and 90s. Several accounts report that Louis Liard, Director of Higher Education, had a conversation with Durkheim in 1886 in which he learned of Durkheim's ardent Republicanism and desire to formulate a secular morality based on science. The next year a fellowship from the Ministry of Education financed Durkheim's study with Wilhelm Wundt at Leipzig and at the University of Berlin. Then, after Durkheim published an impressive series of articles on the new scientific morality in Germany, Liard appointed him, in 1887, to teach social science and pedagogy at the University of Bordeaux. (Clark 1968a: 44; also 54-5, 58-9)

If conceptual and political-cultural conditions were imperative for the founding of Durkheimian sociology, so too were more narrowly organizational ones. Chief among these were first, the character of French higher education; and, second, the team of gifted scholars that Durkheim assembled to advance sociology as a scientific discipline.

Between 1870 and 1914, successive French administrations sought to overhaul the higher education system. Budget allocations to this sector increased roughly threefold between the installation of the

Third Republic and 1895 (Clark 1968a: 58), and the university system was concomitantly reorganized. From its beginnings, Durkheimian sociology aimed to be an academic, university-based, professional enterprise; the new situation favored its institutionalization in at least two ways. In the first place, the highly centralized nature of university funding gave enormous powers of patronage to the Ministry of Public Instruction, and as we have seen, that Ministry looked approvingly on Durkheim's political credentials. And second, Durkheim's appointment in 1887 as *chargé de cours* (a relatively junior position) of social science and pedagogy at the University of Bordeaux

> was in keeping with several aspects of the prevailing reforms in educational policy. This policy included a general attempt to widen the disciplinary range of courses given in the university, specifically in the arts and sciences faculties which were relatively free from the constraints of professional training (unlike the medical and law schools).... Descriptive geography, experimental psychology, and educational science were among the first disciplines that took advantage of such administrative promotion. Sociology merely followed suit. (Karady 1983: 75)

Durkheim and his collaborators were also in an enviable position to exploit, for purposes of intellectual legitimation, their own wealth of cultural capital: their academic background was typically impeccable. The majority of them held the *agrégation*[15] in philosophy, and "a substantial number were educated in the Ecole Normale Supérieure's liberal-arts section." Taken together, this academic profile amounted to "the most prestigious training the French university system could provide" (Karady 1983: 75). It also helped secure a commanding advantage over their rivals from other sociological camps. Conversely, competitors like the Le Playists were in a much weaker position, politically and academically. For so long as the Second Empire endured, Frédéric Le Play himself enjoyed considerable popularity in regime circles. His monographs on the family as the elemental stabilizing unit of social life, and his open support for Napoleon III, with whom he chalked-up an extensive correspondence, secured for his version of social science the necessary political imprimatur (Clark 1973: 105). But with the Empire's collapse, and the coming of the Republic, Le Playist conservatism and Catholicism were no longer in favor, and, for the most part, he and his associates and epigones were treated as marginal figures by the official higher educational culture. Moreover the Le Playists were mostly not "professional" sociologists; they frequently combined sociology with other vocations, and thus invited the anathema of amateurism or eclecticism (Clark 1968a: 54). Dilettantism was not a charge that could sensibly be levelled against René Worms, but his group suffered from a different liability: some of its most notable associates "were Russian emigres—e.g. Kovalevsky, Novicow, de Roberty—and thus excluded as foreigners."[16] Thus, contrasted to their sociological competitors, the Durkheimians were in a strong position, one made even stronger by the twin strategy they adopted of conspicuously ignoring the intellectual achievements of their rivals in France, while engaging seriously with relevant scholarship abroad. As Victor Karady (1983: 82) points out, this strategy conferred on the Durkheimians a double advantage: in by-passing or slighting the internal competition, "the Durkheimians deprecated their rivals' competence; while by acknowledging their counterparts abroad (especially of German *Sozialwissenschäftler* or Anglo-American social anthropologists) the Durkheimians elevated their own status by association with highbrow international companionship."

Yet the most celebrated aspect of the institutional and deliberative founding of Durkheimian sociology is the story of the *Année sociologique*. Established in 1896, and enjoying its halcyon days up until 1913, the *Année* was always more than the great flagship review journal of the Durkheimian school, devoted to an annual compendium and synthesis of the previous year's scientific scholarship insofar as it was pertinent to (the Durkheimian view of) sociology. It also operated as a research institute bringing together some of the most talented figures sociology has ever enlisted. Both as journal and as research laboratory, the *Année* had its precursors and models. During his trip to Germany in the academic year 1885-6, Durkheim had been excited to witness Wilhelm Wundt's Leipzig research institute in action, a testament to the possibilities afforded to scientific work by disciplined, coordinated inquiry (Lukes 1973: 292; cf. 90-1). And closer to home, *Années* had been a common form of publication in France since the foundation of the *Année philosophique* (in 1868). However, the prototype for Durkheim's journal was the *Année psychologique* that functioned, in the 1890s and beyond, as a review periodical and a research laboratory for physiological psychologists operating out of the Sorbonne (Besnard 1983b: 14-15).

Yet to say that Durkheim "founded" the *Année* is itself a linguistic abbreviation of a more complex and collective phenomenon. It seems likely that the idea of establishing the *Année* was suggested to Durkheim by Célestin Bouglé; in any event, the latter played a major role in its founding, a part that Durkheim himself was among the first to acknowledge (Besnard 1983b: 12). And in recruiting the team of scholars that would constitute the *Année*'s "research laboratory," *le maître* heavily depended on Henri Hubert, and most of all on Marcel Mauss, Durkheim's nephew. Mauss (1983: 140) actually described himself as "Durkheim's recruiting agent between 1895 and 1902." Mauss also reveals how closely nephew and uncle worked together. Not only did he actively participate in assembling the quantitative database of *Suicide* (1897), "classifying 26,000 suicides individually arranged on cards and distributed in 75 cases." Mauss also "worked on everything [Durkheim] wrote as he also did with me; often he even rewrote entire pages of my work....Generally, I took part in everything which he did which was not strictly criticism or archaeology" (Mauss 1983 140-1).

Nonetheless, once this research team was established, Durkheim exercised clear authority over it. His outstanding intellect, conceded even by his fiercest critics, formed the decisive component of his leadership. But for such leadership to be effective, he had to persuade, not bludgeon, command respect, not issue edicts and expect automatic compliance from a group of awed disciples. This was particularly evident at the inception of the *Année*, when Durkheim went to great efforts to reach accommodation with those people whom he respected, but who were resistant to key aspects of his vision of sociology (Besnard 1983b: 16-17). Both Bouglé and Paul Lapie, for instance, had grave misgivings about the way that Durkheim had formulated the relationship between sociology and psychology in *The Rules of Sociological Method* (1895); both were convinced of the centrality of psychology to the sociological enterprise. To reassure them, Durkheim was compelled to perform some deft intellectual gymnastics. Hence to Bouglé he wrote in December 1895: "I have never said that sociology shares nothing with psychology and I wholly accept your statement...that it is a psychology *but distinct from individual psychology*. I have never thought otherwise" (Durkheim, 1983a: 41, emphasis in the original). While to Lapie he offered the astonishing emollient: "I see in sociology nothing more than a *psychology, but a psychology sui generis*."[17] With greater consistency, Durkheim constantly protested his view of science as an essentially collective, collaborative endeavour. As he put it, "science, because it is objective, is an essentially impersonal affair and cannot progress except through collective labour" (quoted in Lukes 1973: 293). It was a judgment shared by his fellow *Année* researchers. For Mauss,

A good laboratory depends not only on the person in charge but also on the existence of reliable participants, i.e. new and old friends with a lot of ideas, extensive knowledge and working hypotheses and who, most importantly, are ready to share these with one another, to join in the work of the longer-standing members and to launch the works of the newcomers. We were such a team. (Mauss 1983: 140)

Teamwork, in its turn, required a division of labour; a horizontal distribution of tasks "was a central aspect of the *Année's* structure" (Clark 1968b: 85). Arranged around a six-fold rubric which encompassed General Sociology, Religious Sociology, Juridical and Moral Sociology, Criminal Sociology and Moral Statistics, Economic Sociology, Social Morphology (Clark, 1968b: 76; Lukes, 1973: 291), the specialization of academic labour was explicit and highly organized. François Simiand, for instance, concentrated on economic sociology, while Georges Davy, Paul Fauconnet among others comprised the legal specialists of the team. A "vertical" or hierarchical division of labour was rather less clearly delinated and is a subject of some ambiguity in the literature. Though Durkheim increasingly sought to centralize some functions in his own hands—he would distribute books for review, act as intermediary between the collaborators, "insist on impersonality" (Besnard1983b: 28)—the *Année* had no official office, and Durkheim did not, and could not, rule like a dictator. Moreover, even in respect of the horizontal division of labour, the concepts of "team" and "laboratory" must be used with some caution. Hence while there is evidence to suggest a significant degree of moral density among the collaborators, or, in other words, a union of purpose in affirming the basic "unity of all the social sciences" (Clarke 1968b: 78), the physical density of the "team" was weak. Most of Durkheim's collaborators did not know each other personally; thus the importance of both Durkheim and Mauss in coordinating their efforts. Instead of a strongly knit team, the *Année* was more akin to a network whose nodal-points centred on a few key individuals or "sociometric cliques" (Besnard 1983b: 26). Besnard's own sociogram, figure 3.1, helpfully illustrates the point.

Figure 3.1

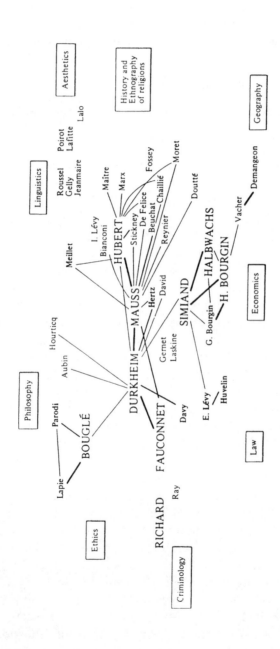

The *Année* sociologique team: realtions and specialisations

The lines between individuals symbolise realtions (of collaborators, teacher-pupil, friends, etc.) known to be of a certain importance. They vary in thickness according to the intensity of these relations. Likewise, the names of the *Année* collaborators are printed in varing sizes of type according to the size of their contribution.

Source: Besnard (1983a: 27)

In summary, then, we can see in the case of Durkheim and the *Année sociologique*, a clear case study of institutional and deliberative founding, one that developed and amplified a certain kind of sociological discourse. Yet even here the matter is not so simply stated: for what did Durkheim and the *Année* actually "found"? They certainly produced a series of stunning analyses of social life and together helped shape a brilliant version of the sociological enterprise. But did they, for instance, provide the foundations of subsequent French sociology? If founding suggests a baseline of continuity, they did not, and this is the case both in institutional and discursive senses. After the Great War, the Durkheim school staggered into decline. The war itself had decimated its ranks, depriving French sociology of some of its most remarkable talents; while, in 1917, the master himself died. Institutional and cultural factors also supervened. Even with the support of prominent Republican figures, and notwithstanding their great intellectual achievements, the Durkheimians' place in the French university system had always been precarious. To some degree this was a result of their own strategy: creating their version of sociology had entailed an open rejection of conventional academic classifications that could absorb and eliminate their distinctiveness. Constituting sociology as a legitimate intellectual endeavour meant carving out a space for it from territories that were already inhabited by other claimants. In the process,

> they violated several fundamental rules that implicitly governed intellectual production in the nineteenth-century university. They ignored the traditional separation of the humanities and law, failed to respect disciplinary specialization, refused to give preference to the culturally established subjects, attacked the ethnocentrism inherent in the choice of scholarly activities and in value-judgements, scorned the exclusiveness of individual (as against collective) work, and gave little credence to the thematic unity of teaching and research. (Karady 1983: 84)

But while this strategy was initially successful in building and promoting intellectual recognition for Durkheimian sociology, institutionally the discipline remained tied, and subordinated, to philosophy (Karady 1983: 77-78). Moreover, an attempt to revive the *Année* in 1927 failed; it was simply unable to draft the necessary talent to rekindle and inspire the enthusiasm of old. Much of its idealism now looked hopelessly *passé*. As Clark (1968b: 90) puts it,

> One basic factor was the shift in national concerns. Before the war the burning national issues—anti-clericalism, socialism, nationalism, the bases for a secular morality—and the questions they raised were, if not resolved, at least clarified and illuminated by

Durkheimian sociology. Not only was there less general interest in these questions after 1918, but to the disillusioned postwar students, the partial answers suggested by the Durkheimians appeared ridiculously optimistic and naïve.

In consequence, the personnel base of the *Année* steadily shrunk, and its ageing core members—Mauss, Halbwachs, Bouglé, Simiand, Fauconnet, Davy—came "to rely on more traditional and bureaucratic modes of domination—through curricula and examination control" (Clark 1968b: 91). To little avail. For the most part, the "generation of the 1930s" (Clark 1973: 229) was guided by theoretical orientations (Marxism, German neo-Kantianism, German phenomenology) alien to the Durkheim school. Raymond Aron, Georges Gurvitch, Marcel Griaule, Georges Friedmann, Jean Stoetzel were sociologists who had little sympathy for Durkheimianism, indeed often opposed its legacy. In social anthropology, aspects of Durkheim—mediated through Marcel Mauss—survived in the work of such writers as Louis Dumont, and in a highly heterodox articulation, Claude Lévi-Strauss. In social history, the *Annales* emphasis on *mentalités* drew on both the Marxian concept of "superstructure" and Durkheim's "collective representations" (Gordon 1993: 201).[18] By the time of the 1950s, however, institutional and cultural changes had attenuated the Durkheimian legacy to such an extent that one of the foremost historians of the Durkheimian school can state that the new sociological research proceeded "according to largely exogenous models and under scholars who paid little more than lip service to their Durkheimian forebears."[19] If archaeological and architectural metaphors have any value at all in this context, it might be to suggest that today French sociology is a terrain supporting many different buildings, including ones that have been standing empty, or at least under-occupied, for some time.

The Founder Idea: A Conjectural Genealogy

There is one last substantial task to accomplish in this discussion of founders, and with its execution we can draw together some threads linking this chapter to the one that preceded it. So far I have offered a critique of the notion that discourse can be founded, and shown, too, that even in the case of institutions the founding metaphor is infelicitous. Most importantly, its individualistic connotations underplay the collaborative nature of innovation. However, what I have failed to explain is *why* the very notion of founding is so closely tied to the idea of individual agency, and why—apart from the legitimating function it enables—the idea of founding has the resonance it does. I have also said nothing of substance about a particular kind of agency that is constantly invoked in the founding idea: founding as paternity. Yet, as we shall, see the expression "Founding Fathers" —an admixture of architectonic and biological metaphors—is anything but fortuitous.

"Founder" is what one might call a performative, or verbally derived, noun: it comes from the verb to found. Inescapably, then, founding suggests an action or a set of actions (usually intentionally) done by an agent.[20] Common to depictions of both discursive and institutional founding is the idea that founding is an "act" of some kind. Wolin, we saw above, presents founding as a "thought-deed" whose "informing intention"[21] harbours an ambition of megalomaniac proportions: the desire to restructure the entire landscape of political thinking and practice. Founding is thus a special kind of "performance" (Wolin 1981: 404) such that "the founder's *action* prepares the *way* for *inquiry*."[22] Foucault, too, informs us that Marx and Freud "created a possibility for something other than their discourse, yet something belonging to what they founded" (Foucault 1984: 114 = 1969: 90). He also writes about "the act that founds" a science (1984 115 = 1969: 90). Similarly, Louis Althusser, an author best known for his opposition to humanism and subjectivism of all kinds, remarks: "If I were asked to sum up in a few words the essential *Thesis* which I wanted to defend in my philosophical essays, I would say: Marx founded a new science, the science of History. I would add: this scientific discovery is a theoretical and political event unprecedented in human history. And I would specify: this event is irreversible" (1976 [1974]: 151).

It is also evident that the performative quality of founding is reinforced by the expression "founding father," because, in Western and near Eastern culture, paternity has frequently been seen as an act of begetting; indeed as the primary act of begetting, with women depicted secondarily as the "field," enclosure or environment in which the "seed" of the begetter is nurtured. There are powerful theological associations here at work. In her discussion of the meaning of paternity, the anthropologist Carol Delaney points out that Judaism, Islam, and Christianity all invoke a "monogenetic" theory of procreation: a theory which suggests that the child issues from a single source—the seed of the man. In turn, this monogenesis complements the monotheism of these religions. For common to Genesis and the Koran is the dogma that "there is only one principle of creation manifested at the divine and human levels and only one God" (Delaney 1986: 502). Similarly, all three religions trace their line of descent to the one founder Abram (meaning "exalted father") or, as he later came to be called, Abraham, a name meaning "father of a host of nations" (Bloom and Rosenberg 1990: 5, 197-8). Modern genetics now accepts as uncontroversial the proposition that the ovum contains half the genetic material necessary for the constitution of the foetus; but the popularisation of this idea, Delaney claims, is no more than half a century old (Delaney 1986: 508).

Monogenetic theory is not, however, the exclusive preserve of the Western or near Eastern world religions. It is also a signal feature of Western political mythology (Pateman 1988: 77-115) in its depiction of the origins of states and constitutions. This is consistent with Carl Schmitt's (1985 [1922]: 36) argument that

> All significant concepts of the modern theory of the state are secularized theological concepts not only because of their historical development—in which they were transferred from theology to the theory of the state, whereby, for example, the omnipotent God became the omnipotent lawgiver—but also because of their systematic structure, the recognition of which is necessary for a sociological consideration of these concepts.

Schmitt's general thesis is exaggerated and controversial (see Blumenberg 1983: 89-102). But one does not have to subscribe to it entirely to acknowledge how entangled theological and political concepts are in Western culture, or to recognise how prevalent a version of monogenesis is in depictions of political (and as we shall see, theoretical) founding. A striking example of political monogenesis is Machiavelli's discussion of founders of states (1972 [1550]: 160-65). It is not just that Machiavelli is specific in crediting Moses, Lycurgus, Solon and others as actual founders of kingdoms and republics. More pertinent is his argument that "to found a state it is necessary to be alone" (Machiavelli 1972: 162). Thus, on Machiavelli's reading, Romulus—the putative founder of Rome—deserves no censure for having murdered his brother Remus, because

> seldom or never is any republic or kingdom organized well from the beginning, or totally made over, without respect for its old laws, except when organized by one man. Still more, it is necessary that one man alone gives the method and that from his mind proceed all such organization. Therefore a prudent organizer of a republic and one

whose intention is to advance not his own interests but the general good, not his own posterity but the common fatherland, ought to strive to have authority all to himself. (Machiavelli 1972: 161)

Romulus was just such a figure. He should be forgiven by history because he was violent "to restore," not "to destroy" authority; because, having restored, he limited his powers to command of the army and the right to convoke the Senate; and also because by vesting the Senate with real powers of its own, and thus sharing responsibility with its members, he left Rome with institutions capable of attracting enduring collective support and commitment.

Machiavelli offered monogenesis without employing religious imagery, though in another version of the "history" of Rome's origins—Virgil's *Aeneid*, the great poem which, politically speaking, was written to justify Augustus's assumption of power—both themes were woven tightly together (Harvey 1984 [1937]: 7.) They are resurrected in Hegel's philosophy of history. For while Hegel viewed "World-Historical Individuals" as people "whose vocation it was to be the agents of the World-Spirit" (Hegel, 1956 [1830-31]: 31), he also emphasised that only some individuals could perform this role, namely those whose practical political ambitions, insight and remarkable talents coincided, albeit unconsciously, with what was ripe for historical development. Moreover, a World-Historical Individual is characterised by a special kind of focus and passion: "He is devoted to the One Aim, regardless of all else" (Hegel 1956: 32). From this perspective, as Shlomo Avineri points out (1972: 230), states come into being not through social contract but through the action of heroic figures. According to Hegel,

All states have thus been established by the sublime power of great men: not through physical strength, since the many are stronger than [any] single person. But the great man has something in his traits which makes all others call him their master; they obey him against their own will...All gather around his banner: he is their God. Such was the way in which Theseus founded the state of Athens...[23]

The idea that the political founder must be a god of sorts was a fairly common one during the Enlightenment. It is prominent, for instance, in Rousseau's discussion of the Legislator (Rousseau, 1973 [1762] 194-6), the "father of nations." Rousseau had argued that the Legislator "being unable to appeal to either force or reason, must have recourse to an authority of a different order" if he were to persuade the multitude of the necessity for wise legislation and gain their consent. The authority that the Legislator claims is "divine intervention." By crediting "the gods with their own wisdom," Legislators could legitimate the laws of the state (Rousseau, 1973: 196). It was a conclusion given a particular twist by Robespierre in his search for a source of absolute, stable authority during the tumult of the French Revolution. Thus his invention of the cult of the "Supreme Being" to channel revolutionary fervour, and his appeal to an "Immortal Legislator" to provide the legitimacy for the "laws of the new body politic" (Arendt 1973 [1963]: 185). During the American Revolution, too, a similar language came to be employed, leading Hannah Arendt to remark on

> the paradoxical fact that it was precisely the revolutions, their crisis and their emergency, which drove the very "enlightened" men of the eighteenth century to plead for some religious sanction at the very moment when they were about to emancipate the secular realm fully from the influences of the churches and to separate politics and religion once and for all ...[T]he need for a divine principle, for some transcendent sanction in the political realm, as well as the curious fact that this need would be felt most strongly...when a new body politic had to be established, had been clearly anticipated by nearly all theoretical forerunners of the revolutions. (Arendt 1973: 185-6)

All of the above gives credence to Wolin's[24] contention that religious creation mythology "has served as the paradigm for one of the most important political myths of ancient and modern societies, the myth of founding or of an original political constitution that brings into being a distinct form of collective life."[25] Still, what has this excursion into political theory got to do with our interest in founders of sociology? My suggestion is that the expression "Founding Fathers" draws heavily on, and substantially reproduces, both the assumptions of monogenetic theory, and its masculine, theological, and political overtones. It extends the authority of the Founder-Father of the world, the *polis*, and the child to the realm of "secular" knowledge; the metaphors of father and founding in theology and political mythology have migrated to the sphere of sociology to become a key source of its collective memory.

Moreover, not only do we have a creation myth here. We also have a related myth of lineage: a series in which descent and succession can be linked to the Original Act. Indeed, the founding fathers of sociology resemble the Christian notion of the apostles—the designation given by Christian theologians to those who had witnessed the "risen" Jesus, or who were commissioned by Jesus himself to carry on his teachings (Küng 1968: 347). The status of apostleship is thus restricted to the first generation of Christians (or, perhaps, "proto-Christians") on which the church is founded (Greinacher 1991: 241-243); the church is "built upon the foundation of the apostles and prophets, Jesus Christ himself being the chief corner stone" (Paul, Ephesians 2:20).[26] This apostolic generation is unique, irreplaceable—and long dead. Nonetheless, its mission remains, since later generations of Christians "are dependent on the words, witness and ministry of the first 'apostolic' generation" (Küng 1968: 354). Accordingly, the apostles are seen by believers to be the original "bearers of tradition," and much Christian theology consists of appeals to the wisdom of these "fathers" (Congar 1967: 45).

Equally, the apparent relationship of sociologists to their founders appears to transpose to a secular register the idea of an apostolic succession, which has both "ecclesiastical" (that is, "institutional") and "doctrinal" (that is, "discursive") dimensions (Higginson 1984; also De Waal 1983). In the former case, the church itself, like a university one might say, functions as the vehicle through which the genetic material of authority is passed on: Yves Congar [1967: 242] tells us that the early Fathers "thought of the Church as a propagation starting from a single seed." In the latter, the teachings of Jesus are transmitted, via the apostles, to believers, providing a "unity of mission" and a source of doctrinal identification (MacDonald 1987: 53-54). And in both cases, the concern with lineage and legitimation is vital, as it is in Matthew 1:1-16 and Luke 3:23-38 which place Jesus in direct line to the throne of David, part of the scriptural requirements of being the Messiah (Bossman 1987; cf. Baigent, Leigh and Lincoln 1986: 39-46).

This can be no more than speculation about elective affinity and meaningful congruence, or about the tendency of models from one domain to shape others. It is notoriously easy to compare ideas; far more difficult to establish causal links between them. Still, this conjectural reconstruction suggests that the founders notion is one example of what Maurice Halbwachs (1992) called "collective memory." A collective memory is not history; it is a way of framing knowledge that invests it with a peculiar emotional saliency. As Peter Novick (2001:4-6, 278-279) remarks, collective memory simplifies the untidiness of history, has little sense of time and ambiguity, "reduces events to mythic archetypes." Such archetypes derive from "choices" not as—or not mainly as—calculated, considered decisions, but as selections from the past that help to define who we are. When such definitions are successful, they become part of the "instititutionalization of memory." Sociology, a struggling discipline from the beginning, beset by disciplinary antagonists who denied its right to exist, had reasons enough to cling to the founders idea and draw on a stock of broader cultural motifs that could be turned to its advantage. The search for founders became part of the search for identity, for symbols of the collective past, a past, as we have seen, and will see again, about which consensus can never be reached.[27]

Founders as collective memory helps explain that peculiar quality of deference that sociologists so often bring to their discussion of their founders, and that leads even the most empirically-minded of them to speak of those "revered" "founding fathers of sociology" who have "begotten a science" (Goldthorpe 1979: 16).[28] It is also consistent with the claim, first enunciated by Vico, that "all major verbal structures have descended historically from poetic and mythological ones" (Frye 1992 [1990]: xii; cf. 82). Or, moving closer to a disciplinary matrix, one might consider the remarks of Paul Bouissac on the development of modern semiotics:

> The migration of models from one domain to another in which they were not previously considered relevant seems far more apt to account for changes in the mapping of knowledge than the progressive and largely repetitive deepening of a philosophical tradition, even though the innovators tend usually to join *a posteriori* a tradition through terminological and conceptual adjustments. One can mention, for instance, Propp's reliance on botanical taxonomy for the reframing of an object of study which was already enmeshed in a scholarly tradition, or Lévi-Strauss's massive importation of models from structural linguistics (especially phonology) into the domain of cultural anthropology. (Bouissac, 1976: 381; also Bouissac, 1990a, 1990b, 1990c)

One should also note that the expression "founding fathers," which in its plurality appears to be in tension with monogenesis, is rendered compatible with it when theorists speak, as they often do, of a founding or classical "generation,"[29] "tradition" (Mills 1959: 22-4), or, of "a single, basically integrated, if fragmentary, theoretical movement" (Parsons, 1968 [1937]: x); or when they seek to link the founders' efforts to an overarching "logic," "deep structure," or "world view." For in these instances, the principle of monogenesis has simply become lodged, essentialized, in another collective actor or abstraction. In any case, the expression founding fathers has not stopped sociologists regularly adopting a serial view of founding in which one person assumes priority in the lineage; hence the disputes about who, exactly, the first real sociologist was. Predictably, this dispute is another example of aporia—of chronic undecidability, of a problem that permits no clear resolution—because there are no stable criteria to adjudicate among competing claims. Jennifer Lehmann (1991: 164) is thus plainly mistaken when she says that "Durkheim is universally recognized as the 'father' of sociology." On the contrary, everything turns on one's definition of what sociology is, and on what one considers fundamental to it. So for instance, while according to Therborn (1976: 156), Adam Ferguson is demonstrably part of sociology's "pre-history," for Macrae (1979 [1969]: 27), Ferguson "was the first real sociologist." Indeed,

> What is certain is that sociology began with Ferguson. He realized its essential nature and from this realization developed propositions new in kind and novel above all in their systematic inter-relationships. (Macrae 1979: 35; cf. Swingewood 1970; and Camic 1982)

Or one might consider Kenneth Thompson's defence of Comte as founder (1976: 3-8; cf. Simpson 1969: v) versus Gouldner's celebration—incongruent when we consider his previous critique of conventional views of authorship—of Saint-Simon "who was not only father of positivist sociology but of utopian socialism."[30] Durkheim, incidentally, offered support for both interpretations when he maintained that while Saint-Simon "was the first to have a really clear conception of what sociology had to be and its necessity, strictly speaking, he did not create a sociology" since he subordinated scientific abstraction to practical, immediate concerns.[31] This distinguished Saint-Simon from Comte, who was far more willing to invest effort in theoretical abstraction, confident that for a science to be effective it must first be sure of its general presuppositions. Comte's orientation helps explain why he was the "greatest" of the "founders of the new science" (Durkheim and Fauconnet 1982 [1903]: 176). Yet even this qualification fails to capture the mercurial complexity of Durkheim's views. As Lukes (1973: 278) points out, Durkheim's assessment of the origins of sociology changed markedly throughout his professional life:

> In 1886 (Durkheim) had written of sociology's always having existed in a "latent and diffuse" form and of the "simplistic" conceptions of Rousseau and the classical economists that the state is artificially conjoined to society, rather than emanating from it. Two years later, in his inaugural lecture, he summed up his account of the history of sociology by observing that the subject had been "born with the economists, established with Comte, consolidated with Spencer, delimited with Schäffle and led to specialize with the German economists and jurists." In 1892 he wrote that it was "Montesquieu who first laid down the fundamental principles of social science...."

And so on. Moreover, the attempt to establish a lineage for sociology, and particularly the attempt to locate the pre-eminent Founder or Founders of the discipline, is not only aporitic, dependent on shifting standpoints on what is considered constitutive of sociological enquiry. It is also frequently accompanied by metaphorical incongruity: the architechtonic and biological imagery, instead of illuminating the process of intellectual innovation, constantly serves to obscure it. This once led Merton (1968 [1957]: 2, n. 2) to observe that

> The nomination of Comte or Marx or St. Simon or many others for the status of *the* father of sociology is partly a matter of opinion and partly the result of an unexamined assumption about how new disciplines emerge and crystallize. It remains an opinion because there are no generally acknowledged criteria for having fathered a science; the unexamined assumption is that there is typically *one* father for each science, after the biological metaphor. In fact the history of science suggests that polygenesis is the rule.

Despite that caveat, Merton himself continued to use the expression "founding father/s" without any visible reluctance (e.g. 1968: 28, 30, 34, 35), and so have countless others since.

Conclusion

In this chapter, and the one that preceded it, I have sought to clarify the various meanings that the terms "founder" and "founding father" assume in sociological discussion. I began by distinguishing between founders of discourse and of institutions, and between founders who deliberately and self-consciously attempted to construct sociological institutions, and those who were appropriated by the discipline retrospectively. I went on to suggest that the most common usage of the term founder, to refer to a discursive icon, is implausible on a number of counts, particularly in conflating an author's work with the discourse around it. Readers were also cautioned against an enticing, but flawed, analogy between founders of states and founders of academic disciplines, though one can readily agree that the founder concept has a pronounced political dimension in as much as it lends itself to legitimizing an academic, or some other, project. Following an extended analysis of institutional "founding" focusing on the *Année sociologique*—designed to show the collective, collaborative and negotiated nature of the innovation process—I turned, finally, to explain why the founders concept itself is so apparently persuasive. Part of the answer lies in the linguistic notation of the term "founding" itself. As a performative, it implies that discourse can be established through, or endowed by, the action of a founding figure. But that response only begged a further question: why has that performative been so attractive a figure in the narrative of sociology? The answer to that puzzle, I suggested, is to be found in the myth of monogenesis (and of lineage), deeply rooted in Occidental culture, and whose influence has been deeply felt in religion, politics, and social science alike. These are the principal sources of sociology's collective memory of founding. Sociology, typically regarded as the social science of modernity *par excellence*, the child of Enlightenment secularism and empiricism, the great debunker of tradition, has been far more influenced by theological ideas and by myth than is often appreciated.

Notes

1. For example, by Lukes 1993.
2. A broadly similar point is made by Collins 1985: 56-62.
3. For a more refined analysis of the Marx-Engels authorial partnership, and its many dimensions, see Carver 1998: 164-179, and Carver 1983.
4. For a more extensive discussion, see Brown 1990b.
5. And Kuhn 1962: 52-65.
6. Elsewhere, Collins (1999: 1) quotes approvingly Durkheim's remark that history should be sociology's microscope. "Not that it should magnify the tiny, he meant, but that it should be the instrument by which structures are discovered invisible to the unaided eye."
7. Ingeniously turning the tables on those who would charge him with theoretical ethnocentrism, Collins elicits the central principles of intellectual networks from Asian civilizations first, and then applies them to the West. As he puts it, "Asian history shows us the basic ingredients of all world history": 379.
8. On the importance of being first in a field, see also 75, 627.
9. The statement is redolent of Collins's relationship to one of his own teachers, Talcott Parsons.
10. See also Schumpeter1967 [1954]: 815: "....we must never forget that genuine schools [of thought] are sociological realities. They have their structures—relations between leaders and followers—their flags, their battle cries, their moods, their all-too-human interests. Their antagonisms come within the general sociology of group antagonisms and of party warfare. Victory and conquest, defeat and loss of ground, are in themselves values for such schools and part of their very existence."
11. Leo Strauss (1952 [1941]: 24-5) once argued that persecution "gives rise to a particular technique of writing" aimed not at all readers but at a highly selective group of them who are especially "trustworthy and intelligent." The technique employed by the persecuted writer is to *compose*, as it were, "between the lines," appearing to support a position while actually deliberately undermining it. The audience of such writing consists of individuals thoughtful and giften enough to *read* between the lines and who, having done so, are tempted by the forbidden fruit of heterodoxy. Collins's theory can easily accommodate such a covert strategy

because it is always possible for someone to struggle for the attention space despite an unfavorable opportunity structure. But the case of artists under and against Stalin is different. There the astute reader could be a member of the secret police. The artist must try and *restrict* the attention space to trusted intimates, not open it up, remain furtive, not visible and public. Collins says hat "creativity comes to those individuals optimally positioned to take advantage" of "market opportunities" (51). But in the case of oppositional poets under Stalinism there was no "market opportunity" yet many of them remained creative just the same. Intellectual motives deriving from disgust, loathing, anger, honor, religious faith or secular principle were, in the case of Stalinism during the desperate 1930s, more salient than the hope of success. Recognition of these motives does not make a theory of creativity any less sociological because it is the society itself that provokes them. (To the objection that a writer who composed between the lines would be deterred by the secret policy or their equivalent, Strauss [25] lamely replied: "As a matter of fact, this literature would be impossible if the Socratic dictum that virtue is knowledge, and therefore that thoughtful men as such are trustworthy and not cruel, were entirely wrong.")

12. The Stalin poem, recited by Mandelstam to his interrogator, Shivarov, at the Lubyanka in May 1934 is worth quoting, among other reasons, for its depiction of the claustrophobic world in which intellectuals had to live.

> We live, not feeling the country beneath us,
> Our speech inaudible at ten paces,
>
> But where there are enough for half a conversation,
> The Kremlin mountaineer is sure to be mentioned.
>
> His thick fingers are fatty, like worms,
> But his words, like pound weights, are true.
>
> His cockroach moustache laughs,
> And the tops of his boots shine.
>
> Around him a rabble of thin-necked bosses,
> He plays with the obeisances of half-men.
>
> Who whistle, who mewl, who snivel,
> While he just yammers and prods.
>
> He forges his decrees like horseshoes—
> Some get hit in the groin, some in the forehead,
> some in the brows, some in the eyes.
>
> Whatever punishment he gives is just like a raspberry
> To the broad-chested Ossete.
>
> (Translated by Laurence Mintz)

13. Roth 1988: xvi; Winkman, 1980: 484-5; cf. Baumgarten 1964: 605.
14. Gilcher-Holtey 1990; Roth 1988; Schwentker 1987; Henrich 1987; Green 1974; Mitzman 1970. Obviously, common sense is required here. Marianne Weber, Mina Tobler and others did not write Weber's work, and could not have written it. To mention the contribution of these women to Weber's ideas is not to deflate his individuality or genius.
15. That is, they had been successful in the annual state competition to recruit teachers for positions in secondary education.
16. Clark 1968a: 54. For other impediments to their sociological advancement, see Clark 1973: 157-159.

17. Lapie's report to Bouglé, 24 March 1897, excerpted in Besnard 1983a: 63, underlined in the original text,

18. "The tension between Durkheimian sociology and the human geography of Vidal de la Blache goes back so far that it might be considered part of the structure of *Annales*. The Durkheimian tradition encouraged generalization and comparison, while the Vidalian approach concentrated on what was unique to a particular region. The founders [of *Annales*] tried to combine the two approaches but their emphasis was different. Bloch was closer to Durkheim, Febvre…to Vidal. In the middle phase of the movement it was Vidal who prevailed, as the regional monographs published in the 1960s and 1970s attest. Braudel did not neglect either comparison or sociology, but he too was closer to Vidal than to Durkheim" (Burke 1990: 109-110).

19. Karady 1983: 88; also, Karady 1981: 42, in an article with the revealing title: "The Prehistory of Present-Day French Sociology" [1917-1957].

    Durkheim is, of course, still often invoked in France though more often as a symbol than as a sociologist whose work is to be actively extended and built upon. A farcical instance is the controversy that accompanied the granting of a Ph.D in sociology to Elizabeth Teissier (a renowned French astrologist whose thesis advisor was Michel Maffesoli). In the ensuing literary furore, Dr. Teissier's supporters claimed that she had fallen victim to what Maffesoli called the "Durkheim current:" French rationalism and quantitative social science. Weber, we are informed, was more interested than Durkheim in the irrational, non-logical, and emotional aspects of human experience, a contrast that will astonish anyone who has read *The Elementary Forms of the Religious Life*. I am drawing on a report in the *New York Times* Internet Edition June 2, 2001.

20. The following discussion largely restricts itself to the notion of "founder." The concepts of "foundations" and "foundationalism" raise other, somewhat related questions, but I do not tackle them here. For a sophisticated analysis of the "foundations" metaphor, and its many uses (and misuses), see Seery 1999.

21. Wolin 1970: 7-8, 4.

22. Wolin 1981: 403, emphasis in the original; cf. 418.

23. Cited in Avineri 1972: 230.

24. Wolin 1985: 230; also Arendt 1973: 125.

25. It may also lend some circumstantial support to feminist speculation that founding represents a masculine version of (political) birth. See Pitkin 1984: 54, on Machiavelli; and Pateman 1988: 244, on Sir Robert Filmer.

26. Paul's authorship of this epistle is, however, widely questioned by New Testament scholars. See, for instance, McKenzie1965: 240

27. Novick (2001:279) makes the point that "collective memory, when it is consequential, when it is worthy of the name is characteristically an arena of political contestation [we could say disciplinary contestation] in which competing narratives about central symbols in the collective past, and the collectivity's relationship to that past, are disputed and negotiated in the interest of redefining the collective present." The implication here is that a collective memory, rather than a simple banality, requires controversy to keep it alive. As I mentioned at the beginning of the last chapter, "Founders of sociology" is both a platitudinous skeleton (the ubiquitous text book account) *and* a bone of contention (wherever sociologists have wrestled with locating the origins of their discipline in relation to one person or tradition or, as today, have sought to make it a more "inclusive" endeavor).

28. In the United States, the collective memory of the Revolutionary "founding fathers" (Washington, Jefferson, Madison among others) adds a special emphasis to sociology's own founders that is attenuated in other national traditions.

29. For instance, the "generation of the 1890s": Stuart Hughes 1974 [1959]: 32; cf. 287.
30. Gouldner 1980 378; cf. Gouldner 1959: viii-x.
31. Durkheim 1959 [1928]: 108.

4

The Utility, Rhetoric, and Interpretation of Classic Texts

Introduction

One feature above all others distinguishes the notion of classics from that of founders, and it is evident in casual speech. "Founders" invariably refers to *persons*—individuals who are deemed to be the elemental source of distinctive social theories, theoretical traditions, or even entire disciplines, religions or states. "Classics," on the other hand, directs our attention, first and foremost, to certain exemplary *texts*. It is true that that this is not always the case. Where the term "classic" is preceded by the definite article, as in the edited collection *The Future of the Sociological Classics* (Rhea: 1981), it is generally a clear signal that the Classics whose future is being pondered are sociology's great figures or "masters" (Rhea, 1981: xi). Similarly, it is not uncommon to read of "sociology's classical founders" (Alexander, 1983b: xvii). In these cases, person and text have been conflated and for an understandable reason: typically, a text will have a determinate author with a name and an identifiable biography.

Typically, but not always. We know little, for instance, about the people who actually composed, revised, and amended the five books of the Hebrew Bible which Jews call the Torah and which Christians, in the version of the Hebrew Bible they call the Old Testament, call the Pentateuch (from the Greek *pentateuchos*, meaning the "book of five scrolls"): Genesis, Exodus, Leviticus, Numbers, Deuteronomy. Lacking the names of the authors, schools or editors responsible for the formation of these texts, Biblical scholars have had to resort to abbreviations such as J or E or P or D to identify their constituent strands.[1] Equally, it is far from certain whether an indi-

79

vidual called "Homer" actually existed. Even if he did exist, the *Iliad* and the *Odyssey* could not have been his unique creation. Composed in a pre-scribal culture, these epics could survive only through recitation; and recitation over long periods of time itself depends not just on memory, but on a host of devices which combine and recombine themes integral or germane to the story.

So texts can be "classics," it appears, without entailing a demonstrable relationship to definite persons who can be posited as their source. And the term "classics" is even more heterogeneous than this. One of its inflections is the idea of venerability—for instance in regard to the classical age of Graeco-Roman antiquity and the great luminaries such as Plato and Aristotle, Cicero and Virgil, which that epoch produced. On the other hand, while an instant classic is a logical impossibility—historical perspective is required to distinguish the great from the sensational—the expression "modern classic" is not necessarily an oxymoron. For here classic can be understood to refer not to a book that has stood the test of time, but rather one by which a time or era is measured. A modern text is considered a "classic," then, (the hyperbole of publishers aside) in virtue of qualities that are seen by a literate and influential public as particularly important—qualities such as aesthetic daring, social significance, outstanding reflection on our current condition, prospects or past. Another connotation of classic is respect and deference—classics, the *Oxford English Dictionary* informs us, alluding to seventeenth-century usage, refers to products "of the first class, or the highest rank or importance." But then again the idea of the classic can also provoke rebellion and acrimony, as in the late eighteenth and early nineteenth century incendiary dispute between proponents of classicism and romanticism in the visual arts and in poetry. The hostility continues in our day with those versions of contemporary cultural criticism that speak derisively of the classics, or the "canon," as the defunct artefacts of DWM, the Dead White Males of Western culture—or, closer to home, perhaps the likes of D(urkheim), W(eber) and M(arx)?

"Classics," then, is a multi-dimensional term.[2] For that reason, it might appear a particularly troublesome one to unravel. Yet the discussion of the idea of a classic is graced by one advantage that was palpably absent in the analysis of founders: sociologists have themselves produced a substantial body of literature specifically devoted

to examining the nature of classicality. Broadly speaking, this literature falls into two parts. The first approach consists of the hundreds
of exegeses purporting to show what the classics actually said. This
is the stuff of the main textbooks on the classical authors, of varying
sophistication, originality and discursive purpose. The second approach, on which I concentrate below, represents the major trend in
current sociology's approach to classic texts. Here, though exegesis
remains important, the emphasis has shifted to determining, not just
what the classical texts say, but what they *are*, what they *do*, how
they are best to be *understood*, and how they came to be *recognized*
as worthy of classical status. More specifically, current discussion
focuses on a range of overlapping issues relating to:

1. the definition of sociological classicality;

2. the functions classics perform for the discipline of sociology;

3. the rhetorical and aesthetic properties that classic texts share;

4. the question of how they are best comprehended;[3]

5. the processes of reception through which certain works and authors acquire classical value.

This chapter focuses on (1) to (4) and defers the study of reception to the chapter that follows.

A Definition of Classic Texts

Most of the writers who have sought to determine the nature of
classic texts have proceeded from the perspective that such texts are
great and dynamic ones. It follows that most definitions of a sociological "classic" entail a set of stipulations that seek to establish, in
varying degrees of precision, in what this greatness consists. Let us
begin our inquiry by quoting, and then expanding upon, the trenchant definition of a classic proposed by Jeffrey Alexander (1989: 9):

> Classics are earlier works of human exploration which are given a privileged status vis-
> à-vis contemporary explorations in the same field. The concept of privileged status
> means that contemporary practitioners of the discipline in question believe that they can
> learn as much about their field through understanding this earlier work as they can from
> the work of their own contemporaries. To be accorded such a privileged status, more-
> over, implies that in the day-to-day work of the average practitioner, this deference is
> accorded without prior demonstration; it is accepted as a matter of course that, as a
> classic, this work establishes fundamental criteria in the particular field. It is because of

this privileged position that exegesis and reinterpretation of classics—within or without a historical context—become conspicuous currents in various disciplines, for what is perceived to be the "true meaning" of a classical work has broad repercussions.

Alexander goes on to argue that classics have a centrality in a discipline such as sociology because the sociological field is inherently discursive. That is, sociology proceeds primarily through argument and reasoning rather than through prediction or attempts at verification/falsification; and through argument and reasoning that are conducted at a greater level of generality and speculation than normally takes place in the natural sciences. This is not because sociology is intrinsically more metaphysical than the natural sciences. All sciences have an a priori basis, that is, they rest on theoretical commitments (definitions, categories, concepts, ways of seeing) and exemplary practices, that lend order to, and render coherent and intelligible, the facts of experience. Rather, it is because the natural sciences have typically been more successful than sociology in bracketing-out of sustained inquiry the nature of their presuppositions, so as to concentrate instead on "questions of operationalization and technique" (Alexander, 1989: 18). At root, this ability reflects the capacity of significant numbers of natural scientists to broadly agree, at least for sustained periods of time, about the presuppositions that inform their practice. This degree of accord is itself predicated in large measure on the nature of the empirical referents of the natural sciences—material objects and organisms that are in principle[4] indifferent to, and autonomous from, the human mind that appropriates them.

In sociology, on the other hand, the object of analysis and the means of analysis both involve some reference, at some point, to states of mind (of observer and observed); while description and evaluation are inter-dependent. Many sociological terms—anomie, alienation, fetishism, domination, rationalization—imply some normative assessment of what they are supposed to denote. Put somewhat differently, the practice of the social sciences is marked by enduring conceptual disagreements (cognitive, political, ethical) that characterize the wider society of which sociologists are part and which they are seeking to explain. Under these conditions, sociological attempts at quantification have limited purchase, often "disguising or promoting particular points of view" (Alexander 1989: 20). Sociology lacks the common, bridging language typically found in the natural sciences, for instance, the periodic table in chemistry, or zoological taxonomy. Its partial substitute can be found in the discursive stature, and pivotal place, of classic texts and their authors in the discipline as a whole. On Alexander's account, then, "the very conditions which make discourse so prominent also make the classics central" (Alexander 1989: 27).

In short, "classics" are those texts that have assumed an exalted position within sociology as sterling examples of sociological discourse and as vital points of reference for the discipline as a whole. Just why and how this is so is the subject of the next section, where I will be concerned with the classics' contribution to the field of sociology as it is practiced and thought about today.

Classics in Common? The Uses of Classical Theory and the Discipline of Sociology

To speak of the "discipline" of sociology is to recognize that over the course of a hundred or so years sociological perspectives have become increasingly embedded in academic organizations. Sociology today depends on, and is mediated by, a series of institutions— university departments, professional associations, journals—that jointly organize, and loosely officiate over, how its practices are to be conducted. Other indices that help us measure the degree to which a discursive activity has become academically institutionalised include the following: formal criteria governing the hiring, promotion, pay—in short, the career—of individuals credentially qualified to teach the intellectual activity in question; the existence of regular funding mechanisms and budgets to resource its specialised teaching and research practices; facilities that offer students the option to "major" in the subject, and pursue research in it at the graduate level; and arrangements that allow for the publication of information aimed at a dual audience of fellow professionals and the interested lay public (Shils 1982 [1970]: 279-284). So what uses do the classics have for the discipline of sociology so defined?

To begin with, a classic "reduces complexity. It is a symbol that condenses—'stands for'—a range of diverse general commitments" (Alexander 1989: 27). In turn, this *condensation* effect offers some standardization in an increasingly specialized and bewilderingly multiform discipline. It allows a sociologist the option to speak to his or her colleagues in a general way through familiar concepts

found in the classic texts (anomie, rationalization, charisma, superstructure, etc). It enables a sociologist through "ceremonial citation
... a conventional means of identifying membership within a particular field and simultaneously signalling at the onset of the article
the particular orientation and direction of the research" (Adatto and
Cole 1981: 149). And it also affords the useful expedient of being
able to argue for a set of "generalized commitments...without the
necessity for making the criteria for their adjudication explicit. Since
such criteria are very difficult to formulate, and virtually impossible
to gain agreement upon, this concretizing function of the classics is
very important." For instance,

> Rather than having to define equilibrium and the nature of systems, one can argue about
> Parsons...about whether his theory (whatever that may precisely be) can actually ex-
> plain conflict in the real world. (Alexander 1989: 28)

Second, classics are important because they embody the various
social logics that comprise the discipline's theoretical substructure.
Let us call this second function *logical mediation*. This refers to the
classics' capacity to represent "paradigmatic" (Sherman 1974),
"presuppositional" (Alexander 1982a) or logico-strategic (Johnson,
Dandeker, and Ashworth 1984) choices and theoretical dilemmas,
with which every social theory must engage in some form or another. Johnson, Dandeker, and Ashworth (1984: 12) put the matter
as follows,

> While it is true that sociological theorising is, at present characterised by its diversity,
> we will argue that an underlying order can, nevertheless, be detected; it has a *structure*.
> This structure is not the outcome of a consensus among sociologists about what the
> nature of social reality is; or about the ways in which our knowledge of the social is
> constituted. Rather, this underlying order derives from the fact that all sociologists have
> to pose certain fundamental questions, the answers to which are a precondition for any
> sociological investigation.

Most evidently, any social enquiry is pressed to answer the ontological question: What is the nature of social reality? and the epistemological question: How is social reality known? Answers to these
questions have generated four logical possibilities: the ontological
positions of materialism and idealism; and the epistemological positions of nominalism and realism. The importance of the classics lies
in their crystallization of logical strategies that are, in effect, permu-
tations of the possibilities mentioned above. A similar kind of logic-
based approach is found in Alexander's four-volume *Theoretical*

Logic in Sociology[5] where, for instance, Marx and Durkheim are depicted as the quintessential representatives of "sociological materialism" and "sociological idealism" respectively.

Johnson and colleagues' argument is not, we should note, that the classics can be exhaustively subsumed under any one theoretical strategy, but only that their work displays a "strategic *bias*" in favour of one set of presuppositions rather than another. Moreover, strategic resolutions are mobile and artful rather than monolithic; they are "the product of the field of tensions that operates across the axes" of the ontological and epistemological positions described above, such that

> Each of the strategies is then a dialogue, a mediative process which attempts to cope with the persistent sociological paradoxes that are generated by the alternative solutions: between fact and theory, freedom and determinism, structure and action, meaning and conditions, and so on...[T]he field of tensions and their associated dilemmas [are]...generated by the recognition that alternative strategies make valid claims which need to be taken into account, as well as the fact that each strategy is confronted by its own internal problems which undermine its capacity to construct a stable position in its own terms. (Johnson et al. 1984: 22-3)

Consider in this context Marx's "substantialism." Marx was a substantialist, according to Johnson and colleagues, inasmuch as he sought to demonstrate and enlarge on two presuppositional claims: the ontological "materialist" claim that social reality is a stratified and structured domain of relations between people and things chiefly characterized by the ways human beings produce their livelihood and exploit the labor power of others; and, the epistemological "realist" claim that this social reality can be objectively grasped in thought by revealing the hidden causal mechanisms that generate the events and experiences of the phenomenal world. The "tension" that emerges within this strategy concerns a problem of validation. How are we to know that that we have grasped something that is hidden from direct observation? Might not the posited causal mechanism be no more than a figment of the investigator's imagination? "Where the problem remains unresolved there is a tendency for the materialist view of reality to become increasingly subordinated to an idealist conception of knowledge; that is to say, the material world effectively exists only in our theories of it" (Johnson et al.: 118).[6]

To sum up: the use-value of classics lies in their provocative embodiment of strategies and creative tensions endemic to sociology more generally.

Third, classics offer *standards of excellence* or "touchstones" (Stinchcombe 1982: 2) for neophytes and established sociologists alike, models of exemplary practice.[7] These standards have less to do with any particular method or concept that the classics developed, than with their habit of their asking the "big questions" (Berger 1992: 12), their articulation of fundamental "problems" or "ideas" (Levine 1981: 64; Stinchcombe 1982: 3; Merton 1968 [1957, 1949]: 36), and "their singular and continuing contribution to the science of society'" in virtue of outstanding powers of empathy, description, and evaluation (Alexander 1989: 29-33). Classics, thus, potentially offer sociology a prophylactic against "parochialism, triviality, rationalism and ideology" (Berger, 1992: 16; also Levine, 1981: 63-64). For instance, the classic authors avoided excessive rationalism through understanding the difference between an empirical science like sociology which must of necessity be rationally oriented, and the empirical world sociology studies, whose agents are frequently guided by non-instrumentally rational motives and moral sentiments (Berger 1992: 17).

In addition, a figure such as Weber tried hard to distinguish the contrasting logics governing social science and solidarity politics. Where the former absorbs the latter, Weber argued, social research and enquiry is ancillary and subordinate to a political agenda that has already been decided in advance. Solidarity politics—incarnated in the role of the advocate—essentially adopts the role of propagandist. Difficult facts are played down to minimize splits within the constituency "represented," and to encourage public credibility. Sociological research, by contrast, is paradigmatically skeptical and interrogative. It is guided by the questions: Why do people do x and not y? What are the conditions under which their activity takes place, and with what likely or unintended consequences? It is not guided by the question: What should I do to promote this particular group's interests?

There is another sense, too, in which the "classic authors" and the sociological texts they produced provide a model for subsequent generations. For, and this is the fourth major use to which such work lends itself, classic texts provide a discipline with a *master heuristic*, or, in other words, with vital perspectives and methods that facilitate the actual social research process. At its most basic, classic texts provide "toolkits" (Coser: 1981) of concepts that may help orient social enquiry and enhance its application. Moreover, these texts are sufficiently rich as to reward numerous re-readings since "you can never exhaust their meaning and their significance for your work in a single reading. If you go back to them, you *always* find something new you did not understand before" (Parsons 1981: 189-90). Equally,

> part of what is communicated by the printed page changes as the result of an interaction between the dead author and the live reader. Just as the *Song of Songs* is different when it is read at age 17 and at age 70, so Weber's *Wirtschaft und Gesellschaft* or Durkheim's *Suicide* or Simmel's *Soziologie* differ when they are read at various times. For, just as new knowledge has a retroactive effect in helping us to recognize anticipations and adumbrations in earlier work, so changes in current sociological knowledge, problems and foci of attention enable us to find *new* ideas in a work we had read before. (Merton 1968: 271)

Fifth, classics are an important source of *authorial legitimation* (Adatto and Cole 1981: 149-51), useful "for purely strategic and instrumental reasons. It is in the immediate self-interest of every ambitious social scientist and every rising school to be legitimated vis-à-vis the classical founders. Even if no genuine concern for the classics exist, they still must be criticized, reread or rediscovered if the discipline's normative criteria for evaluation are to be challenged anew" (Alexander 1989: 31; cf. 38-44).

Finally, classics offer sociologists a sense of *historical continuity* with their past, a linkage to their "traditions," a way of locating their work within the broader stream of social theory. The classics also allow sociologists to view themselves as participants in a project larger than their immediate area of study. To place oneself within the tradition of "Marxism," for example, means not only to employ a version of historical materialism but also to become part of the ongoing political anti-capitalist project associated with Marx's writings. Even where allegiance to a particular project is not involved, the classics give the sociologist an anchor in the past, an assurance that he or she has a scholarly heritage from which to draw both ideas and inspiration.

Classic texts, then, play a number of functions for the discipline of sociology. But will they continue to do so? This is a harder question to answer unequivocally than it once was, and not just because of the growing dispute surrounding the utility and relevance, or lack of it, of the sociological "canon"; I shall examine aspects of this controversy in chapter 6. More immediately pertinent is the argument that changes in sociology's institutional structure have already produced "a discipline in name only, whose members have fewer common ancestors than they did twenty years ago, fewer common concepts, less to talk about and less language to talk about it with" (Becker and Rau 1992: 70). Becker and Rau are talking principally about sociology in the United States; but since the institutionalization of the discipline has nowhere else been more extensive, the U.S. experience may be[8] particularly instructive.

Recent decades, Becker and Rau argue, have witnessed a growth of specialisms quite different from the era of specialization that preceded them. During that latter era, roughly from the end of the Second World War to the late 1960s, a number of specialties emerged, such as demography, criminology, marriage and the family, and with them arose organizations whose aim was to promote scholarly interest in these endeavors and to encourage cross-disciplinary cooperation. Nonetheless, the majority of these specialties "were still closely tied intellectually to a core of sociological thinking. When sociologists wrote about art or science or religion or stratification, they referred to a common body of ancestral materials, the works of Durkheim, Max Weber, Robert E. Park, George Herbert Mead and (later) Karl Marx" (Becker and Rau, 1992: 69). Since then, in contrast, not only have sociological specialisms vigorously multiplied, they have also assumed an increasingly remote relationship to sociology. A "common disciplinary core" is thus becoming ever more a thing of the past, and the profession of being a sociologist is more likely now to be a mere flag of convenience than a valued vocational marker. Equally, "the organization of intellectual work now rewards inter-disciplinary rather than intra-disciplinary border crossing," so that sociologists tend "to invest their effort in work in disciplines with concerns that overlap theirs." In consequence, sociologists of science, for example, find more to talk about with historians and philosophers than they do with the bulk of other sociologists, just as sociologists of culture have more in common with literary critics and humanists, than they do, say, with sociologists of deviance or stratification.

On Becker and Rau's account, this growing organisational differentiation of sociology, and its accompanying theoretical fragmentation, means that "sociology" has become a label for what is in fact a largely dispersed body of activities. What gives sociology the modicum of coherence and unity it vestigially retains is not the presence of any overarching body of ideas to which its members subscribe, so much as the departmental obligations sociologists are minimally required to discharge: their "joint responsibility to provide an undergraduate program for majors, service courses for majors in other fields, and, in research training centers, a graduate program" (Becker and Rau 1992: 70-1). Accordingly, discussion about the "uses" of the classics today requires a great deal of caution, and for a simple reason: it may be referring to a mode of disciplinary formation that no longer exists or, at least, that exists only tenuously. To the degree that Rau and Becker's description is accurate, attempts at "theoretical synthesis" in sociology via the classic texts will be paralyzed, or deemed largely beside the point, as sociology continues to freeze into various sub-compartments. Redundant, too, will be invocations of the classic texts as touchstones of exemplary practice or as disciplinary markers. In short, if Becker and Rau are right, appeals to the classics' uses for sociology are more likely to become an elegy to cherished times and lost standards than a credible rallying point for disciplinary coherence.[9]

So far I have sketched some of the functions the classics are characteristically said to perform for the discipline of sociology. In the next section, I continue this description of what classics "do" by examining a slim, but growing, body of research concerned with the properties of classic discourse. This research envisages the classic text as a kind of rhetorical accomplishment. It asks: what are the linguistic, stylistic and aesthetic qualities of classic works that lend them their persuasive and unusual powers?

Rhetoric in the Classical Tradition

Of all the social sciences, sociology is particularly notorious for its use of repellent and redundant language. So to speak of sociology as a rhetorical or literary form, of a sociological "poetic," is immediately to invite hoots of derision from many quarters. Nonetheless, in recent years, a heightened interest has become discernible in the formal properties of sociological texts. This interest starts from the obvious point that sociology is, among other things, a textual activity. Sociological perspectives, methods, arguments, and facts are enshrined and encoded in books and articles. How is this writing "put together"? What properties does it possess, and what figurative strategies and techniques ("tropes") are employed by an author to convince readers of the force and validity of an argument?

No one explored questions of this sort more acutely than Friedrich Nietzsche, though his principal target was philosophy and theology rather than sociology (for his damning verdict on the latter, see Nietzsche, 1968a: [1889]: 91). His critique of Socratic dialectics sought to demonstrate that the dialectical method, far from avoiding rhetorical tropes, was itself an especially effective, if dissimulated, form of rhetoric, designed to cudgel and humiliate its opponents (the Sophists and their allies) into intellectual submission. The dialectical method's claim to Truth was a rhetorical trick, Nietzsche claimed, a linguistic fiction, as all claims to Truth are. A triumphant discourse is one that mobilizes its "army of metaphors, metonyms and anthropomorphisms" (Nietzsche, 1954 [1873]: 46-7) to best effect, and is able thereby to make its preferred and partisan ideas ("logic") attractive, edifying, obvious, *compelling*. So that in the words of a modern philosopher much influenced by Nietzsche's analysis, "It is pictures rather than propositions, metaphors rather than statements, which determine most of our philosophical convictions." Accordingly, in the absence of "the notion of the mind as mirror, the notion of knowledge as accuracy of representation would not have suggested itself." And without "this latter notion, the strategy common to Descartes and Kant—getting more accurate representations by inspecting, repairing, and polishing the mirror, so to speak—would not have made sense" (Rorty 1979: 12).

With the advent of postmodernism in sociology, Nietzsche's star is on the rise. Foucault's work, too, and that of deconstructionists like Derrida and de Man has also served to amplify his iconoclastic voice. Even so, the surge of interest in the structure of *sociological* texts has not for the most part been Nietzschean in character. Far more important have been the influence of ethnomethodology and speech-act theory. Both perspectives have prompted sociologists to view textuality as an "accomplishment," a rhetorical performance, governed by "rules" that are as amenable to scientific study as any other social activity is. Writers may be no more aware of the conventions and figures of speech they use to get their effects than readers are conscious of why a particular text, or set of texts, has convinced or moved them—or failed to do so.[10] To study this relationship between sociologists and their audience, and the art of persuasion and reception it involves, is to be concerned with what has come to be known as the "poetics of sociology."[11] The relevance of this kind of analysis to the classical tradition of any discipline is clear. Classical texts must perform some kind of work which sets them apart from the ordinary, or even the "interesting" (Davis 1971). Thus, in the case of the anthropological "classics," Clifford Geertz (1988:4) contends that

> The ability of anthropologists to get us to take what they say seriously has less to do with either a factual look or an air of conceptual elegance than it has with their capacity to convince us that what they say is a result of their having actually penetrated (or, if you prefer, been penetrated by) another form of life, of having, one way or another, truly "been there." And that, persuading us that this offstage miracle has occurred, is where the writing comes in.

Moreover, anthropological writers of the stature of Lévi-Strauss, Evans-Pritchard, Malinowski, and Ruth Benedict have not only been able, with supreme mastery, to convince their public that they have "been there" (among the Zande, the Melanesians, etc.), but also that "had we been there we should have seen what they saw, felt what they felt, concluded what they concluded." Equally, great anthropological writing must do this in a way that amounts to more than "mere" travel-writing or journalism; it must present its findings in a manner consistent with academic conventions: "It is Being Here, a scholar among scholars, that gets your anthropology read...published, reviewed, cited, taught" (Geertz 1988: 16, 130).

What, then, of classic sociological writing? The most ambitious attempt so far to decode it was offered by Murray S. Davis (1986)[12] whose level of analysis is a social theory considered as a whole, as distinct from any of the particular texts that compose it. The theories he considers are those of Marx, Durkheim, Weber, Simmel, and Freud. Davis argues that for a social theory to be deemed classic, its truth is less important than its ability to seduce. And since seduction is in good measure mediated by and performed through language, we need to pay special attention to the linguistic techniques that enable this allurement to proceed (and succeed). This is where rhetoric comes in, for

> Rhetoricians have observed that this persuasion occurs especially at certain places in the exposition called "commonplaces"...well-known (today: "clichéd") abstract distinctions where most people clearly prefer one alternative to the other (e.g. the good is preferable to the bad). The arguer tries to convince his audience that his position fits their preferred alternative....Commonplaces are forks in the road where the arguer uses various rhetorical techniques ("tropes") to *turn* his audience one way or the other....What this aspect of rhetoric can contribute to our new mode of investigating social theories is

not that most people prefer one alternative to another but that they have common concerns, common places in their cognitive charts where alternative conceptualizations are possible. (Davis 1986: 286)

What can fruitfully be explored, then, is how "each 'classic' social theorist 'turned' his audience at the same points in their mental maps, even though each turned them in different directions" (Davis 1986: 287). Davis then offers an account of just how this happens, suggesting that the "rhetorical programme" of Marx et al., spoke to a number of "primary" audience concerns in an essentially similar way. First, each of the classical social theorists pointed to the emergence of some "fundamental factor," that is, a unique social force or structure (capitalism, the division of labor, instrumental rationality, etc.) that was both the source of modern society's distinctiveness and the cause of its malaise. By so doing, they managed both sharply to clarify their audience's previously amorphous sense of living in new and disturbing times, and distil into one principal concept the "fundamental factor" responsible for the problem. Second, each of the classical theorists dramatized the uniqueness of this crisis-ridden modernity by contrasting it with "previous or other societies unaffected" by the root cause of today's travails (Davis 1986: 298).

The effectiveness of the classics' rhetorical program is predicated on its ability to grip the attention of the audience to which it is directed. The theory must therefore formulate a problem, and speak to a concern, that is of vital importance to the constituency concerned (see also Lemert 1993: 27-28). And one "would one would be hard pressed to come up with something more highly prized in Western society than the psychological integrity of the individual" (Davis 1986: 290). Hence, and this is the third feature of the classical program, each theory stages a confrontation between the relevant fundamental social factor on the one hand, and its dehumanizing impact on the individual on the other. So, in the case of Durkheim, the unsynchronized character of the modern division of labor undermines the essential need of human beings to live an ordered and morally bounded life by creating normative dislocation—anomie. Equally, and fourth, each "classical social theorist shows how their fundamental factor not only undermines the individual's integrity but also saps the society's vitality" (Davis, 1986: 290). Finally, the classical social theory must provide not simply a vivid and urgent description of the crisis and an explanation for it. The theory must also posit "an agency to challenge the fundamental factor or at least mitigate its harmful effects" (Davis 1986: 293). Thus, for Weber the "iron cage" of rationalization could only be countered by charismatic leaders, whose activity would, at least momentarily, flood the social world with unforeseen possibilities.

To the objection that the above program is a parody of what are in fact complex and ambiguous theories, Davis is in complete agreement. What he questions is the import of such an objection. While it may technically be true, it is phenomenologically and pragmatically naive. Davis reminds us that the audience of classical social theory consists of two basic categories of people: social theory specialists—devoted to the excavation of deeper layers of theory and to the illumination of esoterica—and sociologists whose main interests lie elsewhere: "generalists" working in mostly empirical areas of research. Increasingly, the knowledge of the specialists and the generalists diverges in regard to the classical tradition. While theory specialists see the generalists as being out of date or misinformed, the latter, with other things to do, largely vacate the discursive field. Further, the profusion of specialist interpretations of classical social theory is likely to be more confusing than enlightening for generalists. A typical response will be to stabilize a sense of the classics by recalling their "central" point: "Reducing each classical social theory to the effects of a fundamental factor, therefore, will facilitate the generalists' ability to grasp the essence of the theory by a single handle, an easily remembered central principle around which to derive and organize each of its major concepts" (Davis 1986: 295). Conversely, a theory that does not allow this simplification may well tantalize or intrigue the specialist but will usually be ignored by the generalist as obscurantist and redundant. For a social theory to be "classic," Davis maintains, it must appeal to, and make sense to, both audiences. Finally, it must also be sufficiently ambiguous to allow creative appropriations of it:

> Had each classical social theorist expounded his social theory as single-mindedly as I have tried to do, we might not regard him today as "classical." Ambiguity in social science is not the embarrassment Kuhn finds it in natural science—rather it is crucial to the social theorist's appeal. An ambiguous theory can appeal to different—even hostile—divisions of its audience, allowing each subgroup to interpret the theory in congenial, if mutually incompatible, ways. (Davis 1986: 295-6)

Is Davis's attempt to decode the rhetorical structure of the sociological classics *as a totality* plausible? Critics are likely to counter that the projects and styles of the authors he considers are simply too diverse for his kind of thematic paralleling to be convincing. Yet these critics are probably the very theory specialists whose response Davis has already anticipated. In any case he is surely right in principle to be concerned with the dynamics of audience reception, to which I return in the next chapter, as he is to be concerned with the textual strategies authors employ—and this involves figurative language, literary allusion, aesthetic sensibility, and rhetorical play—to persuade their readers.

It is not difficult to think of some more applications of the so-called poetics of sociology, for instance, the scintillating vampire and fetish motifs in Marx's *Capital* or the occult imagery ("spectre," "haunting," "holy alliance," "exorcise") in the opening paragraph of *The Communist Manifesto*.[13] Or consider Terrell Carver's observations on Marx's *Eighteenth Brumaire of Louis Bonaparte*. Encouraging us to find Marx's ideas "in the choice of words and imagery" he employed, Carver identifies six controlling tropes in the *Brumaire*: "hero/fool, original/caricature, masquerade/parody, downward slope/upward slope, progress/reversion, construction/destruction." Marx was also a master of irony, a technique he used to acidic effect in his *Brumaire* description of the French bourgeoisie's nemesis:

> Finally the high priests of the "religion of order" are kicked off their Pythian tripods, hauled from their beds in the dead of night, flung into prison vans, thrown into gaols or sent into exile; their temple is razed to the ground, their mouths are sealed, their pens broken, their laws torn to shreds in the name of religion, property, family, order. Bourgeois fanatics for order are shot on their balconies by mobs of drunken soldiers, their family gods are profaned, their houses are bombarded for amusement—in the name of property, family, religion and order. Finally the scum of bourgeois society forms the *holy phalanx of order* and the hero Crapulinski [Louis Bonaparte] seizes the [Palace of the] Tuileries as "*savior of society*."[14]

Durkheim's writing, too, was "both polemical and highly metaphorical" (Lukes 1973: 34), and the metaphors he employed were less a matter of cosmetic adornment than a means by which Durkheim sought to gain respectability for his arguments:

> In *The Division of Labour* it was the organic analogy which predominated; subsequently, he was increasingly attracted—far more than any of his interpreters have realized—by the language of "collective forces" and "social currents" and, in general, the analogy of thermodynamics and electricity. *Suicide* is full of such language... (Lukes 1973: 35)

Simmel's literary manner—essayistic, fluid, "impressionistic," seeking to capture nuance and the socially ethereal—was very different, as his contemporary Durkheim once disapprovingly noted (Durkheim 1979 [1900-01]: 328). Weber's writing was dissimilar again, though sharing both Simmel's and Durkheim's penchant for conceptual juxtapostion (see Parsons 1963: xxxix, n. 11; Jameson 1973). With Marx and Simmel, Weber had a great appreciation for literature, particularly the work of Goethe out of which he fashioned his great "daemon" motif.[15] Weber, it is true, was fully capable of composing prodigious quantities of indigestible prose. Yet his work was also full of arresting images—"the cold skeleton hands of rational orders" (Weber 1948c [1915]: 347); violent declamations: "One cannot achieve 'great' deeds against vermin" (1989 [1906]: 676); and lyrical passages.[16] Even the conceptual exposition that opens Part I of *Economy and Society*, a soporific for the uninitiated, can have an austere, sparse beauty for those who have studied its architecture closely. Weber's essays—most notably, *The Protestant "Ethic" and the Spirit of Capitalism*, *The Prospects for Bourgeois Democracy in Russia*, *Interim Reflection*, *Science as a Vocation*, *Politics as a Vocation*—typically deploy a stock of narrative devices whose combination contrives to have a particularly forceful impact on the attentive (and this does not necessarily mean sympathetic) reader. These devices include Weber's tendency to shift illuminatingly between empirical microscope and historical-philosophical telephoto lens; and conclusions, often attended by literary allusion, of great dramatic power and judgment. Those endings are made all the more climactic by the painstaking attention to detail that has preceded them: for without the scrupulousness, Weber's pronouncements would seem merely opinionated, while without the judgment, the concern with minutiae would seem somewhat pointless. Finally, there is the aesthetic pathos in Weber's work that is famously his own: the tension generated by his attempts at intellectual and emotional discipline. For on the one hand, Weber demanded *Sachlichkeit* (matter-of-factness): composed, responsible judgment on and about the state of the world. Yet, on the other hand, this matter-of-factness resonated with the conviction that only such a stance could do justice to the terrible complexity in which human life, and every important decision that emanates from it, hangs tragically suspended.

Understanding Classic Texts

Up to this point I have been concerned to offer a definition of classic texts within sociology, and to examine some of the attributes—functional, rhetorical—that they are said typically to possess. But much of this begs the very obvious question. How can we be sure that we have comprehended these works? Clearly, we must have *some* answer to this question or otherwise the countless exegeses on the classics, and the inducement to read them, would be quite bizarre. Yet since the 1970s it is precisely the nature of our understanding of the classics that has become the subject of a spirited debate between two camps that, with a fair bit of simplification, are often referred to as "historicist" and "presentist." This *is* a simplification both because the parties concerned are by no means monolithic, and because the standards of sophistication that have continued to refresh this debate have resulted in a genuine dialogue between the disputants. Accordingly, positions have been developed and revised, with opposing views accommodated rather than rubbished.

Presentism

The label "presentism," as used in this debate, refers to an orientation to the classic texts that emphasizes their continuing and covenantal importance to contemporary social and political thought. This importance is deemed to lie in the outstanding contribution they made to the clarification of themes or preoccupations that are themselves emblematic of (at least) Western culture, particularly in its "modern" phase. A presentist approach to the classic texts, additionally, is one that tends to assume that the authors responsible for their production recognized these themes and issues as especially salient, sought to formulate convincing answers to them, and did so in ways of such enduring significance and authority that they represent nothing less than the jewels in the crown of the sociological imagination. Because of this achievement, it is perfectly legitimate to interpret classic texts from our own current vantage points (thus "presentism"). We will be wise, of course, to recognize the specific circumstances that prompted the classic authors' arguments, and that, correlatively, may help explain the partial solutions they came up with. But in the last analysis their historical location is less important than the commonality they share with us, their latest generation of readers, in virtue of the fundamental questions they raised concerning the modern Western tradition or, even more grandly, social life as a whole. Accordingly, it might be said that Marx and Weber are especially notable because of their contribution to the "conflict viewpoint," a perspective that "has emerged over and over again wherever there have been politically astute observers," and that stretches from at least the time of the Greek historian Thucydides (c. 460-400 B.C.E.) to the likes of modern writers like Ralf Dahrendorf, Gerhard Lenski, and Randall Collins himself (Collins 1985: 48). Or it might be said that constitutive of sociology as a unique social science is the existence of "unit-ideas" of sufficient generality, continuity, distinctiveness and perspective that

> are as visible and as directive of intellectual effort today as they were when the works of Tocqueville, Weber, Durkheim, and Simmel made these ideas the foundation stones of modern sociology. We live, and we should not forget it, in a late phase of the classical age of sociology. Strip from present-day sociology the perspectives and frameworks provided by men like Weber and Durkheim, and little would be left but lifeless heaps of data and stray hypotheses.[17]

Robert Nisbet (1966: 7) argued that the "unit-ideas" that epitomize the nucleus of the sociological tradition, the categorical framework in which imagination and experience are fused, are the "linked antitheses" of "community-society, authority-power, status-class, sacred-secular, alienation-progress" (Nisbet 1966: 7). It follows that to study the classics is to study their momentous contribution to these antitheses, considered as archetypical of the sociological enterprise more generally, and as relevant to our own time as they were to theirs.

Presentists may disagree in their estimation of what it is, precisely, that gives sociology its coherence. What they broadly share, nonetheless, is a commitment to the view that the sociological classics epitomize a set of problems and dilemmas definitive of the discipline; for this reason they can be studied as if they were, in a very real sense, contemporaneous works. This is what Alan Dawe (1978: 366) affirmed when, in his own version of presentism, he argued that the key quality that gives Marx, Weber, and Durkheim their enduring vitality

> is the continuing relevance of their concerns to our experience. When Weber speaks to us of his bureaucratic nightmare of a world, he is also speaking to us of our world. So, too, is Marx speaking to us of our world when he speaks of his world of alienation and

dehumanization; and Durkheim, speaking of his and our worlds of anomie. Through the *creative* power of their thought and work, they reveal the historical and human continutiy which makes their experience *representative* of ours.

The Historicist Critique and Alternative

Around the middle of the 1970s, an intellectual current in sociology began to gather momentum that was deeply critical of aspects of the presentist orthodoxy. Strongly influenced by earlier developments in the history of science, anthropology, but especially the history of political thought,[18] a growing number of sociologists began to consider a very different approach to the history of sociology in general, and to its classic texts more especially, than had prevailed hitherto.[19]

The counter-approach to presentism has come to be known as "historicism" (a term that itself has enjoyed a very chequered history.[20] Sociologists offering historicist analyses frequently diverge in many respects, substantive and epistemological. Their projects and theoretical agendas are quite varied so that before listing and relating the chief principles associated with "historicism," as I shall do in a moment, a cautionary note should initially be sounded. Not every thinker mentioned to exemplify one or more of these principles would give all of them unqualified assent, or give them the same emphasis. Even so there is sufficient "family resemblance" in these principles to be confident that the following description is not a gross caricature of the lineaments of the historicist persuasion.

Most fundamentally, historicists criticise what they consider to be the blatant anachronism and conceptual befuddlement that plagues much of the discourse on the sociological classics. Historicists claim not only that the presentist approach is guilty of projecting on to the past questions and problems inappropriate to it; but that as a result presentism also encourages a naively continuist attitude to that past. This may not be a "Whiggish" attitude that comprehends present achievements as the progressive, triumphant culmination of previous thought. On the contrary, many presentist writers have a far higher opinion of classical acumen than they do of the pedestrian contributions of the vast bulk of their peers. But in writing of "unit-ideas" and the like, permission is granted to think of the past in terms that, from the standpoint of the historian, looks very much like the conflation of current preoccupations with ones that historical inquiry reveals to have been quite different. More positively, writers who have contributed to the historicist argument insist that statements about sociology's past should be guided by a sensibility to the thought-world and institutional matrices of the period under investigation. Just how this is to be done will become clear in a moment, but it is important at this point to note what historicists do *not* deny, before going on describe more specifically what they wish to affirm.

To begin with, historicists do not suggest that we can study the sociological past without an orientation *from* the present, but this is a very different matter to confusing the past *with* the present. Obviously, both our interest and our topic are given to us from where we are currently situated, the questions and problems we in a specific culture and epoch believe to be worthy of investigation (Jones 1977: 284). Nor do historicists imperialistically insist that an historical approach to classic texts is the only and exclusive orientation that it is legitimate for sociologists to pursue (Jones 1984: 70). As sociologists we can quite properly seek to abstract from the classics the "master heuristic" mentioned earlier. But this is only legitimate so long as we are aware that this is what we are doing; that we are conscious that these are *our* contemporary abstractions, employed for our purposes, and that such abstractions and purposes cannot be assumed to be those of the classics. Finally, historicists are not sympathetic to a vulgar contextualist view that envisages classic texts as principally an emanation of their time. Such contextualism might "explain" Parsons's *The Structure of Social Action* as an outcome of the author's Congregationalist, middle-class upbringing in collision with the strife of the Great Depression years. For historicists this will not do. First, because that kind of contextualism is pitched at such a high level of generality as to be unable to explain the peculiar features of the texts it examines: for instance, why Parsons framed the *specific* sociology that he did, as distinct from some other activity he might have performed consistent with his background experiences (Camic 1989: 40-1). Second, vulgar contextualism is problematic because it is unhistorical. For the point of an historical analysis of texts is not to reduce the latter to their conditions, to see these texts as the cipher of background economic and social forces, impinging on the author, and to which he or she is subject. Rather, it is to recover the intentions that animated the text in question, and to understand these intentions within the extant "universe of problems and assumptions"

(Camic 1982: 165), the material and conceptual resources, on which the author drew—or chose not to draw. So "instead of treating the context as the determinant of complex ideas, it is now employed as the ultimate framework for deciding what meanings, in a society of that kind, it might in principle have been possible for (e.g.) Durkheim to have intended to communicate" (Jones 1977: 297).

More specifically, an historicist approach is guided by the following principles: First, it attempts to understand classic texts in their own terms and in their own right: in short, to work out what the authors intended on doing in writing these texts—what questions they were posing, what audiences they were writing for, what interventions they sought to make. So envisaged, classic texts can be seen as consisting in what J.L. Austin called "illocutionary acts," that is "utterances which have a certain (conventional) force" (Austin 1971 [1962, 1955]: 109). As social actions, they can best be rendered historically intelligible first by focusing "on the conventions governing the treatment of issues or theories with which the text is concerned" (Jones 1977: 297); and second, by studying the contemporaries of classic authors and with whom they were in dialogue. The classic authors' contemporaries and the conventions of their time, then, form the chief locus of interpretation for historicist analysis.

Second, an historicist like Jones wants to grant a classic author

> "'privileged access" to his own intentions—that is, he cannot be said to have meant or done something if *he* could not, at least in principle, have accepted the statement as an accurate account of what he was saying or doing....In other words, our statements about Durkheim must fall within and make use of the range of descriptions which he could have applied to what he was doing; if, on the contrary, our statements are dependent on descriptive and classificatory criteria not available to Durkheim, it is difficult to see how they can be statements *about Durkheim* at all. (Jones 1977: 288)

Third, historicists are wary of progressivist and cumulationist views of sociology's development. They are suspicious on two main counts. On the one hand, such views encourage a perspective in which "the history of sociology is merely quarried to provide spurious pedigrees for current claimants to sociological legitimacy" (Peel 1971: ix). On the other, cumulationism involves an error in which a natural science perspective on theory development is falsely extrapolated to the social sciences. This extrapolation is false because natural sciences such as physics or astronomy presuppose (and demonstrate) the existence of intransitive (independent-of-thought) objects or forces; material things possessed of their own tendential causal powers. Progress and theory-cumulation in these sciences is possible as a series of ever-closer approximations to the objects being examined and ever-deeper scrutiny of the mechanisms that constitute them. The nature of this approximation and scrutiny is, of course, a matter of great contention in the philosophy of science. But both "realist" accounts of science[21] and many "conventionalist" ones (such as those of Kuhn, 1962) are nonetheless agreed that "each revolution in science represents an absolute improvement over its predecessors in its explanatory and predictive power" (Peel 1971: 263).

With sociology, on the other hand, the subject matter of its inquiries—social relations unfolding in time and space—"is not an unchanging stuff, as the basic constituents of physical nature are, and so its development cannot be a growing, overall unidirectional approximation to it, nor can it be a process of simple cumulation" (ibid: 263). Of course, sociology has experienced a number of advances in its own history as a social science. "A large number of topics...are simply better understood than before" and there is "cumulation too in the variety and subtlety of the methods available to sociologists" (Peel 1971: 264). In spite of this, however, it remains true for historicists that

> each new emerging social context, in all its uniqueness, enlarges sociology's subject and provides not only a new subject-matter but new occasions for theorizing. So there is an important sense in which Marx and Dahrendorf, Spencer and Parsons, Weber and Bendix are neither competitors nor associates in theory-building. Very often the theories of the classical sociologists are neither true nor false in the light of the purposes which have led *us* to theorize; because they are in large measure the attempts to grapple with a different reality, the answers to different problems, the upshot of different purposes. Many "refutations" of Marx or Weber are not properly such at all, but the discovery that their theories do not fit twentieth-century stratification or certain types of modern organization. (Peel 1971: 264)

Fourth, the process of historical inquiry reveals that the history of social thought contains within it a series of "lapsed alternatives" (Camic 1986: 1041-3), that is concepts, theories or arguments that were eclipsed not because they proved cognitively inadequate per se but because they fell victim to cultural pressures to discard or marginalize them. An example of a lapsed alternative is the *social* (as distinct from the psychological) concept of "habit." In his richly documented study of this concept—broadly denoting in its social manifestation "a more or less self-actuating disposition or tendency

to engage in a previously adopted or acquired form of action"[22] —
Charles Camic shows how its demotion in sociology was intrinsically bound up with attempts to promote the fledgling discipline
into an autonomous subject in the late nineteenth and early twentieth centuries. Hence, although the idea of habit was an important
one for both Weber and Durkheim's substantive studies in sociology, they felt compelled to downplay (Weber) or jettison (Durkheim)
it in their programmatic statements concerning the discipline's status as a social science. Why? Because the concept of habit had increasingly become colonized by one of sociology's chief rivals, the
heavily scientistic and behavioristic "new psychology" movement,
to refer to "an essentially biophysical phenomenon" (Camic 1986:
1067). As a result, the social scientific usage of this concept gradually fell into disuse as sociologists of many orientations believed
that it was better to cede it to psychology than to risk muddying
sociology's independent program by defending or resuscitating it.

A fifth and final historicist principle can be drawn from the above
comments: namely that preoccupation with the classics, and with
their most prominent concepts to boot, is itself a form of presentism
that is constrictive of historical understanding. To "take sociological
classics as the starting point for the investigation of sociology's past
is to accept present definitions of what past works and authors it is
legitimate to examine. Such a strategy, even when leading to the
rejection of presentist interpretations of Durkheim, still directs one
to Durkheim, rather than, say, Plato or the utilitarians" (Camic 1979:
518; cf. 543-546). To then compound this bias by focusing on "the
issues that are in the *foreground* of their writings...rather than on the
themes, concepts and ideas that remain largely in the *background*
[is to provide] a severely truncated picture of social theories past"
(Camic 1986: 1042). One remedy for this situation, Camic suggests,
is for historians of sociology to identify the "ramifying ideas in the
background" of the classical writers.[23]

Objections to Historicism

The historicist critique of presentism has not had everything its
own way. In fact, it was itself immediately greeted by a barrage of
objections, some of which clearly struck home and prodded historicists in the direction of revision. Some problems immediately suggest themselves. A relatively small one is that the contrast between

the natural and the social worlds invoked by some historicists is over-stated. Most evidently, the "unchanging stuff" of nature to which Peel refers in point three above,[24] and on which cumulation in the natural sciences is supposedly predicated, is in reality immensely permeable to human design and abuse. Indeed, our scientific under-standing of the natural world has come about largely as a result of our ability to manipulate parts of that world: the dissection of living and dead organisms, the isolation of chemical elements, the splitting of atoms. The experimental method in the natural sciences is based not on the passive observation of "unchanging stuff" but on an ac-tive process of intervention, of controlled change within parameters designed by human beings. Furthermore, changes induced by hu-man beings can be permanent and, as we are becoming increasingly aware, potentially catastrophic. While such permanent alterations of the natural world are nothing new (consider the results of genetic manipulation through selective breeding in both agriculture and ani-mal husbandry, or of the diversion of waterways for irrigation), in the early twenty-first century we are faced with a growing litany of ills brought to our attention by environmentalists and scientists, from ozone depletion to deforestation to the dumping of toxic waste, as well as dire predictions concerning such human interventions as genetic engineering. Such phenomena indicate well enough the un-stable, changing character of the natural world as well as of the so-cial. Still, all this might be admitted while nonetheless appearing quite peripheral to the core of the historicist case.

More damagingly, Stephen Turner (1983) has argued that it is dubious to assume that the classic authors' contemporaries were the sole or main audience to which they were directing their arguments. If Turner's objection is sustained, a retrieval of the conventions of the time will do limited interpretive work for us. For not only might an author write with posterity in mind, believing that history, not his contemporaries, will vindicate him. It is also likely that the classic authors were dealing with questions and disputes that form part of the wider tradition of Western philosophy.

For example, although relatively few of the writers in modern sociology have anything to say about the technical problems of applying the notion of causal law to human action, those that do, including Weber and Durkheim, deal with a standard set of issues and examples, such as the nature of "deliberation" before action, a problem made famous by Aristotle and dealt with by Hobbes, and strive to avoid the difficulties Hobbes gets into. (Turner 1983: 277)

Moreover, while this tradition loomed large in the minds of classic authors, coordinating or at least giving some measure of continuity to their arguments, the same cannot always be said of the conventions of the day. And this observation

> is directly relevant to the history of sociology, since mid-nineteenth century social thought is a good example of what might better be described as an agglomeration of mutually regarding viewpoints rather than a dispute or debate governed by common conventions. Thus Marx, Saint Simon, Donoso Cortés and Mill have something to say about the core problems of the day and all wish to give a more general account of the nature of modern social life and its development. But there are neither conventions nor a common substantive policy concern that anchors their "debate". Not only do they talk past one another, but each justifies this talking past one another on the highest philosophical grounds: each, indeed, argues for a different exclusively valid philosophical or theological framework in which the problems are to be discussed. (Turner 1983:276-7)

Consider more closely, too, the manner in which historicists are prone to deal with the key question of intentionality. It will be recalled that a salient principle of the case advanced by Jones concerned a classic author's "privileged access" to his intentions: "that is, he cannot be said to have meant or done something if *he* could not, at least in principle, have accepted the statement as an accurate account of what he was saying or doing" (Jones 1977: 288). A close look at this statement rapidly reveals what is wrong with it. To begin with, "meaning" something and "doing" something are related but distinct activities. This is clear from such everyday phenomena as our tendency to hurt people's feelings, be arrogant, complacent, etc. without meaning to do or be so. In addition, a significant portion of what we were actually and complexly doing at one time in our life, as opposed to what we thought we were simply doing, becomes evident only with the passage of time. This realization comes about not primarily as a consequence of hindsight superimposing factors that never existed in reality (this of course can happen), but as a result of distance and perspective allowing us to see factors affecting us of which we were previously innocent. The implication of the foregoing is that classical theorists may not have been aware of many aspects of what they were doing; or only came to be aware of them after they produced the classic theory in question. In this way, of course, they are no different from other agents. François Furet says somewhere, paraphrasing Tocqueville that "men make history but do not know the history they are making." Theory "making" suffers a similar fate.

Indeed, there is something quite unreal about a conception of intentionality that grants authors sovereign control over their statements. Not only are human beings subject to a number of emotional and psychological forces that they are unlikely fully to understand; their statements are also constituted by "rules of genre" (see Alexander, 1989: 56), composition and metaphor that lie latent in the text and opaque to view. Furthermore, modern debates about the nature of science, for instance, may give us insight into features of classic texts that were present (e.g., certain background assumptions), but passed unacknowledged by their authors. That being the case, "it is not necessary that a classical sociologist acknowledge or describe his or her work as addressing epistemological, presuppositional or ideological topics for us to justify interpreting their texts along these dimensions" (Seidman 1985: 15; also Seidman, 1983).

It was in response to criticisms like these that Jones shifted ground in a later paper. In this revised argument, it is now acceptable in principle to use *terms or concepts* that the classic author failed to use to describe his actions.[25] What remains erroneous and inadmissible is to ascribe *intentions* to that author that are clearly anachronistic because the contextual basis for them was absent. So to say of Marx that he was a "modernist radical" (Crook 1991) may, under some description, be a valid statement, though it is not one that Marx himself employed. To say, on the other hand, that Marx developed this modernist radicalism as an antidote to structuralist philosophies would be arrant nonsense to the degree one could show that structuralism only became available in Western culture some years after Marx died. To ascribe such phoney intentions to Marx would be evidence of our having misunderstood him. But what then, on this revised account, does understanding entail? And how does this affect the question of "privileged access"? Drawing on W.G. Runciman's analysis (1983), and continuing his focus on the example of Durkheim, Jones suggests that "understanding" Durkheim's works "presupposes at least three, analytically separable forms of knowledge"

(1) an accurate *report* of *what* Durkheim did in those works (primary understanding); (2) a valid *explanation* of *why* Durkheim did it (secondary understanding); and (3) an authentic *description* of *what it was like* for Durkheim to do it (tertiary understanding). Finally...both sociologists and historians continually provide *evaluations* of whether (and in what sense) it was *good or bad* for Durkheim to have done it. (Jones 1985: 17)

What Jones then suggests is that the author's privileged access to his own works, and their meaning, "applies only to primary understanding, or 'reportage'" (Jones 1985: 17)—but even there only with a number of provisos to be mentioned in a moment. Regarding (2), Jones acknowledges that Durkheim's reasons for his own action, his explanation of it, could be governed by "motives" of which he was unconscious or only partly conscious. Regarding (3), Jones concedes that Durkheim's description of his action, while being more or less "accurate," may lack "authenticity": that is, the precision of Durkheim's descriptions may cover only a small range of his experiences and may also be framed in terms that exaggerate or misemphasize certain aspects of them. So on this count, too, "privileged access" is not applicable. Nor is it applicable to Durkheim's evaluations of what he did. Whether Durkheim's achievement was (is?) "good or bad" is a matter for the modern scientific community to decide, presumably on the basis of its empirical fruitfulness, logical rigor, and so forth.

So we return to (1): accurate reportage in which privileged access, Jones argues, can certainly be sustained—but only partially and at a price. For in order to sustain the plausibility of privileged access, Jones must continue to dilute dramatically its content, and this by a double strategy. In the first place, what an agent "does" is now to be distinguished from an agent's "actions" i.e. what he or she intended to do, and it is only the latter that falls under the rubric of privileged access. In the second place, Jones also admits that agents may be mistaken about their own action because

> the successful performance of a particular social action (let's call it x) presupposes, not only the intentions constitutive of doing x, but also those physical and social conditions essential to x-ing. Where an agent mistakenly perceives these conditions as present when they are not, even the most sincere and determined effort to x cannot yield the performance of *that* action. (Jones 1985: 17-18)

Jones concludes that accurate reportage "requires close attention not only to the intentions and beliefs of the actor, but also to the social context of the act, and both may be extremely ambiguous" (Jones 1985: 18; see also Jones 1986: 156-8).

Later still, drawing on Richard Rorty, Jones came to grant the legitimacy of "rational reconstructions" of an author's work – imaginary conversations among ourselves and our predecessors. On such an account, Durkheim becomes our contemporary after all as we seek to articulate our projects to his and to justify both accordingly. From that standpoint, the question of what a text means is not reducible to an author's statements but is a rather a question of *"our* interests and purposes." Hence, a text "will have as many meanings as there are contexts in which it might be placed" (Jones 1997: 150). This has not stopped Jones proceeding as a historian by, for instance, reconstructing the intellectual location of Durkheim's concept of *chose* (thing); establishing "to whom and against whom" the injunction to treat social facts as things was addressed. But Jones is now more ready to question, indeed to document, the unreliability of Durkheim's own autobiographical utterances and to proclaim that to learn something historical about Durkheim and his time is also "to learn something about ourselves as well," notably that we, too, are historically located beings.[26]

Jones's reformulation of his earlier historicist claims was a heartening example of a writer willing to respond to criticism rather than dodge it. More than this, by his original provocation Jones put the onus on presentist colleagues to defend their position, and some of these defenses were far more credible than others. It is true that the concept of understanding we are left with from this debate is far more complex than Jones originally thought (for that reason alone the debate was worthwhile). But it is just as true, in fact glaringly obvious, that the intentions of an author, to the extent that we are able to uncover them, offer us one key to understanding the formation and trajectory of his or her texts. Similarly, while the conventions of the time are not necessarily the exclusive locus of texts, they are one locus of them and, as such, call out for consideration. The historicist injunction of writers like Camic (1986: 1043) to examine the overlooked "ramifying ideas in the background" of classic texts is helpful in expanding our range of questions and deepening our understanding of intellectual development. And none of this is necessarily incompatible with the argument of a trenchant critic of historicism like Turner (1983: 285; cf. 280) that in "the classical sociological works there is both the invention of new language and a great sharpening of language, such that the author's meaning can only be properly seen in his own usage, which is to say in the structure of his own argument." Most historicists would be happy to agree with this point. Their claim has not only been that classic writers engage with the conventions of their day but also that they depart from them. Conventionality, in the latter case, becomes a means of calibrating the degree or nature of that divergence.

Conclusion

Preceding sections of this chapter have, with one exception, made it appear that the classics continue to be highly valued in sociology. Alexander's definition of classic texts stressed their privileged status. Their positive functions were rehearsed. The ways to study them—presentist or historicist—assumed that they were worth the effort of study. But this is a misleading picture as it stands. Many sociologists —Robert Merton, James Coleman, Jonathan Turner, Randall Collins, and Richard F. Hamilton are among the most eloquent examples—criticize what they see as an undue deference to the classical tradition of sociology that, ironically, does a disservice to the classics themselves. Comte, Weber, and Durkheim, among others, were iconoclasts. They employed the works of the past to create their own arguments and syntheses. They did not make a fetish out of their predecessors, nor did they engage in footnote scholarship for the sake of it. If sociology is to be credible, on this account, is must be methodologically rigorous, empirically reliable and theoretically productive. The best service one can do for the classical tradition is to adapt those of its concepts that are still fecund, show its errors where appropriate,[27] refuse to engage in textual idolatry, challenge those who indulge in it—and move on.

These critics, who despite their objections continue to recognize the classical tradition's achievement, and would, in its spirit, like to advance social science as a theoretically cumulative endeavor, are to be distinguished from those who entertain a more generalized disdain for what they call the "canon." According to these critics, classic texts epitomize all that is wrong with the Western intellectual tradition: its misguided scientific pretensions, its exclusionary masculinity, and its lack of commitment to the oppressed. Preoccupation with classic works, then, amounts to the veneration of texts long made redundant by history, an antediluvian, elitist and "hegemonic" demotion of the knowledge and "lived-experience" of subordinate groups, notably of minorities and women. I shall address aspects of this critique in chapter 6. Before I do so, however, let me turn to examine how classics come to assume a privileged status within the discipline of sociology.

Notes

1. Bloom and Rosenberg 1991: 4-5; McKenzie 1965: 653-6. Similarly, the Confucian Analects (c. 500 BCE) were the product of many contributors. See Legge 1971 [1893]: 12-18.
2. For other connotations see Kermode 1975, and the very sociological essay by T.S. Eliot 1945.
3. I refer to the debate between those who stress the historical specificity of the classics, and those who suggest that an "underlying continuity between the sociological past and present" can be discerned that, in at least some senses, unites "classics and contemporaries" (Seidman 1985: 13).
4. In practice, of course, matters are quite different, since the experimental method in science depends on the manipulation of nature.
5. Alexander 1982a, 1982b, 1983a, 1983b; also 1987: 1-21.
6. For a critical appraisal of Johnson and his colleagues' "philosophical" approach to sociology, see Mouzelis 1991: 10-24.
7. Mills 1959: 120-3, 129-31; Zeitlin 1987: xii.
8. Then again it may not be. In British sociology, for instance, institutionalization is significantly weaker. Sociology's resultant permeability has allowed it to absorb much of cultural and media studies and recreate itself as "the science of the postmodern": Fuller 2000: 508.
9. For other pertinent assessments of sociology's future, see Abbott 2000 (who refreshingly adds a European dimension); Baker and Rau 1990; and Turner and Turner 1990. On sociology in China (that is, both the People's Republic of China and the Republic of China [Taiwan]), see the contributions of Dai Kejing, Bettina Granslow, Chan Hoi-man and Sun Chung-Hsing (all 1993).
10. An obvious trope in sociology is the list of three—Marx, Durkheim and Weber. Its salience in Western culture is ably documented by Macfarlane (1991: 197). "Threes were everywhere. They still are: three meals; three wishes; three witches; three cheers, three reasons why. There's morning, noon, night; faith, hope, charity; lower class, middle class, upper class; blondes, brunettes, and redheads. Dante divided his universe into hell, purgatory, and paradise. We speak of times past, present, future. There are, according to the ancient riddle of the Sphinx, three ages of man. There are three Graces, three Furies, three bears, three rings in a circus, and three blind mice. Races begin with ready, set, go, and end with win, place, show. In folk stories, it is often the third brother who slays the dragon, wins the princess, finds the treasure. In Christian iconography, there are three crosses on Calvary, three Magi, three temptations, three denials. And there is, of course, the Trinity." On "lists of three" in the speech of politicians, see Atkinson 1984.
11. See R. H. Brown 1990a and 1990b; Atkinson 1990; Baker 1990. Also relevant are Palonen 1999; Peterson 1990; Anderson 1978.
12. See also Davis 1971; Overington 1981, 1977; Jameson 1973.
13. See Carver 1998: 14-20.
14. Quoted in Carver [forthcoming].
15. Albrow 1990: 66-68; Scaff 1989: 67-72; Sica 1985; Prawer 1976.
16. "It is true that the path of human destiny cannot but appal him who surveys a section of it. But he will do well to keep his small personal commentaries to himself, as one does at the sight of the sea or of majestic mountains, unless he knows himself to be called and gifted to give them expression in artistic or prophetic form. In most other cases the voluminous talk about intuition does nothing but conceal a lack of perspective toward the object, which merits the same judgment as a similar lack of perspective toward men" (Weber, 1930 [1920]: 29).

17. Nisbet 1966: 5.
18. Notably Kuhn, 1970 [1962]); Stocking, 1968; Skinner, 1978, 1974, 1972, 1970; Pocock 1972.
19. For major contributions see Collini 1991, 1979, 1978; Lepenies 1988 [1985], 1981a, and the convenient collection in Lepenies, 1981b; Nye 1983; Kuklick 1980a, 1980b; Hawthorn, 1979, 1976; Giddens 1977 [1972]; Peel 1971; Coser 1971; Jones, 1997, 1986a; 1986b; 1985; 1984; 1983a, 1983b, 1981, 1977, 1974; and Camic, 1993, 1989, 1987, 1986, 1983, 1981, 1979.
20. Contrast, for instance, Antoni, 1962 [1940] with Popper, 1961 [1957].
21. Advanced by such writers as Roy Bhaskar, 1975, 1986, 1989a [1979], 1989b.
22. Camic 1986: 1044.
23. For an example of this approach, see my analysis (in Baehr 1998: 223-254) of "Caesarism," the background concept of Weber's "charisma."
24. The passage is also quoted approvingly in Jones 1983b: 456.
25. See also the discussions of Ste. Croix 1981: 35, 69-80, and Collini 1991: 27-35.
26. Jones, 1997: 154, 156, 167-8; also Jones 1999, where the Rortyean influence is even more pronounced.
27. One of the very best examples of evidential scrutiny of a classic text is in Hamilton 1996: 32-106. As Hamilton remarks about the sociological reception of the Protestant Ethic (the reception in history has been quite different): "Criticism is a normal feature of scholarly work. Where problems or outright errors are discovered, they should be signaled in subsequent comments and discussion, but that has not been the case with the Weber thesis." Deference to Weber's "prodigious scholarship"—that appears to accord a higher value to quantity rather than quality—is no substitute for mention being made "about the erratic relationship between text and notes, about the implication of one-person 'samples' for the depiction of world-historical movements, and about the absence of systematic evidence linking religion and economic development" (96-7).

5

Classicality: Criteria and Reception

Introduction

The previous chapter examined, among other things, the growing historical sensibility that informs current sociology's treatment of the classics. In this chapter, I will be summarizing and augmenting another body of literature that is also highly historical in orientation. Essentially, it deals with two related questions. How did the specific body of texts that we today call "classic" come to be recognized as such? And, further, why did some texts achieve that status while others did not? To find answers, we must look at classicality not merely as a function of particular works but as a dialectic in which the text, its evaluation and re-evaluation define what is exemplary.

The Stratification of Classic Texts

A striking feature of "classic" sociological texts is their youthfulness. Contrasted with the longevity achieved by their counterparts in philosophy or political theory, the sociological classics are, in temporal terms, mere parvenus (as, indeed, is the discipline itself). Even so, the works of Marx, Weber, Durkheim, and Simmel and others are not usually hailed as "modern" classics by sociologists; they are thought of as simply "classics" per se. If the term "modern classic" is bandied around at all by members of the discipline, it might be reserved for such works as Harold Garfinkel's *Studies in Ethnomethodology* (1967), Jürgen Habermas's *Knowledge and Human Interests* (1971 [1968]) or many other texts one could mention. Significantly, though, the mention of any one of these texts as classics will invite immediate dissent from many quarters. Hence it will be said that Habermas's *Knowledge and Human Interests* may be a clas-

sic for "critical theory" but not for sociology "as a whole" or, at
least, not for many sociological schools (rational choice theory, symbolic interactionism, structural-functionalism, etc.). In contrast one
can predict that these same skeptics would accept the statement that
Max Weber's *The Protestant Ethic and the "Spirit" of Capitalism*
(1905), or Emile Durkheim's *The Division of Labour in Society*
(1893) are sociological classics, even though these works may be
utterly marginal to their particular areas of specialization or theoretical commitments. This suggests, intuitively, that the classics of the
dead, have something about them that sets them apart from the "classics" of the living—an intuition echoed by Peter Berger (1992: 1).
Reflecting on the twenty-fifth anniversary of his and Thomas
Luckmann's *The Social Construction of Reality* (1967), Berger remarked laconically that while the book's description as a classic was
gratifying, "there is a disturbing downside. The author of a 'classic'
(even a minor one) is commonly assumed to be deceased or soon to
be so, which is a condition to which I do not as yet aspire."

So what is it about the likes of Durkheim and the others that
particularly commends them to the classic stable? This something
cannot be intellectual merit per se, for many people who believe
Durkheim's *Division* to be not a particularly good (persuasive,
methodologically sound, empirically accurate) book would still
accord it the honor of being a sociological classic. I suggest, rather,
that a propitious, though not necessary,[1] condition for the ascent
of a text to classicality is deadness itself: that is, the expiry, or at
the least the silence, of the author who has produced it. This is
important for a number of reasons. When authors are alive, they
are not only competitors in the marketplace of ideas and prestige,
helping to fan all sorts of personal antipathies and rivalries that
may stymie the kind of corporate recognition their creations would
otherwise enjoy. Their work is also too contemporary for their peers
to know whether what they are reading is of classical stature—or
just topical or interesting or provocative. Conversely, as Donald
Levine (1981: 61) observes,

> Like a mountain range, the makers of the sociological tradition become more imposing
> the farther back we stand from them. Dimly sensed as a collectivist mystic, Durkheim
> later flashed into view as a peak of analytic discipline. Max Weber, long a misguided
> economic historian, only slowly emerged as an overarching intellectual summit. Amor-
> phous Simmel eventually came into focus as a genial source of streams of rigorous
> propositions....

Moreover, writers who are still alive *and productive* exert a constant destablizing force on their own *oeuvre*, and this is not conducive either to the acceptance of their work as classic. A classic text, it would seem, must be the collective property of the community that uses it; it must allow multiple readings and articulations. When authors are dead—or at least silent—there is ample scope for doing what one likes with their work. When authors are living, and vocal, on the other hand, they are likely to hinder this process of piratical appropriation and dispersion by insisting on what their work or project "is really about"—through such means as interviews, prefaces or addenda to new editions of their books, and replies to critics that normally cap anthologies devoted to their ideas. To be sure, this will rarely satisfy the audience to whom it is addressed for the simple reason that any work permits a number of divergent readings. Nonetheless, the author's apodictic and proprietorial voice will have the effect of deterring collective appropriation, just as his or her subsequent output will inject volatility into the corpus as a whole. Both aspects will impede the elevation of their texts to a standing that the majority of sociologists can assent to as classic.

It may at this point be objected that such a view fails to take into account a text that, and an author who, would seem flatly to contradict the thrust of the above argument. Talcott Parsons's *The Structure of Social Action* (1937) has been recognized as a classic by people right across the sociological spectrum for at least four decades. (Whether that text, or Parsons himself, will be so considered in a hundred years' time is, of course, something we cannot know.) If Parsons's *The Social System* (1951) was his most notorious book, it never approached the eminence that *Structure*, his first, attained. This explains why Whitney Pope (1973), without stretching credulity, could entitle his critique of *Structure*'s treatment of one of its subjects: "Classic on classic: Parsons's interpretation of Durkheim." It is also notable that of the twelve quotations from Parsons cited in David L. Sills's and Robert K. Merton's *Macmillan Book of Social Science Quotations* (1991), eight are from *Structure*; only one is from *The Social System*.

A constellation of highly unusual factors helps explain *Structure's* unusual eminence. One factor, insufficient in itself, was the type of book it was: namely, one concerned with sociology's theoretical presuppositions. In the professed activity of delineating sociology's deep structure, *Structure* actually helped shape it and thus became a constitutive moment in the discipline's formation and historical memory. Second, Parsons's own intellectual career was not only a long and prodigiously fecund one, spanning over fifty years of intellectual production. It also consisted of a number of discernable "phases" (Hamilton, 1983), or "periods" (Alexander, 1983b). This enabled people, long before Parsons died, to read *Structure* as a kind of disembodied text. Published when Parsons was thirty-five, it had its evident social location in the inter-war, Depression years. From the perspective of the booming sixties, it could already appear as something remote, the product of an era markedly different from the one that replaced it. Moreover, the book's astonishing scope, verve, and critique of what Parsons idiosyncratically called "utilitarianism," could draw commendation from many quarters within sociology while committing none of them to the later project of structural functionalism. Finally, it can be conjectured that Parsons's pioneering and unrelenting role in introducing the classic texts of Durkheim and Weber to other sociologists also helped assimilate his contribution to the rank of theirs. As Habermas (1987 [1981]: 199-2) has justly remarked, "among the productive theorists of society no one else has equalled Parsons's intensity and persistence in conducting a dialogue with the classics and connecting up his own theory to them."

The example of Parsons indicates that the generalization previously formulated—that a pan-discipline recognition of a text's classicality is dependent upon the author's death or silence—is limited in its application. Readers may venture other exceptions,[2] for instance, Robert K. Merton's *Social Theory and Social Structure* (1968 [1957, 1949]) or David Riesman's *The Lonely Crowd* (1950). Be that as it may, we are still faced with the fact that when sociologists talk about "classics," they are usually thinking of texts by authors who are dead.

Deceased classics, however, do not all enjoy the same status. It has often been observed by sociologists that some of their most illustrious predecessors today go largely unread. Herbert Spencer's fate in this respect has become proverbial (yet see Perrin 1976, and Turner 2000),[3] but the same could be said for Montesquieu, Ferguson, Saint-Simon, and Comte. While few would deny that Comte's texts are among the classics of sociology, just as few would want to say his texts are as relevant or as currently important as, say, Durkheim's and Weber's. This suggests a distinction between what we can call "inertial" classics—texts housed, as it were, in sociology's museum (or mausoleum)—and "vital" classics: texts that are constantly read and reflected on, and that continue to animate social research. An example of the former is Spencer's *The Study of Sociology* (1873), which, according to Charles Horton Cooley in 1920, "probably did more to arouse interest in the subject [in the United States] than any other publication before or since."[4] An example of the latter is the texts that make up Weber's sociology of religion and rationality. Still, the distinction between inertial and vital should be thought of as existing on a continuum, not as an exclusive dichotomy, because the fortune of texts is as unpredictable as the environments and discourses that foster interest in them. Although Marx's works, once particularly "vital" in the discipline, have suffered a severe setback with the dissolution of communism, it is unlikely that they will be entombed in Highgate cemetery with the skeletal remains of their author. We still inhabit a world dominated by the capitalist mode of production, in which inequality is rife and economic crisis endemic. Marx's critique, both in its humanistic and scientific aspects, speaks to those characteristics, though how accurately will always be a matter of judgment. It is also conceivable that Marx's theoretical system may possess the protean capacity to live on through being rearticulated to writers, for instance, Weber, whose classical position in sociology is at this time secure (Sayer 1991), and to social movements (against "globalization," for example) and theoretical currents that continue to provoke interest: "modernism" (Berman 1988), "modernist radicalism" (Crook 1991), deconstruction (Derrida 1994) and postmodernism (Carver 1999).

Conversely, works that have long been forgotten may attract attention by writers who believe that the "condescension of posterity" (E.P. Thompson) is not a fate they justly deserve. It may then happen that a sporadic, or concerted, attempt is made by our contemporaries to propel what was deemed inertial towards the "vital" pole. Typically this occurs through arguments that either stress the surprisingly "modern" nature of the texts concerned, or that claim to show that such works constitute a neglected chapter in sociology's history that deserves due recognition and a proper place in its social memory. An illustration of the confluence of such arguments can be found in the body of work that seeks to give proper due to the eighteenth-century Scottish Enlightenment, and particularly the contributions of Adam Smith, Adam Ferguson, John Millar, and William Robertson.[5] Here we have an example of what Wolf Lepenies (1988 [1985]: 4) calls "storage," the fact

> of significance for the history of science, that theoretical programmes at first rejected have frequently not simply disappeared or been forgotten but, having passed a winter in concealment, have returned and re-entered the stream of scientific discussion. These places of concealment may lie within the original discipline itself or in neighbouring disciplines, and one then speaks of inter-disciplinary storage...

It will be evident from this section, then, that the "classics" of sociology are not all of one piece. Beneath a common rubric there actually lies internal stratification, a differentiated order of textual appraisal. Moreover, the properties that ostensibly make a text classic still remain elusive. Faced with this mystery, we might be tempted to generate formal criteria for classicality—a check-list of attributes—that, to the degree they were satisfied by a particular work, would enable us to say with confidence that it was classic. I attempt to show next why such a strategy is likely to end in grief.

"Criteria" of Classicality?

One approach to the question "Why has X become a classic"? is to draw up a list of specific criteria of classicality. We could then say that if X meets all of these criteria, it is to be regarded as a classic work. Yet when we attempt to formulate such a list, we find ourselves at something of a loss to come up with an exhaustive list of specific properties or conditions that are at the same time both necessary (i.e., criteria that must be met by all texts to be deemed classic) and sufficient (i.e., any text fulfilling the criteria is a classic). A brief assessment of three attempts to determine classic criteria will at least help to clarify the nature of the problem.

In a review of three books from the *Routledge Sociology Classics* series, Jem Thomas posits three criteria by which "any text can achieve the status of a 'classic'" and applies them to works by Mannheim (*Ideology and Utopia*), Parsons (*The Social System*) and Weber (the Gerth and Mills anthology, *From Max Weber*). The most straightforward of Thomas's criteria stipulates that a classic is a work that plays "so important a role in the development of [a] discipline or tradition that any history must refer to it" (Thomas 1992: 114). The point seems reasonable enough. It is, for instance, difficult to conceive of a work on structural functionalism that did not make reference to Parsons's *The Social System*. Moreover, according to Thomas, all three of the texts in question fit this criterion. On closer inspection, however, this standard tells us nothing about the element or elements within a text that make it a classic. It tells us that a work has become a classic, not *why* it became one. Counting the number of times a work is cited in scholarly footnotes gauges the importance of a text for a particular discipline or sub-discipline, but leaves us still in the dark about the source of its classicality.

Thomas's second criterion is closer to the target. It holds that a classic text "contain[s] an account of the way things are that is so powerful that subsequent generations are able to shake it off, if at all, only with the greatest intellectual difficulty." What this suggests, correctly, is that a text becomes classic when it becomes "indispensably part of the context required to interpret subsequent works."[6] The final criterion posited by Thomas is that a classic text is one "so *rich* that it is capable of frequent reinterpretation and, moreover, rewards that reinterpretation, making it a worthwhile thing to do" (Thomas, 1992: 114, 115). Again, that point is intuitively plausible, though we should note that what is "rich" and "powerful" will inevitably be a matter of contention and dispute, subject to differing kinds of aesthetic measure. The problem is compounded when Thomas applies his criteria to the three classics under review. While Weber is vindicated, Parsons and Mannheim fail to meet fully the test. But it is not primarily a lack of richness or powerfulness that pulls them down from their pedestal. Instead, Thomas tells us, their classicality is "defeated by one central and overriding point, both Mannheim and Parsons were in important and irrefragable ways *wrong*" (Thomas, 1992: 115). The scholarly world is, however, brimming with people who would say the same about the texts of Marx, Weber, or Durkheim, yet who would still accord them the standing of acknowledged "classics" of sociology.

A broadly similar analysis of classicality is provided by Nicos Mouzelis, albeit under the rubric of "canonization." The texts of Marx, Durkheim and Weber are canonical, Mouzelis (1997: 245-6) argues, for two main reasons. They offer "a set of highly sophisticated and powerful conceptual tools" that are "useful for raising interesting questions, solving theoretical puzzles, and preparing the ground for more empirically oriented substantive theories." In addition, their "conceptual frameworks" together with their "substantive theories" are simply "superior to other writings in terms of cognitive potency, analytical acuity, power of synthesis, imaginative reach and originality." Mouzelis distinguishes between these intrinsic criteria of "cognitive validity," and the extrinsic historical processes that have eventuated in the classics achieving their recognition. Explanation of the latter, Mouzelis believes, can be safely left to the sociology of knowledge. The distinction between cognitive validity, on the one hand, and the historical processes that lead to a text's becoming classic, on the other, is logically impeccable. But substantively it is too neat. As we will see in a later section, there are many contingent factors responsible for the social appraisal of texts as classic, and some of these have *nothing to do* with their being appreciated as potent or acute. Disavowal and rebuttal may be just as important. Texts in good measure become classic not because they are deemed superior to others but because they become controversial and culturally resonant. Equally, these texts must not be useful in solving "theoretical puzzles" but in provoking more of them. Mere solutions to a problem impede a text's ascent to greatness for the simple reason that they offer no challenges for contemporaries to embrace and successors to ponder.[7]

Mouzelis is right to say that the "construction" of the sociological canon "tells us nothing for or against its cognitive validity." But he is wrong to imply that cognitive validity is the explanation for a text's canonical status. It may be one reason but classicality itself is an interface of author and reading community, something that Mouzelis himself suggests when he properly notes (above) that classical texts provide "a set of highly sophisticated and powerful conceptual tools" that are "useful for raising interesting questions." Conceptual tools, however, do not raise questions themselves; they must be raised by others; the intrinsic and extrinsic reasons for a text's becoming classical are fluid. Neither can be reduced to the other *or entirely separated* from the other. This is not to say that any text could become a classic: a text that is unambiguously clichéd, commonplace, and tied exclusively to a local context (thereby allowing little or no room for extrapolation) could not. Nor is to aver that texts that have become classics in sociology owe their prestige to deliberate strategies of exclusion and inclusion, a view that I will rebut in chapter 6. Least of all am I claiming that sociology's classic texts are not remarkable and luminous. My argument is simply that the classics of sociology require us to understand them in sociological ways.

Equally, it is important to distinguish between texts that we as individuals believe are "classics" but have failed to be appreciated as such, and those that actually have received classical status. Failing to make this distinction is essentially to confuse a personal judgement with a collective evaluation, an individual aesthetic contention with a social fact that can actually be corroborated by examining the reception process that eventuates in classicality. (I offer a model of this process in the next section.) In the first case, "classics" means little more than works that have been "unfairly" ignored or marginalized, even though they are ostensibly profound, perceptive and ahead of their time: for instance, "yet to be canonized classics such as Anna Julia Cooper's *A Voice from the South* which appeared in 1892, the year before Durkheim's book [*The Division of Labor in Society*]" (Lemert 1994:88). [8] However, if "classic" is to have any sociological meaning at all, it is quite evident that Cooper's book is not an example of one. A text is not a classic because we think it should be, and has been overlooked, but because it has demonstrated its mettle—that is, "withstood critical attention" (Olsen 1996: 83)— over a period of time with heterogeneous audiences.[9]

Not all texts become classic for exactly the same reasons. To find common criteria for the classicality of Durkheim and Marx, for instance, we must ignore the circumstances by which each found his way into the select circle of sociology's cherished thinkers. While Durkheim's classicality developed *within* sociology itself, Marx's reputation was first firmly established in other disciplines (political theory, economics, philosophy), and within the socialist movement, long before he became, posthumously, a founder of sociology. Even within Marx's own writings, the paths to classicality of, say, the 1844 *Paris Manuscripts*, *The Communist Manifesto*, and the *Grundrisse* were all different.

On another level, fixed criteria of classicality fail to address the divergent readings to which the classics are subject, and the diversity of views regarding what it is about their work that makes them especially valuable. Finally, it is hard to see how any fixed set of criteria could account for the changing fortunes of particular classics over time. If such criteria were fixed as both necessary and sufficient for classicality, then a classic, once established as such, would remain one forever. Moreover, a text that failed to meet these criteria at one time could never expect to become a classic at another.

Classics and their "Reception"

If, as the above argument suggested, the search for fixed criteria of classicality will not take us very far, we are still left with the question: Why is "X" a classic? In the following section I outline an approach designed to answer this question historically and synchronically. My method will be to proceed, not by definitional fiat, but through the provision of concepts best able to describe and explain the main features of the classic formation process. In so doing, I draw on a body of writing that constitutes yet another development in the interpretation of the sociological classics. Historically oriented, it is concerned to examine the processes of "reception" through which texts or individuals have achieved their celebrated status—or failed to do so.[10]

Guenther Roth puts succinctly the main issue confronted in this literature:

> We like to believe that Marx, Durkheim, and Weber survived their times because of the intrinsic quality of their achievement, but their vaunted "influence" has been very much dependent on our own receptivity and our own orientations. (Roth 1988: xv-xvi)

It is not that the genius of sociology's great authors is here in dispute; nor is it being denied that there is a sense in which works create their own conditions of reception by being particularly challenging and insightful. It is more that genius or greatness are culturally defined and are, in any case, insufficient conditions for elevation to the classical pantheon. For texts and authors to become classic, they must not only be challenging but actually *be* challenged. They must attract cultural recognition; and that is a mediated and negotiated process rather than a spontaneous or obvious act of apprehension.

The sociological literature on reception is bringing about a heightened awareness of just what this social recognition entails and its considerable dependence on what Neil McLaughlin (1998: 215-220), modifying Lamont (1987), classifies as climate of the times, geography/national traditions, institutional prestige, and personal characteristics. And it is simultaneously helping to explain why some authors are forgotten (for instance, Erich Fromm, see below) or rejected. Charles Camic (1992), notably, has argued that the typical "content-fit" model of intellectual influence may well obscure the real process through which predecessors are selected. That model assumes that influence is best gauged by examining the fit between the content of a thinker's project and the content of the works to which the thinker refers; the latter is then considered the unequivocal grounds of the former. But there are two methodological problems with such a view. First, we are encouraged to take at face value an author's statements about how his or her predecessors were chosen. The issue here is not that authors will lie or deliberately mislead but that the rhetoric of science tends to discourage the display of idiosyncrasy and that the passage of time may, in any case, cloud accurate recollection. The second problem with the "content-fit" model is that it ignores what Camic calls "the dark side of the predecessor-selection process: previous thinkers who produced work (meeting contemporary intellectual standards) that the thinker under study was aware of, but chose *not* to incorporate, engage, or otherwise draw upon in developing his or her own ideas" (Camic 1992: 424).

Camic's illustrative case study of this process is Parsons's *Structure of Social Action*, a text that explicitly drew upon Weber, Durkheim, Pareto, and Marshall. The conventional wisdom on this choice is that American social science was so dominated by positivism in the period during which Parsons was constructing his substantive-theoretical project that he was perforce compelled to turn to European sources to compensate for that debility. What such an ahistorical wisdom fails to acknowledge, Camic argues, is that Parsons was well versed in a local intellectual tradition that was singularly congruent with the ideas enunciated in *Structure*. As an undergraduate at Amherst College, Parsons was taught by two economists, Walton Hale Hamilton and Clarence Edwin Ayres (so-called "institutionalists"), who were staunch critics of classical and neo-classical (marginal utility) economics. More generally, the institutionalists, following the lead of Thorstein Veblen, insisted that utilitarian or ultra-rationalist models of economic man failed miserably to account for social action. Human beings were more than utility maximizers. They were culturally located agents who pursued "ideal ends," and their social order was decisively dependent on values and social institutions. The young Parsons was fully cognizant of this countermovement. But he was also aware that at his own intellectual base,

Harvard, economic institutionalism was scathingly denounced, as amateurish and unscientific, by such academic senior statesmen of economics as Joseph Schumpeter, Allyn Young, T.N. Carver, and Frank Taussig. It was this department that Parsons joined in 1927 as an economics instructor, and with whose members he retained in close contact once he moved in 1931 to the newly created Department of Sociology. Parsons's credibility among his colleagues, Camic contends, would have been severely tarnished by identifying himself with the minority institutionalist viewpoint. Had he done so, the sociology that Parsons sought to promote would have been associated with "a legacy of defective reasoning, error, misunderstanding, shallow criticism, fruitless controversy, and pseudoscience" (Camic 1992: 435), and his reputation as an acute thinker seriously undermined. Within Parsons's senior circle, in contrast, Marshall, Pareto, Durkheim, and Weber were all in good standing, or at, the very least, were not impediments to advancing a credible sociological argument.

The point here is not that Parsons cravenly sought to mollify his seniors or peers. Parsons was no coward and was fully capable of standing up for himself, as his conflict with P.A. Sorokin attested.[11] Moreover, if appeasement had been his goal, Parsons would have been less robustly critical of neoclassical economics than in fact he was. It is rather that once Parsons "found" his four Europeans he had all the intellectual sustenance he needed to make his analysis, and that invoking the institutionalists, or even comparing them with the four, would have put his project needlessly on the defensive. Parsons's choice of intellectual predecessors—whom he explicitly included and excluded—was thus not simply about content, even if content was important; it was also about social networks and the academic politics of reputation building.

In the next section I summarize and interpret the growing body of sociological work devoted to the reception and reputational process. I also draw on literary analyses of textual recognition, in particular the writings of Wolfgang Iser and Robert Jauss. To Anglophone readers, the field that Jauss and Iser have pioneered is known as Reception Theory; to German, *Rezeptionsästhetik* (that is, work concerned with the aesthetics of reception) or *Rezeptions-Forschung* —literally, reception research.[12]

Classic Reception, Classic Formation

What, then, are the conditions under which certain texts acquire classic standing? In the first place, and most obviously, the work must attract attention; it must have, or be seen to have, *cultural resonance*, which is to say that it must both contain certain "response inviting" properties capable of being "activated" by the reader—and then find itself so activated.[13] What this means above all is that the work in question must possess qualities of sufficient appeal and utility as to be considered vital for a particular cultural project—or properties that are so obviously antithetical to it that the work sparks controversy and gains notoriety.

As an example of appeal and utility, consider the case of Simmel's reception in the United States between 1895 and 1930. During this watershed period in which American sociologists were keen to establish the professional credentials of the new discipline, it was to German universities that many of them looked "for inspiration and legitimation" (Levine et al. 1976: 815). Yet the options available for the fledgling sociologist were limited. For instance, in the closing decade of the nineteenth century, the peripatetic Max Weber was not yet a sociologist and thus was in no position to provide direct and unequivocal inspiration for the new discipline. And, in any case, it was Berlin—where Simmel was based—not Heidelberg, to which the brightest aspirants of sociology were drawn. Albion Small himself had studied with Simmel when both were students at the University of Berlin in 1880; from then on "a close collegial relationship" between them developed.[14] Not only did Small send three of his students to study with Simmel. He also propagated Simmel's ideas as head of the Department of Sociology at Chicago, established in 1892, and through the *American Journal of Sociology*, which Small helped to found in 1895. A string of translations of Simmel for the AJS followed. So did, in 1921, Robert Park and Ernest Burgess's *Introduction to the Science of Sociology* which contained

10 selections by Simmel, some of them new translations made by Park—many more selections than were drawn from any other author. "Park and Burgess" became the most influential introduction to sociology in the United States in the 1920s and 1930s, playing a major role in the exposure of generations of sociology students to Simmel's writings. (Levine et al. 1976: 817)[15]

Small and Robert Park (like other Americans who attended Simmel's lectures in Berlin, including Charles Ellwood, Edward Hayes, and Nicholas Spykman) were unwilling to embrace Simmel's sociological project *in toto*, but they were certainly receptive to response-inviting properties in it. Thus Small "was particularly attracted by Simmel's seriousness about the need to define a proper domain for sociology,"[16] while when Park "encountered Simmel, he was searching for a general conception of society to use in orienting his analysis of the role of the news media in the creation of modern public opinion. Simmel's notion of social interaction was congenial to him both because it avoided the abstract formalism of atomic and organismic theories, and because its stress on reciprocity paralleled the pragmatists' emphasis on reflexivity" (Levine 1985: 129). Later, other response-invited properties in Simmel could be tapped as his studies on small groups, conflict, exchange, and so on furnished useful reference points for a variety of projects seeking to expand the alternatives to structural functionalism.

Simmel also prompted opposition,[17] but as the main example of cultural resonance through notoriety, let us consider aspects of the American and British reception of a single book: Durkheim's *The Rules of Sociological Method* (1894/1895). An acknowledged "classic in sociology,"[18] *The Rules* has engendered throughout its career far more criticism and hostility than praise. As Gane (1988: 12-13) points out, the introductions of both Catlin and Lukes, to the book's 1938 and 1982 translations respectively, argue that the value of *The Rules* is largely negative. We can all learn from the mistakes of the essay, they suggest, for its errors are highly instructive. Indeed,

> The essay is presented by modern commentators, almost unanimously, as a document which points sociology in the wrong direction. The text indeed possesses strange powers, for it seems to call for repeated rounds of denunciation, as if it indicates the wrong direction with admirable conviction, vigour, even plausibility....But, then, curiously...sociologists are not really agreed as to precisely what is wrong with it.

Gane (1988: 98-99) goes on to say that though typically "rejected as an adequate statement of sociological method," *The Rules* nonetheless became "a major reference point for discourse on method".[19] It is just this capacity of a text—to become "a major reference point"—that is critical for its promotion and survival. The implication to be drawn from this is that the greatest impediment to a text's elevation is not hostility, but indifference. Repudiation may at least provoke the din of controversy or engagement. Indifference or apathy, however, fosters *blockage*, silence. Moreover, if that silence persists it will encourage forgetting: and this may be temporary or permanent. Cultural resonance will also be aided by, but is not reducible to, political support and patronage, for instance of the kind Durkheim enjoyed from the Ministry of Public Instruction, which was documented in chapter 3; or, in a much more ambiguous way, which Max Weber secured posthumously from Carl Heinrich Becker, the minister and secretary of state in the Weimar Republic, in his attempt to modernize German cultural life (Lepenies 1988 [1985]: 247-251).

Cultural resonance alone, however, will not get a work, theory or *oeuvre* very far. Such work must also exhibit *textual suppleness*; that is, in the longer term, it must allow multiple readings and adoptions.[20] Durkheim, for instance, has been a great survivor, capable of assuming drastically different significance for different interpreters at different times. In political or moral terms alone, he has been likened to a fascist,[21] a conservative,[22] a Solidarist liberal.[23] His work has been reconstituted in socialist terms (Pearce 1989) and in postmodernist ones (Meštrovic 1988, 1991, 1992), disparaged as irredeemably patriarchal and sexist (Roth 1989-90; Lehmann 1991), and commended for its sensitivity to the feminine side of humanity, especially evident in its characterization of religion as "the womb" from which human civilization derives (Meštrovic 1992: 100). It is certainly true that a number of these authors have emphasized the multiple doctrinal sources of Durkheim's views, and have not wished to hang him on any single ideological peg (see Giddens 1977: 214). But that qualification only gives added force to the argument that suppleness is a critical factor in a work's durability. (On the various renditions of Durkheim's methodological views—again markedly contrasting in form and tone—see Platt 1995;[24] Lemert 1993: 29-30; Levine 1985: 55).[25]

The textual suppleness of an authorial corpus will depend on a number of factors residing in the work itself: the author's sense of play, paradox, and ambiguity; the stages through which his or her work has passed; the rhetorical figures that are employed—and the range, scope, and sheer bulk of their achievement. And with the classics we are talking about some bulk. The 1968 Berlin edition of Marx and Engels's *Werke* runs to forty-one volumes, while the ongoing Marx-Engels *Gesamtausgabe* (the critical edition) will run to over 100. The Max Weber *Gesamtausgabe* venture will amount to around thirty-five volumes; it would have been considerably larger except that, in contrast to Marx, only a tiny proportion of Weber's original drafts and manuscripts have survived. During his lifetime Simmel published twenty-five books, some very lengthy, "and around 300 articles, reviews and other pieces" (Frisby 1984: 22). Durkheim was also remarkably prolific, as Steven Lukes's bibliography of just over twenty-seven pages amply attests (1973: 561-589; also Nandan 1977). Such mass can be important for the very simple reason that it allows a reading community more interpretive options. The more bulky and messy the legacy, the greater possibilities there are for different readers to make different connections with its constituent parts. A craving for esoterica, a marked tendency of the academic temperament, can thus be abundantly satisfied.

Finally, textual suppleness is greatly enhanced by the survival of letters, corrected galley-proofs, manuscripts in the author's own hand complete with crossings-out and revisions, and lectures document-ing the author's cognitive processes. Or, rather, seeming to docu-ment them, for it is exactly the significance of these letters and drafts that can then become a source of scholarly excitement and revision-ism regarding what the author in question meant or was purportedly doing. And such excitement will only be fuelled by the "discovery," or at least dissemination, of work that gives an established writer a new face, particularly where it is congruent with changes in the wider cultural milieu. Marx's *oeuvre* is a case in point. The publication of the *Economic and Philosophic Manuscripts* (the so-called "Paris Manuscripts") in the early 1930s, and their first translation into En-glish in 1959, presented a "new" Marx: ostensibly humanistic, ro-mantic, existential. As McLellan points out (1975: 79), during the "prosperous" 1950s and early 1960s such work resonated nicely with a capitalist system that showed little sign of termination but that could be critically depicted as anonymous, de-personalized, manipulative, morally degenerate, "one-dimensional"—precisely *because* of its affluence. The Marx of the pauperization thesis or of the laws of motion thus gave way to the Marx of alienation. His early focus on the human subject, and its condition, a hardy peren-nial if ever there was one, nicely synchronized with the prevailing mood, and Marx could be brought into dialogue with Zen, with Christianity and with anything else that challenged acquisitive individualism. Equally, the young Marx became a posthumous critic of Soviet-type societies; and the question of continuity or break in Marx's own work became an animated topic of discussion too. Other discoveries or disseminations only raised the temperature of this discussion. The "lost" seven notebooks that Marx drafted during the winter of 1857-8, the so-called *Grundrisse*, surfaced in the 1930s, only became effectively available in German in 1953, and had to wait two more decades for a full English translation. Great claims have been made for it. According to Martin Nicolaus, "The *Grundrisse* challenges and puts to the test every serious interpretation of Marx yet conceived" (in Marx 1973 [1857-8]: 7); while to Terrell Carver (1975: 4), its Introduction "is one of the most deeply investigative of Marx's writings."[26] The emergence and translation or re-editing of other works of Marx has helped fuel further evaluations. These works includes "Results of the Immediate Process of Production," composed by Marx in the mid-1860s; the "Notes on Adolph Wagner," written between 1879-80; and a new Japanese edition, closely following Marx and Engels' handwriting, of *The German Ideology,* Part I.[27]

Another way of putting all this is to say that cultural artifacts prove supple when they are able not only to mean something to an audience but also to assume significance in markedly different situations (Iser 1978: 151). Texts, theories, and authors, too, must enjoy this chameleon capacity if they are to become and remain classic. But one should not press this point too far. In the academic sphere, it may be hard to shake-off classics *once* they have become firmly established. This may have little to do with their suppleness, resonance, and vitality, and everything to do with the ingrained habits of academics reluctant to change core theoretical curricula on account of lack of imagination or laziness.

Next, cultural resonance and textual suppleness imply the possibility of *reader appropriation*, and this appropriation will take the form of both integration—that is, attempts to harness texts and theories to various projects—and selective repudiation or "disavowal."[28] Appropriation in its turn will frequently involve a number of related hermeneutic activities. Language and conceptual translations may be required, for instance, and these will be generally domesticated in such a way as to make sense to the recipients' cultural conven-

tions and traditions. In some cases this domestication may be purpo-
sive and strategic. One thinks of Karl Mannheim, who orchestrated
an English translation of *Ideology and Utopia* (1936) that differs
considerably from the 1929 German version. Mannheim did not want
to capitulate to Anglophone empiricist and pragmatist traditions. But
he did want a sympathetic reading from an English-speaking public
for whom post-Hegelian or neo-Kantian metaphysical allusion is
rarely intelligible, let alone congenial. Because of this (among other
factors) Edward Shils's English translation witnessed a significant
"transformation of the theoretical vocabulary" found in the German
version. Thus:

> "Spirit" (*Geist*) becomes "mind" or "intellect;" "consciousness" (*Bewusstsein*) be-
> comes "mental activity" or "evaluation;" the various terms for the objective directedness
> of the will, its tendency towards one or another state of things, become "interests,"
> "purposes," "norms," or "values;" "primaeval structures of mind" become "irrational
> mechanisms;" and "false consciousness" is divided between "erroneous knowledge"
> and "invalid ethical attitude." (Kettler, Meja and Stehr, 1984: 114; also 107-128).

More often than not, however, changes in meaning are the result
of translators being unaware, or having little interest in being aware,
of the conceptual matrix in which the original terms are located.
This is the contention of Gisela Hinkle in her paper on "The Americanization of Max Weber":

> By "Americanization" we mean an interpretive transformation of Weber's writings
> through the process of translation. Translation from one language to another and more
> specifically from one intellectual and linguistic context to another, entails not merely a
> substitution of words but a transformation of ideas, styles of thinking, modes of expre-
> ssion, indeed a whole context of mental imagery and assumptions many of which may
> be unnoticed by the writer, the translator, and the reader." (Hinkle 1986: 89)

This has led in Weber's case to "insufficient awareness of his neo-
Kantian inclinations (and) has repeatedly distorted the meaning of
the text" (Hinkle 1986: 89; cf. 101). One salient example of mis-
translation—very important for the history of sociology – was
Parsons's rendition of Weber's *stahlhartes Gehäuse* as "iron cage."
(See the Appendix for a full treatment). Equally, appropriation of
texts or theories will always face the task of what Iser calls "consistency building" and it is this process that in good measure forms the
dynamic of textual interpretation. Iser's point is that any text contains "gaps" (he also refers to these as "blanks," "vacancies" and
"places of indeterminacy") that create an imbalance between text

and reader. This imbalance, moreover, cannot be definitively speci-
fied, because each reader or community will perceive a different set
of gaps in a single text. The varied meanings that can be attributed
to a single text are a result of the difference between the ways in
which different readers fill the gaps in the text. It is this ongoing
activity of consistency-building that enables sustained dispute among
readers while allowing all of them to claim authority in the text itself.[29]

Cultural resonance, textual suppleness, and reader-appropriation,
then, are all critical factors in a text's trajectory to classic status. So,
too, is the process of *social transmission and diffusion* whereby a
text, theory or author find vehicles or, better, agencies committed in
some way to their promotion. Typically the author, theory, or text
will be dependent on what Levine et al. (1976: 814-822) classify as
agents (interested individuals), media (books, articles, publishers,
etc.)[30] and centres of diffusion (e.g., academic institutions). In addition, it is useful, I suggest, to distinguish analytically between institutional and interstitial paths of transmission. The distinction is more
one of emphasis than sharp opposition. By the former I refer to the
primary role assumed by organizational factors in the ascent of an
author to classic stature. In this instance, figures owe their fortune
not only to their extraordinary intellectual gifts, but also to their leadership of a "school," and to the success of that school in promulgating
a theory, perspective, or method that penetrates the discipline's curricula or professional core, simultaneously advancing the status of
the theorist-leader at its head. Durkheim and Parsons are examples
of authors who benefited from this kind of transmission.[31] So, too,
did Paul Lazarsfeld[32] who, unlike his colleague Samuel Stouffer,
was not only an adept institution builder but was also renowned for
his ability "to recruit others to work on problems he was interested
in" and to facilitate a network of dependents and colleagues (Platt
1996: 259).

Interstitial transmission, on the other hand, refers to a rather different phenomenon, partly incubatory in character. Here an author's
work attains classical prominence not because it profits from the
organizational backing that a school affords, but primarily because,
in capillary fashion, it is carried by the tenacity and commitment of
a few dedicated admirers—often in unfavorable cultural and disciplinary circumstances. Interstitial transmission occurs, so to speak,

between the gaps and spaces of schools and current fashions, rather than being the hostage of these. The Anglophone transmission of Simmel after the Second World War is a particularly instructive case of this route; the German transmission of Weber during the Weimar Republic and beyond by the indefatigable devotion of Marianne Weber is another. However, even in these instances, some degree of institutionalization was necessary, not only for the advancement of Simmel's and Weber's fame but for their very survival as figures worthy of sociological consideration. Let us pause to consider this issue in more detail.

On the basis of research conducted by Helmut Fogt (1977), Dirk Käsler points out that the early reception of Weber's ideas—during his own lifetime and the Weimar Republic—was highly selective and, considering his work as a whole, mostly weak. For that reception "concentrated above all on the Protestant ethic writings and the printed versions of the lectures 'Science as a Vocation' (1919, 1921, 1930) and 'Politics as a Vocation' (1919, 1926)" (Käsler 1988 [1979]: 144). It is also sobering to recall that, between 1922 and 1947, *Wirtschaft und Gesellschaft* sold less than 2,000 copies. In contrast, between 1900 and 1920, Gustav Schmoller's now largely forgotten *Grundriß der allgemeinen Volkswirtschaftslehre* sold around 12,000 (Käsler 1988: 209).

How, then, did Weber's ideas survive and spread in German-speaking territories during the period of the Weimar Republic? There was no Weber "school" aggressively asserting itself in the universities during this time and Weber's cultural legacy was largely muted. All the same, it benefited from extant institutional forms. Most evidently, the continued vitality of Weber's ideas depended on the willingness of fellow academics to make them a major reference point in disputes about science and reason (Turner and Factor 1984; Lassman and Velody 1989), and this they did using a standard organizational device of promulgation—the scholarly article or book specifically devoted to his work. Moreover, the *Archiv für Sozialwissenschaft und Sozialpolitik*, the journal for which Weber assumed joint editorial responsibility in 1904, "continued to be the most influential social science journal until it was closed down in 1934" and "presented social science in the broad Weberian sense" (Stölting 1990: 118). At the same time, even though Weber the sociologist made limited headway in the curricula of German universities during this period, his reputation was promoted nonetheless by "popular educational initiatives such as the Hochschule für Politik in Berlin or the Volkshochschule in Cologne, of which Honigsheim (a student of Weber) was president from 1919 to 1933."[33] Weber's legacy was also buttressed by more elite initiatives: the Ludwig von Mises Seminar, for instance, in Vienna between 1920 and 1934, in which Weber's methodological writings in particular were communicated to a younger generation of economists that included Fritz Machlup, Friedrich von Hayek, Oskar Morgenstern, Gottfried Haberler, and Paul Rosenstein-Rodan. "Hayek would later initiate the translation of *Wirtschaft und Gesellschaft* into English; and Machlup, who ended up as a well-known expert on international economics at Princeton, was preoccupied with Weber's concept of ideal types into the 1970s. Alfred Schutz was also a member of the Mises Seminar" to which he delivered a lecture in 1930 on ideas that received extended treatment in *The Phenomenology of the Social World* (1932) (Swedberg 1998: 204-5, 301-2).[34]

The reception of Weber's work in America, up until the late 1930s, was also irregular and idiosyncratic, despite the efforts of writers such as Theodore Abel, Alexander von Schelting, Pitirim A. Sorokin, Talcott Parsons and Howard P. Becker to draw attention to it. Thereafter, powerfully fortified by the German-Jewish emigration from Nazi Germany, Weber's ideas radiated out from the key centres of New York (Columbia and the New School), Harvard, Wisconsin, and, later, Berkeley (Platt, 1985: 448-52). Still, by as late as 1949 only fourteen articles had been published on Weber in American sociological journals: five in *Social Research*, four a piece in the *American Journal of Sociology* and the *American Sociological Review* and one in *Social Forces* (Hinkle 1994: 286; *Social Forces* and *Social Research* were the first to publish articles on Weber in 1934). In Japanese universities, by contrast, Weber was an important presence from the mid-twenties onwards, scrutinized, above all, as a theorist of modernization. By 1998 there were "more than 160 translation of his works and more than 2,000 Japanese books and articles dealing with every aspect of Weber's writings" (Schwentker, 1998a: 171, drawing on Schwentker, 1998b).

Simmel's work enjoyed some institutionalization, of course, when it became part of the research program of the Chicago School. Yet it is Simmel's interstitial trajectory that makes him such an interesting case to examine. Having enjoyed a fairly strong appropriation during the early years of American sociology, Simmel's voice became much more subdued between approximately 1930 and 1955. Granted, his work continued to be canvassed at Chicago, was also a presence at Columbia University, through Robert Merton among others (Jaworski 1997: 69-77), and was also trumpeted and disseminated by a host of European scholars studying at the New School of Social Research in New York.[35] On the other hand, mainstream American social research was strongly positivistic during this phase and Simmel's philosophical, "impressionist" cast of mind repugnant or irrelevant to its sensibilities. For that reason, his legacy depended on the efforts of a relatively small band of enthusiasts. Standing against the current, they sought not to form a Simmel school or movement, but to insist again and again on Simmel's critical contribution to the sociological imagination. Of notable importance in this effort, aside from scholars I have already mentioned, was Everett C. Hughes, a student of Small and Park, who canvassed Simmel's ideas in Chicago during the 1940s and 1950s and who stirred such figures as Hugh Dalziel Duncan, Erving Goffman, and Donald N. Levine. Hughes was also a key broker of Simmel translations (see his own rendition of Simmel 1949) and was responsible for recommending Kurt H. Wolff to Jeremiah Kaplan, the youthful co-founder of the Free Press (Jaworski 1997: 22). According to Levine and colleagues, Wolff's "translation of a substantial amount of new material from the Simmelian corpus, published by the Free Press in 1950 as *The Sociology of Georg Simmel*, was more than any other single factor responsible for the revival of American students' interest in Simmel in the postwar years. It was followed, in 1955, by the translation of two more chapters of *Soziologie* by Wolff and Bendix" (Levine et al., 1976: 819). Yet still Simmel's place in sociology remained precarious. In the 1960s, "efforts to recover Simmel were eclipsed...by the surge of interest in Marxian writings, which led to Marx's joining Durkheim and Weber to form a canonized trinity of sociological founders" (Levine 1997:174). Following the work of Michael Landmann (a German philosopher), David Frisby and Donald Levine in the 1970s (Levine's own studies on Simmel stretch back to the 1950s), a renewal of interest ensued; and today, with the consolidation of postmodernism and of cultural studies, Simmel is more "classic" than ever.[36]

Instititionalization is thus a subterranean process as well as a highly visible one; it can be more or less dense, more or less "hard" and "soft"; it can also be episodic or continuous. Moreover it cannot be assumed that interstitial figures are inherently more vulnerable to the passage of time than their institutional counterparts, even if that is often the case. Erich Fromm's reputation – vibrant in the 1940s and 1950s as "a major psychoanalytic thinker, sociological theorist, and public intellectual" (McLaughlin 1998a: 216)—suffered in the longer term because he created no psychoanalytical school of his own (unlike, say, Adler or Klein), secured only a precarious institutional base in various universities, and straddled heterodox appropriations of Freudianism (critically anti-hagiographic) and Marxism (humanistic) that became increasingly repellent to later Freudians and Marxists. Moreover, as Neil McLaughlin argues, Fromm is one of those thinkers who have been "obliterated by incorporation" (Merton) as many of his ideas became absorbed into mainstream institutional settings without due recognition of their source. Perhaps Fromm's very heterodoxy will make him one day ripe for revival as a major thinker.

Conversely, institutionalization can severely damage a figure's reputation in the longer term. Interstitial figures, it is true, face the potential liability of being forgotten or of not enjoying the "influence" others better institutionally placed may profit from.[37] But they do possess the advantage of flexibility and agility. Being positioned obliquely to schools, their fate does not rest on them; when under attack, they are moving targets. Conversely, the leader or "representative" of a school or perspective resembles nothing so closely as a sitting duck. Marx's reputation, for instance, stands far greater chance of surviving in societies that were spared Soviet ideology than it does in societies in which Marx was the official icon of the regime, the pagan saint of one party rule. In contrast, Parsons, another figure whose work became highly institutionalized, has survived the sustained assault on his standing that began to mushroom in the 1960s. This is not only because structural functionalism never became the church of sociology, or a state-backed ideology, and from the beginning was openly contested. It is also because Parsons was always more than the bogeyman of normative functionalism. Had he just been this, the collapse and discrediting of normative functionalism would have meant his own theoretical annihilation too. This has not happened; and although the assimilation and critique of Parsons's work today is incomparably weaker than it was in the 1950s and 1960s, the majority of theoretical syntheses in sociology continue to confront it.[38] The work of Lazarsfeld, particularly following the demise of his Bureau of Applied Social Research, offers a somewhat different case. As Jennifer Platt (1996: 260, n. 10) remarks, Lazarsfeld "will not be forgotten, but his special association with method, and in particular a method so successful that it has become universal and has been worked on by many successors who have developed it in their own directions, leaves his memory at some disadvantage compared with those especially associated with a substantive specialism."

Finally, diffusion and transmission are marked by patterns of import, export—and re-export, that is the re-introduction of authors or texts, now suitably transfigured as "classic," into the host country that produced them. The case of sociology in Japan during the Meiji Restoration (1868-1912), and in the early part of the Taisho period (1912-26), can serve as an illustration of the import phenomenon, for in those years sociology developed under a strong British and American impress. By the early 1880s, Spencer's *Principles of Sociology* (1876) was already circulating in a Japanese translation; and Spencerian ideas were being canvassed by Japanese academics like Nagao Ariga—and Shōichi Toyama who, in 1893, was the first incumbent of the newly created chair of sociology established at the Tokyo Imperial University (Steiner 1936: 708-709). As Steiner reminds us, this "early recognition of sociology by the Japanese government antedates the establishment of professorships of sociology in England, France, and Germany, and is only slightly later than the beginnings of sociology in American universities." And indeed American sociology itself found particular resonance in Japan. As early as 1876, an American from Massachusetts, E.F. Fenollosa, was teaching sociology in Tokyo University, doubtless expounding (and exporting) Western ideas. But as Japan's rulers searched for models of modernization, the desire to import and inspect American concepts was the critical factor behind their reception. Copies of Lester F. Ward's *Dynamic Sociology* were available for purchase in Tokyo's Maruzen Book Store only a year after its original American publication in 1883 (Morioka and Steiner 1959: 606); and translations of Small, Giddings, Cooley, Ross, Ellwood, and others were soon to follow. Later on, in the twenties and thirties, American sociology fell from grace as growing regional rivalries saw Japanese social scientists turn increasingly towards French and especially German traditions—until, that is, the Allied victory when American sociology was embraced once more, though with some ambivalence towards its strongly quantitative and ahistorical tendencies (Morioka and Steiner 1959: 607-9; also Watanuki 1975).

As an example of export, and re-export, consider once more the case of Max Weber. Weber's position as a classic author of *sociology*, specifically, owes itself to a number of sources. During the 1930s, Weber's ideas were carried into exile (exported) by a remarkable group of scholars, who gave them various forms of expression: Mannheim from his base at the London School of Economics; Alfred Schutz, Albert Salomon, Karl Mayer, Emil Lederer at the New School of Social Research; Theodor Adorno, Max Horkheimer, and Herbert Marcuse at Columbia; and, at other places, scholars that included Reinhard Bendix, Hans Gerth, Paul Honigsheim, Paul Lazarsfeld, Alexander von Schelting among others (Kivisto and Swatos 1988: 30). Still, it is now widely acknowledged that Max Weber's position as a sociological paladin first took firm shape as an American appropriation, particularly by Talcott Parsons in the 1930s and thereafter. In the forties and fifties this was given further impetus by the American-based translations and interpretations of Hans Gerth and Reinhard Bendix, but also by such scholars as Edward Shils and C. Wright Mills. And in Germany itself it appears to have been Parsons and the school of structural functionalism he led that was decisive in "promoting Weber, the 'classic,'" (Käsler, 1988 [1979]: 211).[39]

The four factors that I have assembled to describe the process of classic reception/formation—cultural resonance, textual suppleness, reader-appropriation, transmission and diffusion—are best envisaged both diachronically and synchronically. Synchronically, because each of these elements to some extent implies the others; they are "moments" of a single process, rather than discrete entities or stages through which a text or author must pass (see figure 5.3). Diachronically, because classic-formation obviously requires time, particularly as regards diffusion and transmission. A temporal process is not, however, a foundational, continuous one. If it were, the ascent of writers and texts, once underway (whatever this means), would be smooth and cumulative. Yet as we have seen, with regard to Simmel and Weber, this is far from being the case.

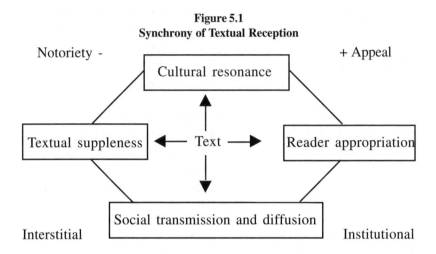

Figure 5.1
Synchrony of Textual Reception

Notoriety -   + Appeal

Cultural resonance

Textual suppleness ← Text → Reader appropriation

Social transmission and diffusion

Interstitial   Institutional

Books, works, and authors are compelled to climb a slippery slope to become classic—*and it is not their slope.* Success is contingent on a whole range of conditions and projects outside of their "influence," and the dimensions of these are complex. Since the end of the nineteenth century, sociology has been an international phenomenon. Originating in Europe and America, it now traverses the globe. But the peculiarities that mark sociology's path have, like the other human sciences, been manifestly conditioned by changes in the wider society in which it is practiced, and by the position of that society itself in the still wider geo-political web in which it is caught. By the same token, the esteem in which particular sociologist have been held is quite clearly related to these extradisciplinary factors.

The Classics, Gender, and Sexuality

In the previous section I noted that reader-appropriation is always selective, not just in terms of what *in* a text is rendered significant, but which *particular* text or texts are deemed especially significant too. We might now underline this contention by adding that selectivity is itself strongly conditioned, not just by cultural resonance in some nebulous manner, but by the impact of very specific social movements on reader-focus. In particular, the growth of feminism, and the wider explosion of interest in gender and sexuality associated with the rise of the women's movement, has had important consequences for the reception of classic texts. Because of these developments, essays and passages in the work of Comte, J.S. Mill, Marx and Engels, Spencer, Tönnies, but especially Durkheim, Max and Marianne Weber, and Simmel on sexual difference, eros, patriarchy, and women's culture are presently being given far more attention than previously they were.[40]

It is "of course" easy to forget just how divisive the gender question could be in the early days of sociology for those who chose to raise it. The Comte-Mill correspondence in the early 1840s, for all the studied courtesy and apparent mutual good will displayed by its interlocutors, effectively foundered on the issue—and the related one of biological determination. Mill, in November 1841, may have awaited each new volume of the *Cours* "with real intellectual passion," as he confessed to its author, but initial enthusiasm quickly cooled as he came to recognize the gulf between his own gender theory and Comte's insistence (in this stage of his thought) that "the female sex is constituted in a kind of state of radical infancy that makes it essentially inferior to the corresponding organic type." Mill's argument against this position invoked cultural explanations for women's subordinate status that have since become commonplace. But more important than the details of the argument was the recognition, shared fully by Comte, that their disagreement on the biology and sex questions amounted to "the most fundamental which social speculation can raise."[41]

The new reception afforded to the classics' approach to gender and sexuality has similarly reaffirmed their "fundamental" character. In sociology, Marx and Engels's contributions were the first to attract sustained and elaborate attention, either to co-opt them to a feminist politics or to jettison them from it.[42] At first—in the late sixties and early seventies—this had relatively little impact on, or resonance for, sociology more generally, both because of the highly self-referential character of Marxist discussion in much of that period, and the oblique and discomfited relationship of academic Marxists to sociology itself. Their congregation in sociology departments, either as faculty or students, coexisted with a widespread, though not universal, rejection of sociology as a bourgeois, normative, ideological, and hence largely bankrupt endeavour. In the past three decades, on the other hand, a decisive change has taken place. Now the work of all the classic figures is mined for gender comment and analysis; and, consistent with changes in the wider society, gender is treated as basic, as distinct from residual, in the writings of the great sociologists. For this reason, statements that would have until recently occasioned astonishment and incredulity are today sounding increasingly prosaic. Thus Klaus Lichtblau (1989-90: 89) can claim, and then seek to demonstrate, that when "the 'founding fathers' of German sociology set about to create a theory of cultural modernity, they treated gender as crucially important;" while Roth (1989-90: 71) can aver that "In the American canonization of [Durkheim], sociologists have almost completely overlooked the fact that gender plays a constitutive role in his theory of modern society."[43]

Moreover, the prevalence of modern gender politics has also undoubtedly prompted other research of relevance to sociology's classical legacy: for instance, on the contribution made to sociology by women in the early stages of the profession (Platt 1996; Deegan 1988; cf. Bulmer, 1989, 1984); or on incidents previously ignored or unknown, as in a study of Karl Mannheim that identifies "a surprising parallel" between his theory of intellectuals and of women, and which also establishes, the appreciative, but heterodox, relationship that existed between Mannheim and some of his most gifted female students—notably, Nina Rubinstein, Margarete Freudenthal, and Viola Klein (Kettler and Meja: 1993b). "Their achievements long hidden by the neglect imposed by cruel times that silenced voices and destroyed texts, as well as by the anti-feminine bias of intellectual history, Mannheim's women students produced exceptionally robust responses to his intellectual initiatives" (Kettler and Meja 1993b: 19). Even so, while the responses may have been "robust," it took the labor and scholarship of Meja and Kettler to exhume them; and this effort, in turn, would have been most unlikely without a sensitivity to the place of women in modern culture that the women's movement has helped promote.

At the same time, it is also becoming noticeable that the reception of the classical sociologists as gender theorists has produced an appraisal hierarchy in which the works of Weber, and especially Simmel, draw the most commendation from pro-feminist writers, and Durkheim the most animus.[44] Either way, the classic status of these authors is confirmed and consolidated by the continued attention—positive, negative, ambivalent—that they receive across yet another axis of their thought. Durkheim's case is proving to be particularly troublesome, even provoking somewhat contrasting responses from the same hand. Thus Jennifer Lehmann, in her critique of Durkheim's theory of the structures and functions of sexuality, can deplore the "widespread and profound theoretical violence [sic] and violation which Durkheim is led to commit, in a sense, to women." Moreover, "Durkheim is more than the father of sociology. He is a quintessential theorist of neo-liberalism, a quintessential articular/advocate, ideologist/apologist for welfare capitalism" (Lehmann, 1991: 165; also Lehmann, 1993: 1-11). Durkheim, one might think, could scarcely be expected to survive such a harangue. Yet in a companion piece it appears that he is not so easily dispatched:

> Feminism must continue to study Durkheim: to attempt to understand his theory of women, his general sociological theory, and the relationship between them as well as their impact on contemporary social thought and practice. Two objectives can be served by such research. First, a comprehensive feminist critique of Durkheim's work can be formulated. Second, a critical feminist appropriation of Durkheim's work can be effected. Several efforts along these lines have already been undertaken. (Lehmann, 1990: 185)

In addition, the implications of Durkheim's findings in *Suicide* that "the wife profits less from family life than the husband," that, "in itself conjugal society is harmful to the woman and aggravates her tendency to suicide" (Durkheim, 1970 [1897]: 188-9) are for Lehmann "radical," even "explosive," however much Durkheim himself sought to defuse them.[45]

Durkheim's treatment of gender, as Lehmann suggests, has by no means been negatively evaluated on all dimensions.[46] Yet it is also true that much of the commentary is damning. Mike Gane may rescue some interesting stray theorems of Durkheim—for instance the law that "under determinate conditions a group perceiving itself morally superior to another *normally* inflicts violence on the lower group," but for the most part the emphasis falls on the curious and dubious dilemmas Durheim's theory created for itself, as well as the ingrained "paternalism" and "conservatism" it displayed (Gane 1983: 260, 266). Roth's judgment is harsher still: Durkheim, "the patriarch of academic sociology" "accepted conventional bourgeois views of gender inequality, reinforced them with the pseudo-scientific arguments of physical anthropology, and elaborated a defensive ideology of unequal gender complementarity which was part and parcel of an evolutionary theory of organic solidarity." From this perspective, Durkheim is portrayed as continuing the "backlash against radi-

cal feminism" that emerged in France in the 1850s in response particularly to the "Saint-Simonian women's movement of 1848/49"
and to the later Comte's cultish idolization of Clotilde de Vaux (Roth,
1989-90: 72, 74).

In contrast, the retrieval and scrutiny of Max Weber's and Simmel's
gender theory has in general been far more positive and sympathetic. In Simmel's case this has been facilitated both by the striking
resemblances between his ideas on "objective culture" and the concerns of modern cultural feminism (van Vucht Tijssen 1991: 215;
Oakes 1984), as well as by the fact that Simmel bequeathed for interpretive excavation a significant corpus of work (fifteen essays or
so)[47] devoted to such issues as women's psychology, women and
militarism, female culture, the male and female "principles." Simmel's
focus is at once familiar: the obstacles to women in spheres and
institutions of "objective culture" (science, technology, government
in particular) whose ethos and rules of the game are distinctively
male in orientation and structure.[48] However, before Simmel's essays on women could be linked to cultural feminism, they had first
to be unearthed, and, as Lewis Coser points out (1977), there was
nothing automatic about this process. On the contrary, they were
largely ignored through all phases of his reception, in both America
and Germany, until the 1970s. The most prominent members of the
Chicago School did not discuss them, nor did later interpreters like
Kurt Wolff, Donald Levine, Robert K. Merton, or Coser himself in
earlier days. Yet, in Coser's later opinion, these essays "rank...among
the few major analyses not only of women's position in society, but
of the male-dominated culture which over the ages has been a powerful obstacle to women's ability to make contributions to the common culture" (Coser 1977: 870). However, if men ignored these
essays, the psychoanalyst Karen Horney did not. As early as 1926
she was championing their importance in an essay entitled "The Flight
from Womanhood: The Masculinity Complex in Women as Viewed
by Men and Women."[49] During the 1970s, Horney's essay reap-
peared in a number of anthologies (e.g., Miller 1973; Strouse 1974)
devoted to feminine psychology and the roots of the women's moment. According to Coser (1977: 871) "It seems incontrovertible
that without the peculiar sensitivities of these women writers Simmel's
essay(s) would not have become a contribution to our present debates."

Weber wrote far less specifically on women than Simmel, but both his concepts and his epistemology have earned critical feminist appreciation. For Sydie, (1987: 51) "Weber's ideas are very relevant to feminist concerns, particularly with regard to the definition of patriarchy," while Sylvia Hale (1992: 144) remarks that "Weber's view of sociology has the potential to provide a radically different and subjective interpretation of social reality." Still, for sheer exuberance, nothing matches Roslyn Bologh's paean to Weber in her book: *Love or Greatness: Max Weber and Masculine Thinking—A Feminist Inquiry* (1990). On the "new world...of men who struggle for power, men who strive to dominate their world, to give meaning to and find meaning in that world... I have no one to thank more for my entry and introduction ... than Max Weber.... His wealth as a man long part of that world enriches me" (Bologh 1990: xiv, xiii). Further, while "Weber's generally overlooked discussion of erotic love relationships is brief, embedded in his examination of the 'religious rejections of the world and their directions,'"

> the discussion is suggestive and provocative. Although he describes the joy and meaningfulness of erotic love in a disenchanted, rationalized world, he also describes erotic love in terms of conflict, coercion and brutality. His analysis resembles the analysis made by some modern-day radical feminists of all heterosexual relationships. (Bologh 1990: 195)

Bologh's comment that the aforementioned discussion has, until recently, been "generally overlooked" is certainly true. But why has this been its fate? Forming only a small part of Weber's "Zwischenbetrachtung"—that is, his "Interim Reflection," first published in 1915, and conceived as part of the unfolding project on the sociology of religion—one might suppose that it would be easy to miss. But this cannot be the whole story. The essay of which it forms seven pages in the English translation is reprinted in the most accessible and widely used of all Weber anthologies: Gerth and Mills' *From Max Weber*, available since 1948. Moreover, its strategic location—following immediately after Weber's essay on "The Protestant sects and the spirit of capitalism"—can hardly be said to give it a marginal position in the book as a whole. Yet how many cohorts of students and faculty simply skimmed this essay? How many social theorists, who are not Weber specialists, would be able to summarize its argument? How many people even knew Weber wrote about erotic love? Today this essay, which Gerth and Mills translated as

"Religious rejections of the world and their directions," has received a major fillip because of its resonance with certain postmodern motifs—particularly, its description of the life-world as consisting of various spheres or orders (economic, political, aesthetic, erotic, etc.) each subject to their own immanent principles and tensions. Increasingly, the essay as a whole is gaining the stature that "Class, Status and Party" or "Bureaucracy" also enjoy. "The light of the great cultural problems moves on," Weber once wrote (1949 [1904]: 112). To which we might add: and with it the enrichment of our understanding of the classics themselves.

In short, the feminist reception of the classics offers yet another angle on them that, until relatively recently, was largely absent. Feminist writers have sought both to engage critically with this work and, to varying degrees, incorporate it within their own agendas and concerns. The defects of the classical legacy, far from being impediments to its appropriation, give interested parties something new to chew on and debate. The inspiration or infuriation the classics provoke protects them from the greatest danger to their reputation—apathy and indifference.

Excursus on Classic Appraisal in Sociology and the Arts

Before closing this chapter, it may be useful to elucidate a key difference between the reception of classics in sociology and those in the arts—particularly the visual arts and the novel. This will help us appreciate, and re-emphasize, the point that the nature of classicality is stratified among branches of knowledge as well as within them. It will also reaffirm the contention that the search for an Archimedean point from which to judge a text as classic fails to recognise the historical complexity and specificity of classic formation and appraisal.

Alan How (1998: 830) has suggested that one major distinction between classics in, say English literature, and in sociology lies in the following peculiarity: whereas "the object of analysis for the student of literature is the classic literary text which makes up the canon...for the sociologist the canon is the medium through which the object, society, is viewed. As a result, for critics of the literary canon, theory has become the medium for liberating the discipline from the dead hand of classic authors; for critics of the sociological canon, theory *is* the dead hand of classic authors." This characterization is broadly accurate though we should note that some historians of sociology are concerned with classical sociological theory *itself* as a field of research (Camic 1997) and that some defenders of the literary canon, such as Harold Bloom (1996 [1994]: 30), insist that its "aesthetic power enables us to learn how to talk to ourselves and how to endure ourselves" – how, in other words, to confront our own existence. To that extent, the literary classic extends beyond itself to touch on the most poignant aspects of the human condition. Be that as it may, I suggest that there is another distinction between classics in sociology and in the arts that is even more telling than the one to which How draws our attention, one that helps to explain both the ferocity and the hyper-theoretical orientation that today characterize so many departments of English.

Sociological information is typically consumed by three, somewhat overlapping, publics[50]: scientific peers who are, above all, interested in recent advances of the discipline and new methods of investigation, institutional clients who want useful marketable data or politically convenient facts, and a discerning public that wishes to keep abreast of social issues and events. Yet who is it that affirms and sanctions in sociology that a text is a classic? The answer is surely other sociologists, who act as both judge and jury of the matter. Classic appraisal in sociology, then, is an internal and self-validating process, arrived at by specialists of the discipline invoking what are essentially esoteric criteria. Sociologists tend to believe that the people who are entitled to judge sociological merit are not "outsiders"—on what basis could they do so?— but members of their profession or "academic community." Moreover, this community is extremely exclusive, and essentially amounts to academic faculty who are, simultaneously, the consumers of the books they read and the estimators of their merit. It is true that, throughout the world, sociologists teach hundreds of thousands of students each year. But this is a subaltern audience. Though students are in a position to challenge the authority of what are introduced to them as classic texts, they are not in a position to *ignore* them if, for instance, Classical Social Theory is a mandatory course for their degree. And even the challenge will depend upon engagement with the classic texts. A challenge that does not do this will be treated as arrogant or dismissive, and will incur the appropriate penalty.

In contrast, a classic in the arts is not simply or always a function of the appraisal of culture specialists, such as literary or art critics. Neither is public recognition of a classic a necessary consequence of the compulsion exerted by these connoisseurs.[51] Rather, both potentially and in fact, there are two audiences available to a text awaiting judgment of exemplary greatness—the culture specialists and the non-academic public (or publics). This creates a unique problem for the former that is absent in sociology: the need to construct a "dividing line" between what Plato, in Part 7, Book 6 of *The Republic*, famously called "knowledge" (in which an agent really understands the nature of the object apprehended) and "opinion" or mere belief (in which understanding is shallow and impressionistic). This need arises because, without it, the authority of culture specialists would be usurped by a mass audience. It would also be difficult to sustain the distinction between pap and quality; and, without that distinction, anything that was massively appreciated, however "vulgar" or "trashy," would threaten to become a classic.[52] Sociology does not face this problem in regard to classic texts[53] for the simple reason that it has no public rivals, no, so to speak, "external" competition to defend itself against.

Put differently, the opportunities for popular contestation about matters of merit are much greater in the arts than in sociology. It is, of course, true that literature counts among its classics works that are immensely complex and opaque and that have "never had a life in the actual culture of their society; never, like Dickens or Shakespeare...had an existence in what we might call the marketplace, never had ordinary readers." Exemplary here are modernist texts like *Ulysses* and *The Waste Land*. Yet precisely because "there was no intervening process whereby they lived an authentic life in the ordinary culture of society," these texts may be "much more vulnerable than some of the older" ones in the longer term (Thorburn 1991: 312).

Nonetheless, the stratification of literature into different sorts of classics does not undermine the main point that, in literature, classics are open to being negotiated in a way that is simply not possible in sociology, whose classical texts have only a tangential relationship to "the ordinary culture of society." This is not to say that authors like Weber and Durkheim had an exclusively academic audience. They also wrote for the press, and made interventions into matters of wider political and cultural concern. But the point remains that it was not a non-social scientific public that accorded their work *classical* greatness. That was secured by culture-specialists, often from countries other than those in which the classic authors had flourished. (The case of Marx is obviously somewhat different because of his involvement in the workers' movement—for instance, the First International—and because of his symbolic importance for millions as the theoretical founder of communism.) With the classics of fiction, matters are very different, as John Sutherland (1993: 24), commenting on the British case, makes plain:

> Jane Austen, the Brontës, Thomas Hardy and Dickens sell (in World's Classics and Penguin Classics editions alone) up to fifty thousand copies a year of their most popular works in volumes costing 5 pounds or less....Cumulative sales are incalculably large. Thackeray currently sells twice as many copies a year of *Vanity Fair* as he did at any point during his lifetime.... Obviously much of this output is sopped up by traditional middle-class readers, many prematurely "retired," and by rising generations of schoolchildren and students entering adult literacy. But a good proportion must also be reaching self-improving readers.

Moreover, it is not just that non-academics play a continuing role in the appraisal and endorsement of classics in the arts. They have also made a major contribution to lifting them to the classical pedestal in the first place. The classic works and authors of sociology, on the other hand, were created by other sociologists. Accordingly, there is wide agreement that the person who is more responsible than anyone else for making Max Weber's texts classics of sociology is Talcott Parsons. In contrast, consider Botticelli's ascent to the classical (or "canonical") pantheon. Frank Kermode (1985: 6; cf. 17, 30) observes that Botticelli

> owed his promotion not to scholars but to artists and other persons of modern sensibility, whose ideas of history were more passionate than accurate, and whose connoisseurship was...far from exact. At this stage exact knowledge had no part to play. Opinion, to some extent informed, required, at this modern moment, a certain kind of early Renaissance art; Botticelli, along with some contemporaries—though first among them—provided it. Enthusiasm counted for more than research, opinion for more than knowledge.

In England, Botticelli's fame was established in the 1860s and early 1870s by the likes of A.C. Swinburne, the poet and critic, and Walter Pater, the essayist and critic. Neither was a professor, and though Swinburne had entered Balliol, he left without finishing his degree. The role of scholars like Herbert Horne and Aby Warburg was to "reinforce and secure" Botticelli's reputation; they were both "affected by a movement of taste over which they had no control," namely, "a new appropriation of Greek art, of Dante, of the newly valued Quattrocento" (Kermode 1985: 6, 29, 5). Sociologists also respond to changing taste; but the fame of Durkheim or Simmel was established by other academics, not by a lay public.

Literature's openness to lay publics has triggered in recent times two related kinds of response from those professors of English who deride the "canon." One has been to demote all literary artefacts to the same level or, if you prefer, to promote in the interests of "democracy" the meanest graffiti to the status of artistic expression worthy of humanistic study. The other, by means of which the first is often conceptually articulated, has been to manufacture forms of high-octane theory (poststructuralist, post-colonialist, feminist, semiotic) whose language is all but incomprehensible to the lay reader. As a result, the democratic rhetoric of anti-canonicity is itself couched in terms that actually preclude genuine democratic (public) intervention. The Platonic line between knowledge and opinion is thus sharply reinforced. Radical critics of the literary canon protest that their chief objective is to challenge the authority structure that decides the canonical list of authors and texts. In fact, there is no such authority, "no authoritative organ within the institution of literature which could constitute a universally valid canon of literature through a decision similar to the one taken officially by the authoritative organs of a worldwide church" (Olsen 1966: 76). If there were such an analogous body in literature, a literary equivalent to the Council of Trent, no canon debate would be permitted. That there is such a debate in literature is the clearest demonstration that literary classics are not the product of a single powerful constituency or a coalition of such constituencies, a source of regret, perhaps, for those with coup d'état ambitions.

Conclusion

My chief objectives in this chapter have been twofold: to show that the quest for fixed criteria of classicality is probably a hopeless task, second, to elicit from the expanding volume of sociological research on reception a set of concepts that will enable us better to understand the classic-formation process. These concepts offered not evaluative criteria of classicality, which, I argued, can only be question-begging, but rather an analytical schema that enables us to understand *sociologically* how certain texts come to achieve their standing. As such, the analytical categories are no substitute for the empirical studies that alone will be able to explain why and how a determinate text achieved "classic" status—in any of the multiple, stratified meanings associated with that term.

The next chapter turns away from classic reception to classic rebuttal. Increasingly today, one hears voices questioning the value and legitimacy of the classical legacy. These voices have not been harmonious; it would be simplistic to speak of a clear demarcation between friends and enemies of the classics. Besides, criticism of the classics, or of over-preoccupation with them by sociological theorists, is nothing new. For decades, advocates of applied research have complained of classical infatuation, deflecting sociologists from their real substantive task of explaining modern times or of attending to novel theoretical developments. Yet out of the cacophony of recent dispute, one theme stands out with particular audibility: a critique of the classics as, or as part of, a "canon." I now turn to examine the nature of this controversy and its implications for the practice of higher education.

Notes

1. I put it this way to acknowledge that a text may be deemed classic by an influential public during an author's lifetime, and be judged similarly by later generations. The point remains, however, that one cannot know that a contemporary text *is* classic. One can only know, from the standpoint of a later generation, that a text has become one.

2. Again, with the proviso mentioned in the previous endnote.

3. Jonathan Turner (2000) argues that Spencer has been unjustly forgotten and deserves "another reading as an important sociological theorist."

4. Cited in Lukes 1973: 392.

5. See Camic 1982; Hawthorn 1976; Swingewood 1970; Schneider 1967; Meek 1967 [1954]; Macrae 1979 [1969]); Macrae 1961.

6. I am grateful to Anne Furlong (2000: 10) for this insight and formulation. As she puts it, "classics are works which must be read, or whose implications must be incorporated into the global inferences of a discipline, in order to work in that field in the present."

7. For a similar view, see Randall Collins 1998: 32. Wilhelm Hennis (1988 [1982]: 31) has called Weber's *Protestant Ethic* writings a "didactic catastrophe." He adds that this is "perhaps the basis of their indestructible attraction."

8. Lemert introduces a further confusion when he seeks to explain why Durkheim's *Division of Labor* is "*still* a classic, its errors notwithstanding." Among the reasons he adduces "is that this book was powerfully successful in defining and solving the foremost moral dilemmas of *his day*." Yet then Lemert goes on to observe that "We,

however, in 1993, face a different set of moral concerns" (1994:91; my emphasis). This does not make sense. How can a book still be a classic because it defined and solved the moral dilemmas of Durkheim's day, particularly when these moral dilemmas are no longer our own?

9.   Olsen (1996: 78) says that "A literary work cannot, and this cannot is logical, be recognized as the work of art it is except through a process of appreciation." One might adapt this as follows: "A sociological work cannot, and this cannot is logical, be recognized as the work of sociology it is except through a process of assimilation."

10. Olsen 2001; McLaughlin 1999, 1998a, 1998b; Platt 1995, 1996, 1985; Aschheim 1992; Kettler and Meja 1993a; Meja and Kettler 1990; Kettler, Meja and Stehr 1984; Roth 1992, 1988, 1971; Camic 1992; Lamont 1987; Megill 1987; Tribe 1989, 1988; Käsler 1988 [1979]; Kivisto and Swatos 1988: 28-39; Gane 1988; Hinkle 1986; Lang and Lang 1988; Levine 1985, Levine, Carter and Gorman 1976; Frisby 1984; Brauns 1981; Rüschemeyer 1981; Weiss 1981; Riemer 1981 [1959]; Sprondel 1981; Cahnman 1977; Coser 1977; Shils 1982 [1970].

11. See Johnston 1995: 84-165 for details.

12. For useful accounts of the field see Holub 1984; Link 1980, [1976]; also relevant are Klein 1985; Holub 1983; Hohendahl 1977.

13. Iser, 1979: 15; Iser 1980: 62; Jauss 1982: 21.

14. Levine et al. 1976: 815.

15. Abel 1965 [1929] opens with a chapter devoted to Simmel. Of the three other thinkers Abel believed to have made major attempts to establish sociology as an independent science, only Weber has survived to be read and re-read. The sociology of Alfred Vierkandt and Leopold von Wiese is today mostly forgotten.

16. Levine et al. 1976: 816.

17. Levine et al. 1976: 818.

18. Catlin, in Durkheim 1938: xi.

19. Or as Stephen P. Turner (1995: 12) remarks, *The Rules* is a "classic", because it poses "questions of enormous difficulty and centrality." For a not so ironic counterpoint to Durkheim's "Rules," see Giddens 1976.

20. Conal Condren argues that classic status is not an outcome of such inherent properties as "originality," "influence" or "coherence," but is rather the result of the adoption of particular texts by political or other movements seeking authoritative support. Of particular importance to the ascent of texts to classic status, to their "appraisive field," is textual ambiguity because

> By virtue of the ambiguous [the theorist] can bypass, or mask, politically divisive issues among the audience to which he would appeal. By virtue of the ambiguous he thus gives the different sections of his audience the creative opportunity of deciding for themselves ways in which they may identify with him. The ambiguous, then, can provide an important mechanism by which otherwise different groups can find salvation under one banner and share a common vocabulary for the variety of future actions and expressions of belief. (Condren 1985: 243)

21. Catlin, in Durkheim 1938: xxvii.

22   Zeitlin 1987 [1968]: 48 and passim.

23. Bellamy 1992: 74-104.

24. Jennifer Platt's article on the American reception of *The Rules* is particularly valuable in identifying four problems that all reception research encounters. She mentions (a) the problem of untangling the reception of one text (in this case *The Rules*)

from that of others by the same author, particularly where references to the former are oblique; (b) the problem of "whether to count only explicit, referenced use as part of the reception of the work" (such a limitation might miss cases of what Merton calls "obliteration by incorporation" and, relatedly, might conflate direct influence and mediated influence; (c) the problem of "where to look for the reception," given that texts like *The Rules* are pertinent to a very broad area encompassing theory, metatheory and methods; and (d) the problem, for those reading translations, of distinguishing between Durkheim's impact on a readership and that of the translator's (Platt 1995: 77-79).

25.   And on aspects of Durkheim's reception during his own life time in France, see Lukes 1973: 296-319; and Gane 1988: 75-86.

26.   See also the estimate of Hobsbawm, in Marx 1964: 9-11.

27.   For details of publication and translation of these texts, see, respectively, Mandel, in Marx, 1976 [1867]: 943-947; Carver, 1975: 161-178; Carver 1998: 104-107. The re-edited version of *The German Ideology* Part I is a result of the meticulous labors of the Japanese Marx scholar, Wataru Hiromatsu, details in Carver 1998: 117, note 26.

   Reinvigorated speculation on Durkheim's intellectual trajectory was provoked by the discovery in 1995 of around 600 pages of notes, in the hand of the philosopher André Lalande, recording Durkheim's lectures a the Lycée de Sens between 1883-4. According to Jones (1999: 112) , this lecture course "reveals a Durkheim so dramatically different from the one with whom we are familiar that he might be reasonably described as the 'earlier' Durkheim. Most important for our purposes, this earlier Durkheim was in no sense a social realist—in fact, he seems to have possessed no sociological sensibilities whatsoever."

28.   On the latter, see Levine 1985: 89-141.

29.   Iser 1978: 18, 167; Iser 1974: 282; Freund 1987: 146; see also the pertinent remarks of Collingwood 1946: 241-243 on the " a priori imagination."

30.   See also Naumann, 1976: 120, on "mediating organs."

31.   For models that seek to depict this process, see Wiley 1979, Tiryakian 1979; Szacki 1973; Mullins, 1973, 1983. Also relevant are Oberschall 1972; Meyer 1970.

32.   I am not invoking Lazarsfeld, and was not previously invoking Mannheim, as instances of "classic" figures, though many people might believe both authors should be so credited. (Can anyone write seriously about the sociology of knowledge without having read *Ideology and Utopia*?) Lazarsfeld's case is rather illustrative of the school-building phenomenon more generally, as Mannheim's is of the relationship among author, translator and reading public. For a *classical* example of that relationship see the Appendix on Weber, Parsons, and the reception of the "iron cage" metaphor, below.

33.   Tribe 1988, summarising Lepsius, 1987 [1981]: 5; more generally, Lepsius, 1981.

34.   On Hayek's role in initiating the English-language translation of *Wirtschaft und Gesellschaft,* see Parsons 1980: 42.

35.   For Albert Salomon's estimation of Simmel, whose Berlin lectures he attended in 1910, and also for a physical sketch of Simmel as a lecturer – "fascinating and repellent alike, as if surrounded by a halo of solitude and disgust," see Salomon,1997 [1963]: 91-108).

36.   Weinstein and Weinstein 1993. For a critique of postmodernized Simmel, see Jaworski 1997: 116-123.

37.   See, in this regard, Shils on the contrasting fates of Mannheim and Horkheimer, in Shils 1982 [1970]: 303-9.

38.   Just as practically all the major textbooks devoted to modern sociological theory continue to describe it.

39. On Parsons's importance for the German reception, see Stölting 1990: 125; and more generally, Kivisto and Swatos 1988: 31; Shils 1982 [1970]: 317.
40. Pickering, 1997; Gane 1993; Lehmann 1991, 1990; van Vucht Tijssen 1991, 1988; Bologh 1990, 1987a, 1987b; Erickson 1989; Roth, 1989-90, 1988; Lichtblau 1989-90; Scaff, 1989; Kandal 1988; Schwentker 1987; Sydie 1987; Vromen 1987; Dahme 1986; Dahme and Köhnke 1985; Oakes 1984; Tiryakian 1981a; Wityak and Wallace 1981; Coser 1977; Thompson 1976; Besnard 1973; Johnson 1972.
41. I am drawing on the Comte-Mill correspondence in Thompson 1976: 193, 198, 201, 205.
42. For relevant material, see Allen et al. 1974; Rowbotham 1973; Leacock 1972; 7-67; Mitchell 1971; Firestone 1971 [1970], Reed 1970 [1969]); also Barrett 1980, and the papers collected in Malos 1980
43. See also Gane 1983: 236, on the "pivotal" nature of Durkheim's research into "the separation of the sexes"—pivotal, that is, in "the reorganisation of the general theory."
44. A notable exception to this generalization is the work of Stjepan G. Meštrovic (for instance, 1991 and 1992). See also Ramp 2001.
45. Lehmann 1990: 177, 164.
46. She cites Kandal 1988; Gane 1983; Tiryakian 1981; Besnard 1973 as evidence of writers who have sought, despite their criticisms, to salvage something of value from Durkheim's gender analysis.
47. Comprising 253 pages of small print in Simmel 1985 [1890-1911].
48. Simmel 1985 [1890-1911]; Simmel, 1984; cf. van Vucht Tijssen 1991: 203; Dahme and Köhnke 1985: 12-22.
49. The essay was published in the *International Journal of Psychoanalysis* 7 (1926): 324-39.
50. I am adapting Joseph Ben-David's (1975) discussion of the three publics of social science.
51. Though public recognition will be affected by curriculum control in the schools and universities: students are first told *Hamlet* is a classic, and then are expected to see and show why it is.
52. This is an oversimplification. The public culture soon sheds popular works that do not measure up to aesthetic/artistic standards of a great text. Hence the term "classic," in this context, is a misnomer, part of the stock hyperbole of book publishers.
53. Though it often does in relation to the social world more generally: "good" theory, after all, is supposed to be counterintuitive.

6

Canons

Introduction

Over the last two decades, the term "canon" has become something of a buzzword in cultural circles. In the humanities—particularly in literary theory and the study of religion—the "canon" dispute has spawned a truly gargantuan body of writing. The social sciences, too, have increasingly adopted this concept, though its meaning remains very much in flux. However, two features of the term's physiognomy have become particularly noticeable in the short period of time it has been in vogue.

The first is the largely (but not exclusively) polemical dress in which it has been clothed. Second, and relatedly, the word "canon" is largely used in a specific context: the battle over the university and college curricula. This battle encompasses such issues as how best to teach the "great books" or "classic texts" of the social sciences, which of them to teach, whether they should be taught at all, what their relationship to modern texts should be, and whether the prestige accorded them is defensible or desirable in a late modern, ethnically plural, gender-conscious, economically and politically divided social world (Parker 1997). Over these matters tempers are liable to fray, and for an understandable reason: the teaching curriculum is the key institutional mechanism through which sociology as a discipline continues to be shaped.

This chapter outlines and examines the multiple meanings the "canon" has assumed in sociological, or sociologically relevant, discussion. The argument can be summarized as follows: Broadly, the term "canon" has little sociological value as applied to secular "classic" texts. Though some limited meaning can be rescued from cur-

rent usage, the term helps promote a caricature of political disagreements about the classics in the academy; and erroneously implies
that secular classics and religious canons have fundamentally similar properties. Even so, while the terms of the debate on humanistic
and social science education are muddied by references to the canon,
the issues raised by the debate itself are a pertinent index of changes
within these disciplines more generally—particularly in regard to
teaching practices and the growing divisions of sensibility that
characterise those engaged in academic work.

"Canon" in Current Social Theory: Usages and Appraisals

What, then, does the term "canon" embrace in sociological discussion and in social theory more generally?

1. Most important, it is employed of the "great" texts and, though
less often, great authors of sociology; canon and classic are thus
used synonymously. Three versions of this conflation can be identified; each of them, but especially the first and the third, are redolent
of discussions in contemporary literary criticism and evidence of
the osmotic effect on sociology those discussions have had in recent
years. The first derives from those who see in the classical "canon,"
not greatness at all, but, as they express it in their vernacular, op-
pressive logo-centrism, sexism, Eurocentrism and other kindred trans-
gressions and omissions of hegemonic Western culture. In other
words, the canon is excoriated for its intellectual exclusiveness and
the stranglehold over cultural institutions it exerts; its monumentalist
world-view in which the "canon of Western culture's great works
[are] understood as enduring, sacred objects of worship" (Rosaldo
1989: 219); its exclusion of texts and authors from non-Western, or
domestically subordinate, cultures; its related complicity in the per-
petuation of social injustice visited on oppressed or marginal groups
by ruling elites.[1] This attack by many academic feminists, leftists,
and so-called multiculturalists is evident not only in texts devoted
specifically to a deflation of the sociological canon (e.g., Connell
2000; Connell 1997),[2] but also, and more usually, in conference
caucus banter, newsletter polemic, departmental discussion on what
graduate students should read as part of their comprehensive exami-
nations or on what kind of faculty should be hired, attempts by sociologists engaged in women's studies programs to challenge the "male"
curricula, and so on.[3] In an extreme form it surfaces in remarks of

an English professor, offering an obituary to Audre Lorde. Proclaiming Lorde a feminist theorist, the author continues:

"What does it mean," Lorde asks "when the tools of a racist patriarchy are used to examine the fruits of the same patriarchy? It means that only the most narrow perimiters [sic] of change are possible and allowable." Lorde is speaking about a university. (Fulton 1993: 11)

Feminist theory, "to create lasting change, requires the skill of the poet to resist the master's tools and to articulate our lives and our knowledge." Failing that, the bleak "alternative is 'to make a graveyard for our children'" (ibid.). With greater sobriety, but with the same adversary in mind, we are also instructed,

The standard models of the university curriculum are profoundly exclusionary. When the origin of the traditional curriculum is traced, the reason for this version of reality is not difficult to understand. As feminist pedagogy has pointed out, today's monastic models of the university were initially forged for an elite: male students who were white, able-bodied, and heterosexual....Programs and courses in Women's Studies are attempting to change this atmosphere and fill the exclusion protected by the canon. (Forbes 1993: 3, 8)

In this first version, then, the canon is an object of denigration. The canon encompasses the classic texts of Western civilization, and typifies a broader cultural oppression. The implication is that the canon so defined is largely irrelevant to the modern world, and lacking in radicalism. In the second key usage of the term, conversely, the classical tradition and the core values of liberal humanism are vehemently affirmed. Often, "canon" appears in this variant in scare-quotes, indicating a dislike for the pejorative and tendentious connotations that this term often assumes. Essentially, this second rendition is a response to what its protagonists portray as the current assault on the liberal university as a whole, and the Enlightenment values of reason, discipline, and independence that, for over a century, have nourished it. Typically, the roots of this assault are located, by its opponents, in the rapid growth of higher education during the postwar boom, and the "expressive revolution" of the sixties' counter-culture. Its "single minded, often fanatical onslaught on boundaries and structures," and its associated "crusade to release infinite, expressive modes of being and cognition into the world of everyday life" (Berger, B. 1991: 321) have done profound damage to the university. A stratum of disgruntled academics is the insincere beneficiary of that period and its aftermath. It is a beneficiary because it was university expansion, a product of the very capitalist society the critics habitually condemned, which gave them their comfortable, tenured positions. It is insincere, because the obsession with "power" that courses through the writings of the self-styled radicals —the power of men, whites, Europeans, capitalists, etc.—bespeaks not a genuine egalitarianism, but a profound *ressentiment* towards those with more resources and wealth than they have themselves (Alter 1991: 285-6). Such a stance, and the genuflection to "political correctness" that is its corollary—ideological conformity to a radical or "progressive" program—threatens to "destroy an inheritance of timeless value," namely, "the achievements of the classics, both as icons of permanence and ... index of change." Defending "what has come to be derogatorily called 'the canon'" thus becomes tantamount to defending the liberal university and society against the ravages of its detractors (Berger, B. 1990: 324, 315). For the "late sixties" have not disappeared; "they have become institutionalized, both culturally and politically" (Berger, P. 1992: 13; and Bloom, A. 1987: 313-335). As Irving Louis Horowitz puts it,

> Sociology is now an ideology, instead of what it had been in an earlier epoch, a study of ideology. Under such circumstances, the flight of serious scholarship and scientific research from sociology is inevitable....Sociology is thus a residue of what it once was. Its core is no longer theories of society patiently built up from empirical investigations; instead it consists of crude caricatures of society. Sociology has become a series of demands for correct politics rather than a set of studies of social culture. Theoretical differences are evaporating as gentle intimidation displaces intellectual inquiry, and the result is an advanced form of decay disguised but not removed by the plethora of ideologists who have invaded this once omnibus "science of society."[4]

Horowitz himself does not use the term "canon" in this piece, probably because he believes the term to have been so theoretically compromised by the classics' detractors. But the atmosphere that pervades the article, and its general argument too, is unmistakeably part of the ongoing culture war in which discussion of the canon has become a salient motif.[5]

The equation of classic and canon is not always as pugnacious as these first two versions may make it appear. For notable also is a variant which may be called the "qualified canonicity" position. From this standpoint, both critique and support of the canon are legitimate, *sotto voce*. The critique, for instance, may be that "inculcation into a canon is an intellectually restrictive identity forming process which makes it difficult for students to think critically about 'sacred' texts" (Gubbay 1992: 9). Or it might be said that canonicity does not connect with the "life-experiences" of students, is restrictive, and that theoretical learning should be more issue-centred. Still, there is no denial of the greatness per se of the canonical texts, indeed that greatness may be robustly affirmed, and of the need of sociology students to have some relationship to them (Calhoun 1996). Conversely, while defenders of canonicity rehearse the functions such texts perform for the discipline and for students (canonical texts are exemplars of creative thinking, etc.), there is recognition of the costs previously mentioned. Where these costs are especially emphasized, qualified canonicity may be said to shade into, but is only analytically separable from, "critical canonicity." Contemplating the experience of his department's review of teaching theory at Britain's University of East Anglia, Howard Caygill puts it this way:

> So, we reflected on why we had a canon—what did it do—this trinity of Marx, Weber and Durkheim? As literary critics tell us in their more sociological moments, a canon of texts obeys a logic of inclusion through exclusion; they are identity forming practices of exclusion. So a particular religion, or discipline, identifies itself by the possession of texts which belong to it, and to no-one else. At UEA we were concerned about this aspect of canonicity which...worked against the students developing radical critical skills in dealing with them....But then we realized that in working within a modular system we might not be producing the kind of identities which would be recognisable by the profession as a "sociologist." (Caygill, in Gubbay and Caygill 1992: 4)

Faced with this dilemma, the department's compromise "was to produce a course which obeyed the principles of canonicity, but which also deconstructed that principle." This "critical canonicity" is in keeping with those who "want to keep a canon, even if it's a different one" (ibid.).

So far I have dealt with one major usage of canon, canon as classics, and I have traced three verdicts on it: against, for, ambivalent. Yet, as this discussion stands, matters remain ambiguous on a particular point. Is it the classics as authors that are the canon (drawing on the analogue of the canonized figures of the Roman Catholic church: the saints)? Is it their texts that are canonical? Or is it a *portion* of their texts that are to be characterised as such? A perusal over the last few paragraphs indicates that those who employ the term "canon" are disposed to skate over both of the first two usages, but a more restrictive one, what might be called super-classicality, may also be implied. Guenther Roth (1992: 454) states it explicitly:

In American social science it may be feasible to use the term canonical to refer to writings that are ritually cited and assigned, and given standardised, routinized treatment in textbooks. Only a small part of the work of a so-called classic author attains that status. In Weber's case, this involved at least the Gerth and Mills translation [*From Max Weber*, which has sold over 200,000 copies], including the two speeches ["Politics as a vocation," and "Science as a vocation"], as well as *The Protestant Ethic and the Spirit of Capitalism*.

2. Canon, we have seen, can be applied to both classic authors and texts. But there are also more general usages of the term that embrace the classics, but that insert them into a broader intellectual and social environment. One such general usage is covered in the German notion of *Bildung*, "that untranslatable word denoting, in Hegel's words, a 'rising towards the universal,' a transcendence of the tribal pieties towards a vision of the whole" (Scruton 1993: 213). In Germany, *Bildung* was procured through the learning of foreign languages and through familiarity with "the classical humanist curriculum. You were expected to recognise quotations from, or allusions to, Dante, Shakespeare and Goethe.... Today political journalists in Germany are still supposed to know that Weber spoke of politics as a strenuous slow boring of hard boards," and French graduates from the Ecole Nationale d'Administration are expected to have read the two speeches on science and politics as a vocation" (Roth 1992: 453). Or, to express the idea of *Bildung* in an Anglophone idiom, we can say that it is concerned with cultivation, a receptivity towards "high culture," which the canon itself makes concrete: the "canon defines what one ought to have read and understood, at least in reasonable large part, if one is to count as an educated person" (Quinton 1993: 15).

Accordingly, *Bildung* suggests a strong and enduring relationship to tradition and history, and it is this nexus that has also occasioned discussion of the canon. In literary and aesthetic theory, for example, the canon has been envisaged by writers such as Ernst Gombrich and Northrop Frye "as a total narrative, a work of art made out of other works of art that tries to tell the 'whole story' about the origins and transmission, the interrelationships between, and the final worth of a culture's valued works of literary or visual art" (Gorak 1991: 254-5).

So far as I am aware, no parallel to this usage exists in sociological discussion. What does exist, and this is the second of our general usages, is a notion of canon that refers not primarily to a list or series of "classic" texts so much as to the principles of excellence and standards of achievement that such texts establish or represent. A commitment to canonicity, in other words, entails a cultural appreciation of what greatness has come to mean within a particular tradition, a "good" towards which action can be oriented (Turner 1990; MacIntyre 1988: 31). Tradition and canon are thus closely tied notions (as are tradition and "classic"),[6] but remain distinctive nonetheless. Canons exist within traditions, but not every tradition necessarily enshrines a canon. For a tradition that harbored no injunctions to be excellent, and that encouraged simple repetition, or thoughtless, slavish compliance and conformism would be bereft of a canon. Moreover, the authority that a canon embodies is open and discursive. It persists as engagement, not genuflection; is not immune or indifferent to novelty, but rather becomes the context in which, and the means by which, novelty is measured and assessed; is not static, but an expanding interface between a set of standards and particular interests; is not transparent but requires interpretation by a community of enquirers.

Another way of putting this is to say that a "friend of the canon" (Turner 1990) departs insistently from two other kinds of standpoint towards it: that of the "contemporary," and that of the "philistine." The former values only the present, the immediate, the relevant, the concrete, the instantaneous, equating this with the authentically new. For the "contemporary," tradition is bunk, history unedifying, and the dominant emotion is the desire to be without (to be "free" of) precursors or heritage. It is John Cage stating that "Beethoven is shit" (Turner 1990: 239). From such a perspective, the canon represents an intolerable infringement on self-creation and self-expression, the "self" here being envisaged as a *tabula rasa*. Equally, the canon's intimation of boundaries and limits is deemed out of place in a democratic culture. For those whom Nietzsche called "philistines," a rigorous sense of canon is also uncongenial. While the philistine will happily endorse the greatness of what is past, and revile as vulgar or declinist what is present, this is not, for Turner, the same as appreciation of canonicity. The canon is a formative moment of an activity, not a set of monuments or an object of complacent idolization. Or, rather, the canon is the sedimentation of past practices and achievements that are recognized to be superlative, and that inspire apprentices to match or surpass them.

Translated to the classics of sociology, one might then say that the "good" to which the classics orient us, the standards they ask us to meet, are what they themselves embodied: independence of mind, the comparative method, the discovery of big questions, the formulation of pregnant concepts, scholarship, the spawning of hypotheses and fruitful provocations.

3. Finally, the notion of canon in sociological discussion extends to two other meanings that are general and specific simultaneously: general in referring to more than the classical tradition; specific in referring to what on the face of it appear fairly concrete objects of cognition. In the first place, "canon" denotes a broad area of disciplinary instruction. This is the sense conveyed in James Dowd's article "Revising the Canon," in which the author's zealously over-quantitative colleagues are urged to make room in their graduate programs for interpretive, hermeneutic sociologies, and, by so doing, expand the present canon. According to Dowd:

> A graduate training program constitutes a type of canon. It specifies, although not always explicitly, an authoritative, approved list of courses, authors, works, and ideas....As discussed here in this essay, the canon of sociology includes a set of texts written by the sociologists of the classical period, a set of procedures for conducting the research and for analyzing the data that it produces, and a set of ideas (that is concepts, generalizations, and theories) generated by empirical research undertaken in this century. (Dowd, 1991: 317)

More crisply, the canon for graduate students consists of "a curriculum of required courses and related performance tasks, most especially the dissertation" (ibid.).

In the second place, canon refers not specifically to the curriculum, but to works that may well help to shape it, especially those that aspire to be a kind of sociological audit, a codification of where sociological research currently stands. A salient use of the term canon in this context, perhaps drawing on associations with Canon Law, is found in the 1989 Symposium in *Contemporary Sociology* devoted to assessing Neil Smelser's (ed.) *Handbook of Sociology* (1988). Many of the contributors to that Symposium were less concerned with the accuracy and perspectives of the text's many and diverse chapters, than with the nature and function of handbooks themselves. Alan Sica (1989: 504) thus asked whether a handbook is "to be taken as canonical so that scholars not mentioned in it do not exist sociologically" (1989: 504), a question answered in the affirmative by the somewhat troubled Symposium editors, Craig Calhoun and Kenneth Land (1989: 475). In their view,

> A handbook is a statement of some significance for a discipline...a powerful statement of the disciplinary canon (i.e. an authoritative presentation of problems, concepts, theories, methods, and findings that are central to the discipline, its major contributors, and important texts).

Smelser's *Handbook* was thus "a momentous event, potentially very helpful to the discipline but also an exercise of considerable power." As such, the editors wondered whether "revising or reaffirming a canon...is too important and difficult a task for a single editor." They concluded that it was, and that such an enterprise in future should be subject to "stronger institutional mechanisms," so as to "promote as much catholicity of representation of sociological subject matters" as was humanly possible (1989: 475-7).

Straddling both of the usages above is Pierre Bourdieu's discussion of what he calls "canonical disciplines"—he mentions in this context the history of French literature, classics, and philosophy—and the "canonical professors" who teach them, exerting "cultural power" by superintending the standards of academic judgement through curriculum control. For Bourdieu, the production of textbooks and surveys that "consecrate" the canonical mentality "perpetuate an outmoded state of knowledge, instituting and canonizing problems and debates which only exist and subsist through the inertia of academically objectified and incorporated syllabuses" (Bourdieu 1988 [1984]: 100-2).

Conflicting Terminologies

Having now reviewed the major usages of the term "canon" in sociological discussion, what are we to make of them? Clearly, a number of these usages are irreconcilable not only in tone (canon can function both as a term of disparagement and of commendation), but also in meaning and import. For instance, in the usages dealt with under 3 (canon as curriculum and codification) a canon seems to be something open to rationalistic manipulation. A graduate committee can "revise the canon," a disciplinary committee can determine what is to be considered the state of the sociological art. The implication is that canons can be formulated in an almost bureaucratic manner, becoming little more than the application of certain rules and formulae that have been organizationally endorsed. In sharp

contrast, the notion of canon as an excellence to which human endeavour is oriented (see 2) emphasises the limits of proceduralism.
As Alasdair MacIntyre (1988: 31) puts it,

> What can never be done is to reduce what has had to be learned in order to excel...to the
> application of rules. There will of course at any particular stage in the historical devel-
> opment of such a form of activity be a stock of maxims which are used to characterize
> what is taken at that stage to be the best practice so far. But knowing how to apply these
> maxims is itself a capacity which cannot be specified by further rules, and the greatest
> achievements in each area at each stage always exhibit a freedom to violate the present
> established maxims, so that achievement proceeds both by rule-keeping and by rule-
> breaking. And there are never any rules to prescribe when it is the one rather than the
> other that we must do if we are to pursue excellence.

Moreover, the concern articulated by Calhoun and Land (1988:
477) that a Handbook should reflect "canonical representation of
the field," and that, to facilitate this objective, "editors of future handbooks would be well advised to form advisory editorial boards composed of members from diverse specialities of the discipline, schools
of thought, and geographical regions" is not only instrumentalist
but also plays on a democratic notion of representation flatly at odds
with the idea of canon invoked by MacIntyre and Roy Turner. On
their account, a canon is not to be envisaged as an aggregate or a
mean of current practice, so much as an apprehension of what is
best—to which current practice can then be oriented, and against
which it can be measured.

But incompatible usage is not the only problem that emerges from
discussion of the canon. Just as evident is a certain redundant grandilo-
quence that graces the term. Why not call a spade a spade? Why, in
other words, employ the term canon at all when "curriculum" or
"codification"—or "excellence" for that matter—would appear to
serve just as well? More serious still is the tendency towards caricature that the term encourages. This is especially true of those treat-
ments that dismiss the classics as "hegemonic." For not only does
this distort the complex processes that eventuate in classic status
being accorded to texts and authors. It also homogenizes into "the
Western canon" what are in fact diverse theoretical traditions. Moreover, it is not always clear what critics of "the canon" are intending.
Is it the abolition of canonical thought per se which is the objective;
or is it the creation of a new canon? If it is the latter, then by their
own argument this must lead to new exclusions; a new "hegemony"
will replace the old. If it is the former, then we are entitled to ask
how this is to be done.

Conversely, opponents of the anti-canon factions are prone to push their case too far. From as early as one can discern, sociology, like all the other social sciences, has had the closest relationship with ideological notions and projects—liberal, republican, Marxist, nationalist, conservative among others. In addition, sociology in the United States (to restrict ourselves to the principle canon battleground) has been a highly contentious discipline, professionally and intellectually, since the foundation of the American Sociological Society (later re-dubbed "Association") in 1905. "Fights among its leaders and their followers were intense" and, "unlike the situation in the great majority of other discipline organizations, contested elections for the presidency and other offices of the association go back at least to the 1920s" (Lipset 1994: 213). The animus between Sorokin and Parsons, and then Homans and Parsons, at Harvard is the stuff of legend, so too is the bitter division in the Chicago department between Ogburn on the one side and Wirth and Park on the other. Was the era inaugurated by the 1960s any different? It appears that it was.

In America, sociology has always attracted a disproportionate number of people, both faculty and students, who are left-leaning politically and dedicated to social reform. But for much of its history, American sociology's political commitments were complemented and checked by an equally strong partisanship of science and scholarship, at least by American sociology's brightest lights. While disputes arose over appropriate methodology and theory (for instance, positivist or broadly phenomenological), enthusiasm for sociology itself was a constant as was the belief that scholarly rigor was required to nourish the sociological vocation. Seymour Martin Lipset (1994: 203-4) recalls Columbia's Robert Lynd, a revolutionary socialist, being "greatly offended by some left social scientists…who, he thought, were not as committed to scientific integrity – to reporting data that contradicted their beliefs, as he was. He brought that sense of rectitude to his evaluations of students and refused to support at least one subsequently prominent student because he changed his position on academic issues in tandem with reversals in the Communist Party line." Equally, for other major figures of American sociology of the 1940s and 1950s such as Parsons, Merton, Lazarsfeld, Riesman, Bellah, and Bell, "methodologically rigorous social science" was considered to be a "prerequisite for effective social reform, often radical change. This meant that basic research and theory had to come first, they should not take priority over activism." By contrast, the 1960s student movement tended to consider sociology as irredeemably bourgeois, was suspicious of "conventional" social science and of other Western institutions, prioritized social advocacy over scholarship, and in the attempt to combine theory and practice ended up with a strongly anti-rationalist position (Roth 1990: 404-5). As late as 1950, sociology was a small discipline in America whose senior faculty "all knew each other in an immediate, personal way" (Abbott 1999: 82). The booming fifties and sixties, in which the disciplinary population doubled, and then doubled again in two decades, saw the end of the earlier intimacy and directness, and with it the erosion of a moral density in which sociology as a vocation was especially highly valued.

At the same time, one must be cautious of broad-brush depictions of the 1960s, and of demonizing what was in fact a highly complex set of movements and legacies. One indication of this complexity is fairly obvious: many of those active in the sixties are themselves today highly critical of the new self-styled radicals, while just as many, disenchanted with earlier simplifications and current sloganizing, have become politically weary or lethargic. Also, the ethos of the sixties counterculture movement—libertarian and hedonistic, inimical to a regime of rules and regulations and the strict enforcement of moral standards—is a far cry from the new prissiness of political correctness, with its authoritarian and ascetic regimen of language codes, censorship, and sexual scare-mongering.[7]

Besides, and contrary to an impression that is often given, feminists, critics of the Enlightenment or of liberal rationalism (clearly, a very mixed bag) are not invariably hostile to the classical heritage. Sydie (1987: 216), for instance, concludes her book on the classics by averring that "In many ways, the feminist discourse of sociology continues the traditions of the 'founding fathers'"; while Dorothy Smith (1990: 218-219) situates her analysis of narrative organization and suicide "in the methodological and epistemological debate stemming from Durkheim's work." Bologh's (1990: xiii-xvi) praise of Weber and Marx is as fulsome as one can find in the literature on these authors. And, for Porter (1993: 3), "a little re-claiming of the history of radicalism in Sociology" will place Weber and Durkheim, as well as Marx, as exemplars of engaged social theory (see also Seidman 1991: 131-3).

It transpires, then, that what Merton (1972: 40) once called "selective inattention" is an all too present danger in the canon dispute—a fact that is explicable in sociological terms. For

> Under conditions of acute conflict, each hostile camp develops highly selective perceptions of what is going on in the other. Perspectives become self-confirming as both Insiders and Outsiders tend to shut themselves off from ideas and information at odds with their own conceptions. They come to see in the other primarily what their hostile dispositions alert them to see and then promptly mistake the part for the whole....In the process each group becomes less and less motivated to examine the ideas of the other, since there is manifestly small point in attending to the ideas of those capable of such distortion. The members of each group then scan the outgroup's writings just enough to find ammunition for new fusillades.

Can the various usages of canon that I have described so far in this chapter be seen as applications of a core, more elemental and coherent category? I think it doubtful. However, one theme appears to be especially resonant, an analogy in which secular great texts are compared with religious canonical ones.[8] The implication seems to be, particularly on behalf of the wilder critics, that by equating secular classic texts with religious ones, one has thereby debunked the former. But how plausible is this equation? Focusing on the formation of the Christian canon, I will argue below that it is basically untenable because classic texts diverge in quite fundamental ways from their putative religious counterparts. Even the asymmetrical grammar of classics and canon indicates that this is the case. As Joel Weinsheimer (1991: 130-1) observes, while "canon" is a "collective noun denominating a group of works with a common author or authority," there is no noun, but only an adjective, denominating an individual canonical text. "The reverse is true of the classic" where there is a noun for each individual text but none for the whole that composes the totality of all individual classics. "All we have is the plural." Moreover, "while there is a verb 'to canonize,' no such verb exists to name the process whereby a classic becomes a classic." From that grammatical irregularity, Weinsheimer infers that in contrast to a canon that is plural but determinate, the classic is "singular but indeterminate."

The Christian Canon and the Classics of Sociology[9]

The term "canon" derives from the Greek word *kanōn* (Hebrew, *kāneh*), meaning "reed," that is, an instrument of measure (McKenzie

1965: 118). The earliest usage of "canon" in a Christian context was as a term to describe ecclesiastical pronouncements and rules (i.e. Canon Law).[10] Later, "canon" also came to refer to that group of individuals who have been exalted to the status of sainthood, the process of elevation being called canonization (Scholes 1992: 140). In its most general application, however, the theological term "canon" refers to the list of texts recognized as sacred by a particular religion (Bruce 1970: 129). It is this third sense that has clearly become most important in secular usage—though in a manner that adds and tends to conflate the other two. Let us now turn to examine the distinctive features of canonical texts, concentrating on the Christian case.

The formation of the Christian canon seems to have begun in earnest during the early centuries of Christianity. The emergence in that period of "heretical" movements, that claimed knowledge of secret authoritative books, was a major impetus for the canonization of authorized texts (Guthrie 1987: 189). Threatened by persecution, apostasy, and general fragmentation, it became necessary to forge a clear sense of identity for members of the church. The canon emerged principally as a symbol of the church's unity, something that "cemented and expressed [a] new sense of what it meant to be a Christian" (Radcliffe 1989: 62-63). "Canon" was first used as a term to describe the church's body of authorized texts in 367 c.e., when Athanasius designated twenty-seven New Testament books as canonical. These books were, incidentally, the same twenty-seven books that make up the New Testament canon today (Harrington 1978: 158). It has been argued that most of them had already been accepted as authoritative by the majority of Christians before there was a *de jure* canon. If that is right, canonization consisted largely of a codification of what had become the traditional practice of Christians, and was thus a process of reorganization rather than of creation (Grant 1970: 286).

In respect of the Old Testament canon, the situation was somewhat similar, although the general process that led to canonization took much longer. The ancient Hebrews held a certain body of texts to be sacred, but this body was not as rigidly defined as the later Christian canon was to become. In fact, the Hebrews did not have any term in their language that was equivalent to "canon," although some have argued that they possessed the concept (Kraemer 1991:

614-615). In the Roman Catholic Church, the Old Testament canon (including the Apocrypha) was not fixed as dogma until the sixteenth century, when the canon became a major issue for Reformers. Since the Council of Trent in the 1540s, Catholic theologians have viewed the question of canonicity as closed (Bruce 1970: 135; Neuenzeit 1975: 168). And while the canon of the Reformed churches rejected some of the texts of the Roman Catholic canon as apocryphal, they did not claim canonicity for any text outside of that older canon. Hence, the process of forming the Protestant canon was one of exclusion, not inclusion (Kermode 1987: 600).

It is worth noting that the authority of scripture predates the term "canon," indeed the Old Testament (Hebrew biblical) texts were invoked as "scripture" by New Testament writers centuries before the word "canon" designated a body of texts (Kermode 1987: 601). Moreover, the formation of the Christian canon was not a process of assembling a body of texts that would then be considered "inspired." It was instead a process of evaluating an existing corpus of texts and then rejecting what was deemed *not* inspired (Kermode 1987: 604). It has been pointed out by biblical scholars that although "canon" is not necessarily part of the idea of "scripture," "scripture" is necessarily part of the meaning of "canon" (Kelsey 1975: 105). As such, the canon as an historical entity may be said to have a "prehistory" as a generally accepted body of scripture. Canonicity, thus, involved the further delimitation of what was already a limited body of scripture, not a creation of scripture. Texts that became canonical were already authoritative for the community of believers that revered them.

While usage seems to have been the primary criterion for the canonization of a particular text, it is likely that other factors played their part. Compatibility of a text's content with church doctrine, relevance of its content to the day-to-day practice of the church, belief that that content was divinely inspired, and association of the text with apostolic authorship were all conducive to canonization (Harrington 1978: 158-159; Bovon 1988: 35). Nonetheless, it must be acknowledged that lack of firm historical evidence makes the identification of criteria other than usage difficult to ascertain. What actually constitutes canonicity (other than membership in the canon) is in fact still officially undefined. Vatican II, while stressing the continued importance of the canon as "the soul of sacred theology," produced no criteria for canonicity other than that the canon as a whole is known through tradition. As such, Christian believers tend to see the development of the canon as the work of "the mysterious guidance of the divine Spirit in the Church" (Neuenzeit 1975: 168).

This brief overview of some pertinent aspects of the Christian canon allows us now to bring into sharp relief the senses in which a religious canon can be contrasted with the great or classic secular texts of the social sciences that are its supposed counterparts.

First, and as we have seen, it is possible to establish with some precision the actual moments in which the Christian canon formally came into being. Similarly, the process of canonization of saints in the Roman Catholic Church can be accurately and unproblematically described by examining the deliberations and procedures of that committee of Vatican officials, The Congregation of the Causes of Saints, whose job it is to oversee this canonization (Woodward 1990: 87-126). There is no strict equivalent to these processes in sociology. On the contrary, far from them being the product of formal deliberation, classic texts are *emergent*, the result of cultural resonance, textual suppleness, reader-appropriation and social diffusion. In the excursus of the last chapter I noted that classic appraisal in sociology is a largely exclusive activity, led and directed by the judgments of professional sociologists. That notwithstanding, sociology has no "Classic Makers" in the sense of a body of people explicitly charged with the professional responsibility for deciding what will, and what will not, become a classic text.[11]

The Christian canon exists as a *totality*. To call a collection of books "the canon" is "to say that *just these* writings are *sufficient* for the ends to which they ought to be used in the church" (Kelsey 1975: 105). Moreover, once a religious canon is fixed, it must be accepted as a whole (see Bruce 1970: 143). This idea of an exclusive canon, entirely sufficient for all purposes required of it, is the second salient feature that distinguishes the religious concept of canon from the secular use of the word to describe any list of books. In sociology, classics exist as a collection or series or aggregate of texts, but not as a comprehensive or integrated totality.

Third, once a canon is fixed, it is considered *unalterable*. True, the question of whether or not all canonical texts are of equal authority is a matter of some debate; indeed some theologians have claimed that there is a "canon within the canon." And since Vatican

II, the Roman Catholic Church has appeared to accord greater importance to Matthew and to the Pastoral epistles than to some other New Testament books—this despite the Council of Trent's official insistence that all books in the canon were equal in value (Neuenzeit 1975: 168; Harrington 1978: 159). There has also been resistance to the idea that every statement in every canonical text is "the word of the Lord" (such as God's orchestration of various murders and massacres in the Old Testament). Nonetheless, such discomfiture does not mean that the Bible "collapses like a pack of cards." This is because believers recognize that reading the Bible requires "not the swapping of texts, but a consensus of tradition and reason, faith and prayer, individual and corporate insight, learning and conscience, to truly 'know' it and discover its meaning" (Smith 1989: 137-138).

Moreover, not only are the canonical texts fixed in number, but in their *order as well*. Ever since the New Testament canon was established in the early centuries of Christianity, the order in which the New Testament books appear in the Bible has remained unchanged. This order is not chronological. Thus, theologians generally agree that Mark was the earliest of the synoptic gospels to be written, but this gospel always follows the later gospel of Matthew in the canon (Grant 1977: 183-5). The fixing of the sequence of texts was as much a part of the initial establishment of the canon as was the selection of the texts themselves, and this sequence is an important factor in the interpretation of the canon. (Bovon 1988: 20). Again there is no parallel in secular texts such as the sociological classics. Moreover, while canonical texts are closed and fixed, the status of classic texts is open. No one, so far as I know, has ever claimed that the particular texts we regard as classic today are fixed in stone, or that *only these* texts are eligible to become classic.

A fourth distinction between religious canons and secular texts that are dubiously referred to as canonical concerns their respective epistemological character. The books included within the theological canon are considered by believers to be both of a unique character and interrelated as parts of a whole. That whole is the canon itself. Books outside the canon are considered to be of an entirely separate order, to be "understood differently" from those within it (Kermode 1987 605-609). There is an important distinction here between texts that are understood to be different from those outside the canon and texts that are to be understood differently. This is not mere pedantry. Instead it is an indication that the canonicity of a text does not mean that it is more authoritative than non-canonical texts according to a particular standard, but that it is judged according to an entirely different standard. Texts within the theological canon are thus to be read in a different way from texts outside of it. Arguably, this is redolent of classic texts too, but there is an important difference. Canonical texts seem impregnable to, and entirely indifferent to, the possibility of critique. They can be interpreted, but not rationally evaluated. And this is because their divine inspiration means that they are quite simply True (Gorak 1991: 36). Indeed, so potent is this belief that even "non-authentic and pseudonymous" texts can still be accepted as canonical (Guthrie 1987: 190). Today, many canonical books are recognized as "pseudo-epigraphical," that is, written by someone other than the person whose name is assigned to them. This does not lead, however, to a necessary diminution of their canonical value (Anderson 1970: 157-158). Even those theologians who wish to develop an understanding of canonical texts in a more critical, historically oriented way generally make it clear that their intention is not "to threaten the integrity of the canon" (Bovon 1988: 21).

In sum: the comparison between sacred and secular texts under the concept of "canon" is highly misleading. If this is so, it is mistaken for conservatives to claim canonicity for these texts, and just as erroneous for so-called radicals to debunk them for being canonical. In each case the claims are misguided because they involve a mistaken view of what classic texts are. For unlike religious canonical texts, classical texts are emergent, not the product of calculation; heterogeneous as distinct from existing as an integrated whole; open and fluid, not closed or fixed; and as amenable to discussion and criticism as other secular texts. There is also a fifth, less quantifiable, factor, at least in the case of most Christian canons: their extraordinary endurance in the face of changing historical circumstances. The Roman Catholic canon, as mentioned above, has remained unchanged since the mid-sixteenth century. This canon also appears largely impervious to shifts in political ideology. A Catholic liberation theologian and the very conservative Pope John Paul II both accept the same canon, even though they apply that canon in different ways.[12]

Significance of the Canon Debate: The Controversy Over Higher Education and the Purpose of the University

Terms and concepts do not disappear simply because they are illogical or misleading. They endure as long as they have some value and meaning for the constituency that employs them. Proving that analogies of canon and classic are unsound will largely be beside the point if the canon debate enshrines something I have so far failed to address: namely, a tenacious conflict of ideas of which the "canon" dispute is itself a token, a conceptual cryptogram for a larger, more inclusive set of preoccupations. And that is, indeed, the case. As the first two sections of this chapter sought to demonstrate, the argument about the canon is linked to a wider debate about the reach and purpose of higher education in Western societies. The "great books" dispute helps make this debate palpable but does not exhaust it. Those who criticise the canon (in any of its many senses) often do so at the same time as they stake their own alternative—radicalism and relevance. This, we are told, is what the university should offer its students if it is to be a vibrant institution. I end this chapter by examining that alternative and by offering a more cautious view of the purpose of the university.

Of all the claims that academics are inclined to make, that of radicalism is the most questionable—especially as framed by the concept "radical social theory." Common to its usage in botany, linguistics, and mathematics, the term "radical" denotes the idea of arriving at the "root" of some thing, discerning that entity's primary, fundamental, hence non-derivative, element. In social theory, the concept straddles two meanings. The first is that of "reflexivity."[13] Reflexivity concerns the attempt to identify and reflect on the conditions of one's own social scientific practice. A reflexive social theory subjects the sociologist's own work—its assumptions and practices— to systematic scrutiny. The purpose of engaging in this reflection is to be apprised of the possibilities and limitations of what one is doing and to be aware of one's responsibilities to those one studies. The "root" at issue here is thus the reflective self, enquiring into its own activity, prejudices and presuppositions.

From the standpoint of ordinary language, the equation of radicalism with reflexivity might seem somewhat strained. After all, radicalism normally denotes not individual introspection or theoretical practice, but partisanship and engagement rooted in the world outside the academy. And that is the second meaning of radical social theory. Radical social theory is theory in the service of social change.[14] In principle this social change could be in any direction, but normally it is associated with some version of leftist or "progressive" politics. Social theory becomes radical where it identifies the agents of social change, encourages, guides, and educates their activity; and/or where it theorizes the grounds for some project of empowerment, "consciousness-raising," or "emancipation." Accordingly, it is a theory for a given constituency or cause (local or global), not simply a theory of that constituency or cause (academicism). Its purpose is to interpret the world as a prelude to, and as a basis for, (in the favoured jargon) "strategising social and political change." Relevant also is the implication that agents may be unaware of the sources of their predicament, or mistaken about their real interests and thus in need of educative enlightenment.

Now the injunction to be radical in the latter sense is extremely problematic because it seeks to impose on theory ambitions it can never fully realize—if by theory one means, minimally, a set of systematically related propositions, open to being empirically tested, or rationally appraised, the purpose of which is to explain a course of events or a situation. More specifically, the injunction to be radical is problematic for at least four reasons.

In the first place, and most obviously, people outside the academy rarely come into contact with social *theory*, and when they do they often find its language incomprehensible and repugnant, its ideas outlandish, and the moral authority of academics to champion radical social change (to be the conscience of humanity or, in Frantz Fanon's chilling phrase, to engage in "the invention of new souls")[15] highly questionable. In particular, the chasm that separates academic discourse from the discussion of non-academic publics is today so vast that the claim of university intellectuals to speak "for" any non-academic constituency must be dubious in the extreme. A figure such as Tocqueville, was read not only by his nineteenth-century intellectual peers; he was also "intelligible to any educated reader. Today's specialized academics, with notable exceptions, write with a set of intellectual assumptions and a vocabulary shared only by their colleagues" (Bellah et al.: 1985: 299; also Alter 1991: 286). While Dorothy Smith, for instance, may proclaim that she is writing "a sociology for women," what this means, ultimately, is that she is writing with a definite end in mind: to improve women's lot and to explain women's situation to other intellectuals, to "formulate a sociology from the standpoint of women," to preserve "the presence of subjects as knowers and as actors," to give "voice to women's experience" (Smith 1987: 1, 105, 225). What she cannot sensibly mean is that this sociology will be "for" women in the sense of being understood by the bulk of them—and having been understood be a guide for their practice. Most women will fail to comprehend Smith not because they are unintelligent but because they are not feminist sociologists equipped with the appropriate background of terms and concepts. As such, they will not be in a position to judge the merit of her work about them. A sociology "for" women that most women do not understand, and even do not care to understand, is a very strange notion.

Second, it is just as clear that a theory does not become radical—capable of effecting far-reaching social change—by being a theory. In order to have an impact on the world it must secure a bearer, most importantly a social movement or a state. Marx's social theory became radical when parts of it were taken up by certain groups and executed by certain states. Whether they did, or how they did, was beyond his control. The theories of Friedrich Hayek, marginalized for a generation, became radical when they became inspirational and convenient for, e.g., the British and American Right. Anthony Giddens's ideas about the Third Way occupied a similar position in Tony Blair's first Labour administration. Social theory is thus faced with the situation that its radicalism is of necessity always vicarious and conditional. Theories that aspire to be radical are in a very real sense hostages to fortune—and often this means oblivion or grotesque unintended consequences (the Gulag Archipelago).

Third, social theory that yearns to be radical is additionally faced by the irony that in the very process of being adopted it starts to lose its theoretical qualities. It begins to transmute into a creed. The theory's subtleties, qualifications, dynamism, tensions—the very features that help constitute it as a theory—go by the board because theoretical complexity and ambivalence are not productive of the enthusiasms necessary to build commitment, and to translate ideas into the world. Marx's work became a political force when it stopped being a complex theory and became a dogmatic set of postulates—Marxism. Later it became a legitimating ritual of, and apologia for, Soviet-type societies. To really "take root," then, theories must be reduced to a few simple and concrete ideas—ideas that are effervescent, not intricate. The gap between social theory and political practice is a result of the nature of theory and politics themselves.

Finally, one observes in much that passes for "radical social theory" an educative model of politics, a species of what Hannah Arendt (1978:23-26) called "two world theory." Two world theories, of which some brands of Marxism and academic feminism are only the more obvious examples, open up a divide between those who claim to have understood Being, or at least aspects of it, and those who remain ostensibly "trapped" in the illusion of appearances. Duly translated to the register of social science, the job of the theorist is then conceptualized as that of the debunker, tearing away the veil of life-as-it-is-lived to reveal its hidden core. Such language made Arendt shudder not only because of its Olympian conceit, and its implication that those who lived in the world of appearance were ignoramuses. She was also struck by the uncanny and disturbing resemblance of that discourse to the idiom that characterized the Stalinist purges in which it "was always a question of uncovering what had been hidden, of unmasking the disguises, of exposing duplicity and mendacity" (Arendt 1973 [1963]: 100; also 11, 19, 99, 263, 290). Furthermore, the claim of theorists to know a hidden *political* realm, denied to the senses, also encourages them to envisage their task as emancipation: enlisting reason or science to enlighten or "educate" those who have still some way to go on the royal road to enlightenment.[16] Against such a perspective, Arendt believed that politics could never be plausibly given a scientific or rationalist warrant.

In a *political* dialogue, people argue in principle as equals. Such equality is based on the citizenship conferred on them in virtue of being a member not of a species but of a polity. Communication proceeds through discussion and accommodation as actors seek to persuade each other of their case. Conversely, whenever a scientific argument is invoked in the political realm, as it is in many naturalist philosophies, discussion and accommodation become subordinated to an educative model of politics—Arendt would have said anti-politics—that is fundamentally asymmetrical in character: *instruction* displaces discussion; people are not simply "wrong," but benighted. Education, after all, is a social activity that is vertical and unequal by its very nature. It rests on the authority of the teacher to teach, and that authority is based not on the goodness or even the wisdom of the teacher, but on his or her accredited competence in a particular area, and responsibility to the world of fellow citizens. Wherever the educative model underpins a conception of politics, disagreement is seen as the result of error or mystification; consciousness has to be "raised," opinions corrected. The citizen is envisaged as a child to be taught. Education is extended to a sphere where it has no business to be, while politics becomes a sphere bereft of free and equal citizens.

Does this mean that political education is a contradiction in terms? Not necessarily. Clearly one can be taught political history and be instructed on the nature of political structures and constitutions. One can also be taught "civics," though this is no guarantee that people so taught will become civil. Moreover, when historians talk about the political education of, say, the working class in the nineteenth century, they are typically referring to the growing knowledge that its members attained through participating in trade unions and seeking political influence. Political education in that sense proceeds reflexively through experience rather than instruction. Similarly, one might consider political education as the kind of learning that results from the "slow, strong drilling through hard boards, with a combination of passion and a sense of judgment" as Weber put it at the end of *Politics as a Vocation*. Arendt's strictures are aimed not against these ideas, but rather against those currents of modern thought that continue to depict citizens as children, and that mistake the world of politics for the teacher-student relationship. In that sense, she remarked, "Education can play no part in politics, because in politics we always have to deal with those who are already educated. Whoever wants to educate adults really wants to act as their guardian and prevent them from political activity. Since one cannot educate adults, the word education has an evil sound in politics" (Arendt 1993 [1958]: 177).

The University and the Jargon of "Relevance"

These arguments against the notion of radical social theory should be clarified in two further respects. First, while I have argued that radical theory is a misnomer, it is no part of my intention to deny that theory has an important "critical" potential: the potential to assess and evaluate current social practices. On the contrary, social theory becomes most profound when it challenges platitudes, prompts us to think in new ways, exposes ideology. This is a highly significant power of theory and its cumulative personal and social effects can be great. Nonetheless, such effects (increased wisdom, readiness for social action, etc.) are perforce indirect, indeterminate, and contingent. One can no more directly will or produce such effects by a theory than one can directly become happy or fall in love. Nor am I denying that "ideas" more generally can be radical, can deeply affect people's lives and the life of society. In conjunction with other features of social and psychological reality—crucially, an individual's receptiveness and desire to change—they often are and do. But again, "ideas" are not the same as "theory." Theory refers to a sub-set of the cognitive realm, not ideas in general that encompass all the products of consciousness.

Objections to the canon, I have claimed, are part of a wider debate on the purpose of higher education. Those who negatively evaluate the canon often simultaneously articulate their alternative: radicalism and relevance. I have argued thus far that radicalism in the guise of academic social theory is largely a non-starter. Does the doctrine of relevance hold any more cogency?

In one sense, of course, the demand for relevance in the curriculum follows on from that of the demand to be radical. Academics who think of themselves as radical typically also think that the curriculum has value to the degree to which it promotes personal empowerment and social change; the curriculum is thus envisaged primarily as an instrument of social and political agitation. But "empowerment," the benchmark of relevance, is itself a highly loaded concept. Critics of the canon and the liberal university tend to have their own definition of it: someone is empowered insofar as he or she comes to share the project and worldview of the radicals themselves. A woman who decides to enter a women's studies program but who, in the process of study, comes to the conclusion that modern academic feminism is patronizing to other women, or that heterosexuality is not intrinsically coercive, or that patriarchy is an incoherent concept, is unlikely to count as an empowered, let alone enlightened, person by the teaching faculty who inspect and grade her class journal. A Native Canadian who is against aboriginal land-claims and self-government, and concludes that the best bet for

Native peoples is assimilation will clearly have gotten hold of the wrong end of the stick. "Empowerment," it often turns out, means: "accept my ideology and do what I say."

However, the demand for relevance in the curriculum is by no means confined to feminist and multiculturalist critics of the canon. It is also widely shared by enterprise administrators in the upper management echelon of higher education. Bizzare ideological hybrids and political alliances are the paradoxical result. Since the mid-1980s, many administrators—some of whom are former radicals themselves—have been implementing a strategy as ingenious as it is proving to be effective. They are employing the radicals' own rhetoric of equal opportunities, access, engagement with the community, to reshape the colleges and universities along market lines. The language of high principle and community inclusion thus becomes a semantic vehicle by means of which some of the custodians of higher education cut back resources, diminish the opportunities of their faculty and staff, dismantle the trade unions. That aspects of academic radicalism have been co-opted by the new university entrepreneurs is not as surprising as first it may seem, for what binds the fate of each together is a strongly instrumentalist view of university education. Hence both constituencies have a marked tendency to envision scholarship as largely elitist, remote, and quixotic. Both consider the quest for intellectual independence as a chimera, a concoction of the liberal Ivory Tower. Both thirst for The Deed. And both, accordingly, conceive of a university education not as an intrinsic good, possessing value in its own right, the locus of a singular set of qualities and practices, but as a tool of some project extraneous to it. The intimation that there is "a kind of utility that comes only when utility is set aside," that a university education performs one of its distinctive tasks when it pursues "knowledge severed from its present purposes and pursued wherever it may guide us" (Scruton 1993: 211) is largely alien to these doctrines. So it is that the language of empowerment now greets the newspeak of "mini-modules," "learning-packages," "student customers," "consultancy," "clients," "just-in-time" production, in sum, "the corporatized university."

If relevance means providing an education that will enrich students with possibilities hitherto *un*imagined by them; if it means fostering some of the intellectual and moral conditions that will promote the individual's growth; if it means furnishing analytical skills that will help an individual materially to thrive and enhance his or her native capacities; if it means encouraging flexibility and openness of mind, and strength of character; if it means analyzing topics and issues that people need to understand if they are to act intelligently in the world today; if "relevance" means all this, then who can reasonably object to it? But consider that even here our ability as educators to be relevant is limited by the fact that we do not know what a student will come to imagine, what exactly will promote his or her future growth, or what indeed the future more generally will be. If, on the other hand, relevance means drumming into the heads of students a particular ideology (market, Marxist, feminist, postcolonialist, post-normative or some other) and seeking loyalty tests to this ideology, then most sensible people will oppose it. For they will recognize that in this instance education has betrayed itself by descending into propaganda.

My description of the concepts of radicalism and relevance has sought to reveal their lack of intellectual substance. As a counterpoint to that description, let me now summarize what I take to be the unique capacities of the liberal university and their relationship to the classics as a whole (and not simply sociological classics).

To begin with, the university enshrines within it the traditions and anti-traditions of the past. Universities are places in which these forms of life are transmitted, questioned, amended. The commitment to tradition is not a commitment to simulate the past or to venerate it. It is a commitment to learn from it, to understand one's historical location, to comprehend that "coming to be a person is in part appropriating certain material of one's culture, and (that) continuing to be a person...means working through, developing, and extending this material" (Fay 1987: 162). Moreover, the commitment to tradition has nothing essentially in common with a view of history as one seamless web. On the contrary, a university education in the humanities and social sciences will reveal that "our" history is a record of conflict and controversy. The great works of European civilization that are derided or inflated as canonical actually help us appreciate this conflict because they represent *rival* traditions and cultures—"Homeric versus Platonic, Judaic versus Christian, biblical versus classical, Aristotelian versus Augustinian, the Enlightenment versus the Christian" (Macintyre 1990: 229)—discoursing on vital questions of agency and the ends of humanity. Bernard Knox (1993: 15) reminds us that though the ancient Greeks are today assailed by some "as emblems of...enforced conformity," a more realistic picture would portray the "subversive, even revolutionary" role they have played in Western history. It is thus instructive that rebels of the stature of Nietzsche and Freud (and Marx) felt bound to study them—as we now feel bound to study Nietzsche and Freud and Marx. By their very rivalry and intractability, the classic works and the traditions they encode, suggest that no single doctrine can hold a monopoly of wisdom; and that, by the same token, no single ideology can be the sole font of praxis and relevance.

Second, a university education in the social sciences offers a testing-ground for ideas produced within and outside of the academy. I emphasize the notion of testing-ground, rather than originality, in recognition that many of the most innovative and challenging ideas that are generated in a society do not arise within the university itself. The most momentous ideas in the modern world come from diverse sources: the laboratories and workshops, often independently funded, producing the new technologies; the new social movements articulating commitments to community, religion, nation, ethnicity, gender, ecology. Concepts of rights, obligations, justice, liberty, emancipation, inclination, preference, form the armoury of these movements. What the university allows us to do is to trace and document over long stretches of time the impact of these forces and actors, and to scrutinize their arguments. And this scrutiny, in turn, is unlike that which is normally available in other forums, for instance those of radio or television where comment must be brief and truncated, and where sustained argument is constrained by a communications culture of dramatic images and sound bites. The university, in contrast, has the capacity to offer a very different forum, governed by three principles that help jointly to define it: cognitive rationality, open inquiry, and reciprocal elucidation.

Abiding by the principle of cognitive rationality, to use Talcott Parsons's apposite expression, means accepting the priority of logical argument over *ad hominem* attack, intellectual method over spontaneity and impulse. It means accepting that a legitimate argument is one in which reasons are formally stated, and that such reasons are internally consistent. It means providing evidence for one's position that can be checked and disputed by other people. And it means allowing that, in principle, one's own reasoning and evidence could be wrong. The latter commitment is important because without it analysis can always be self-confirming, self-serving, circular. Moreover, cognitive rationality, like the application of all principles, also involves discipline. It requires the effort of balance and circumspection, a decentring of the self that enables one to distinguish among one's own ego, desires, and values and the world beyond them. It also entails a willingness to pursue structured conflict, that is, disagreement refracted through the "discipline" or disciplines one works within or across. Such discipline is not a procrustean bed designed to impede creativity, any more than the chromatic scale, differential calculus, a poetic meter, impede it. Rather it is a structure, or set of structures, that enables the play of a certain kind of creativity, methodical reasoning, to take place.

The second principle, open inquiry, is also distinctive of the university. Many organizations outside of the university today pursue social research. Their various clients include the state, business, social movements, and interest groups. Each of these interests is also served by the university to varying degrees. But where one has a client, one's research will typically end at the point at which its results clash with, or become irrelevant to, the interest of that client. Uncomfortable facts are suppressed; complex arguments and dilemmas are skirted over to avoid offense or difficulty. In contrast, the freedom to engage in open inquiry means that, in principle, no view or fact is prohibited from the discussion. It means, too, that the predominant orientation is experimental not utilitarian, independent not conformist. Moreover, it is worth remembering that the pressure towards ideological conformity in the university can come from the culture of one's own department, as much as, and often more so, than pressures emanating from the administration. (It is not unknown for high-ranking administrators to defend the freedom of academics to say unpopular things when the latter's own faculty colleagues would be more than happy to curtail that liberty.) Universities remain vibrant only so long as they accord open enquiry more importance than any other research consideration, including that of "conspicuous benevolence" (Coleman 1990-91: 20-2): the tendency among egalitarian-minded academics—the majority in sociology— to disapprove of research findings that are considered to buck the egalitarian ethos.

Cognitive rationality and open inquiry, in turn, are nourished by the further principle of "reciprocal elucidation." I take the term directly from Michel Foucault (1984: 381).

> In the serious play of questions and answers, in the work of reciprocal elucidation, the rights of each person are in some sense immanent in the discussion. They depend only on the dialogue situation. The person asking the questions is merely exercising the right that has been given him: to remain unconvinced, to perceive a contradiction, to require more information, to emphasize different postulates, to point out faulty reasoning, etc. As for the person answering the questions, he too exercises a right that does not go beyond the discussion itself; by the logic of his own discourse he is tied to what he has said earlier, and by the acceptance of dialogue he is tied to the questioning of the other.

Reciprocal elucidation is thus a commitment to dialogue, to *disciplined* conflict with those one disagrees with, and to the idea that wisdom emerges from such a dialogue. And with this we return to the classical works. For ultimately the value of the great works resides in their exemplary contribution to a conversation about who we are, what we can know and of what we are capable (Levine 1995). The university is a place in which we can preserve and extend that conversation. For while it is delusive to believe "that all later philosophy is a series of footnotes to Plato," much of it

> is a *dialogue* with Plato, if only to refute him or fight the undesirable consequences of his views (or others' misstatements of those views). If we heed only the later philosophers, we are hearing just one side of the conversation, a frustrating and dangerous deprivation. Virgil and Milton are engaged in a dialogue with Homer. If we hear only Milton and not Homer, we are not even hearing Milton. Though some have tried to use the classics to close discussions, the Greeks, properly understood, are the great conversation openers. They are not torches shining upon our darkness. They are more like the street lamps of history, near which people have recurrently gathered to argue with others. (Wills 1993: 39)

Conclusion

In this chapter I have outlined the meanings of canon in contemporary social theory; shown the difference between classical secular texts and religious canonical ones; and offered a perspective on the meaning and purpose of higher education. Since that last perspective is likely to be misunderstood, let me clarify it. My argument against academic radical theory and against the jargon of relevance is not an invitation to complacency; nor does it attest to an Olympian indifference towards the many injustices that assail our epoch. On the contrary, it is precisely because social and political questions are so important that academics should not mislead themselves, and others, by professing an authority they cannot realistically discharge. My claim is that the university has a distinctive but modest role to play in the modern world. We would be wise not to inflate that role. We would be just as wise to defend it against its detractors.

Notes

1. See Gorak's fine summary of critics of the canon in Gorak 1991:1-8, 221-260, and the literature cited there.
2. "The continuing influence of the canon in defining what counts is one of the main reasons why gender and race, though now institutionally important for American sociology (as shown by affirmative action programs or the sections of the ASA), have still not reestablished themselves as central concerns of sociological theory" (Connell 1997: 1546). Connell's thesis is that the development of the sociological canon "can only be understood in the framework of global history, especially the history of imperialism" (1545). For a forceful rejoinder to Connell, see Collins 1997.
3. See Rosaldo 1989: ix-xii, 218-224; Conway 1991; Long 1993; also the comments of Roth 1992: 454.
4. Horowitz 1992a: 32, 38; also, Horowitz 1992b and, for the broader context of his argument, Horowitz 1993.
5. See, for instance, Bloom, H. 1994 on "the school of resentment"; Bromwich 1993; Kimball 1990, 1987; Hirsch 1989; Helprin 1988; Bloom 1987; and the comments of Ryan 1993; Griffiths 1993; Hodges 1993; Sanders 1993; and Wilkinson 1991).
6. See Gadamer (1989 [1975/1960]): 285-290) and the application to sociological classics by How 1998.
7. For analysis and reports of these phenomena in American and British tertiary institutions, see Jacoby 1994, MacGregor 1993, Tysome 1993. The polemical literature on this is now huge and too obvious to require extensive citation.
8. See the objections, respectively, of Chafetz 1993:1, and Gottdiener 1990: 461, to "Talmudic" or "Biblical" exegesis of classic texts.
   It is no great objection to my argument to say that the real model for the sociological canon is the literary canon because the latter concept itself is typically based on an analogy with the canon of scripture. For reasons why such an analogy is misleading, see Olsen 1996.
9. This section was principally researched and mostly written by Mike O'Brien. See the acknowledgments, above p. xi.
10. See Guthrie 1987: 189.
11. For interesting sociological analyses of the canonizing process, see Goodich 1983; Delooz 1983; and on the passing of the saint and the significance of this for modernity, see the beautiful essay by Coleman 1987.
12. Stein Olsen has pointed out to me (personal communication) that there is a qualitative jump when a body of texts, the scriptures, is recognized as canonical. The whole point about a "canon" and "canonization" is that we pass from process to act, an act underwritten by formal authority. What is lacking in secular contexts (such as in sociology) is the necessary institutional framework that would make it meaningful to talk about canonization.
13. For an influential statement, see Gouldner 1970: 488-504.

14.   Radical social theory is a staple of sociology conferences devoted to questions of social justice, marginality, patriarchy, colonialism and sexual post-normativity. A recent variant of it in print, under the rubric of "democratic sociology," can be found in Connell 2000: 294-6. Opposed to the "market agenda," and convinced that "we now live in a world where the normal content of mass communication is lies, distortions, and calculated fantasies," Connell enjoins sociology to cast off its exclusionary professionalism and embrace a "democratic project." By cooperating with "union organizers, with teachers, with broadcasters, with community activists, with bureaucrats," sociology can become "the self-knowledge of global society," a weapon against "the motivated self-ignorance of market society," an instrument that "serves the goals of broad participation in decision making, mutual respect among social groups, and social equality."

Radical social theory overlaps considerably with what Arthur Stinchcombe (2001:6-8) describes as the "new social movement, or populist" style of writing in American sociology. Stinchcombe is principally concerned to identify two contrasting modes of sociology book reviews and their respective markets. The first, aimed largely at colleagues, emphasize a text's disciplinary, scientific qualities (notably, methodological rigor and explanatory sophistication). The second, recommended mainly for undergraduate use, is more concerned with a book's contribution to identifying social oppression and to offering prescriptions to remedy it. The new social movement style of review "is especially likely to characterize a few subject specialties, notably, gender studies, gay rights, and community and ecology studies, as well as that part of political sociology whose key words are political economy or globalization. The overall structure of the argument is that multiple diffuse features, often a power structure, tend to maintain or advance some bad feature of social life, often domination or discrimination. Only activism and consciousness raising, to which the book may contribute, can undermine this stability—or this retrogession." Books of this kind are often recommended by reviewers for their accessibility. But what is accessibility to one person may be banality to another, particularly where issues are constantly recycled in almost identical, formulaic prose. Musing on the state of cultural studies, Meaghan Morris (1990:21-22) once remarked that "the sheer proliferation of…restatements" conveys the impression that "somewhere in some English publisher's vault there is a master disk from which thousands of versions of the same article about pleasure, resistance, and the politics of consumption are being run off under different names with minor variations." Class, Race, and Gender get a similar treatment in North American sociology, particularly at sociology conferences.

15.   The phrase is quoted appreciatively by Charles Lemert (1997: 138) in his review of Edward Said's *Representations of the Intellectuals* 1996. Said (1996:41) remarks that Fanon borrowed the expression from Aimé Césaire. Fanon himself, of course, was not an academic but a revolutionary, psychiatrist, and public intellectual.

16.   For a historical account of the "radical fallacy" among French intellectuals (many of whom were academics) between 1918 and the mid-1970s, and the three kinds of irresponsibility it produced, see Judt 1998. For a review of Judt, see Baehr 2001.

7

A Concluding Look at the Three Concepts

In this book, I have analyzed three concepts—"founders," "classics," and "canon"—and examined their significance for sociology today. My attempt to identify and unravel the metaphors of founders and canon was not done for its own sake, an exercise in deconstructive pyrotechnics, but to show what happens when people mistake these figures of speech for something literal. In those instances, metaphor lapses into a pseudo-description of (what purports to be) an actual event or entity. Thus, despite being widely and uncritically accepted by sociologists, the concept of "founders of sociology" does little to enhance our understanding of the emergence and growth of sociology, either as discourse or as a discipline. It tends, on the one hand, to portray "founding" as an act rather than as a historical process, and, on the other, to focus almost exclusively on individuals at the expense of the wider intellectual and social milieu in which they operated. At its most crude, the mythology of Founding (Fathers, Mothers, Sisters) deteriorates into hagiography as it seeks to legitimate some project or obsession. At its most sophisticated, it draws on associations that are provocative but misleading and ultimately confusing.

"Founder," I concluded, is at root a mythological and theological notion, and in this latter respect there is a parallel to the notion of a "canon." The object of heated debate, the canon caricature has nonetheless failed to make plain the signal differences between sociological texts and religious ones, and the complex circumstances in which sociology's great works are defined and redefined. Canon is a misleading metaphor and a bad analogy. Still, as we saw, the dispute around the "canon" is part of a larger struggle: canon is a codeword for a variety of concerns regarding the nature and purpose of a university education. This struggle will doubtless continue, but I hope at least to have shown what is serious about the canon dispute, and what is frivolous about it.

While the concepts of "founder" and a "canon" are unhelpful in understanding the nature of sociology's outstanding figures and writings, the notion of "classic" has much more to commend it. When used sparingly, it helps us appreciate the value and vitality of a select group of texts. Continued membership of this group is not guaranteed; nor is position in the pantheon the result of deliberate powerbroking stratagems of insiders. By the same token, it is unrealistic to envisage the classics of sociology as timeless cultural icons whose endurance is based solely on their reputed intrinsic value. Instead, since their vibrancy depends on an interface of authorial brilliance and interpretive appropriation, classic status is unstable, contingent in the last analysis upon sociologists continuing to deem texts important and useful. As I demonstrated, in order for a text to achieve the accolade of classic, it must typically overcome a variety of cultural hurdles; while to survive as one, it must be subjected to continual critical engagement, its concepts reformulated to meet new problems and trials. Not many texts can survive, or attract, such scrutiny and productive reshaping. Those that are able to do so are quite properly described as "classic."

Appendix on Translation and Reception

The "Iron Cage" and the "Shell of Steel": Parsons, Weber and the *stahlhartes Gehäuse* metaphor in *The Protestant Ethic and the Spirit of Capitalism*

"...Look within my Vail,
Turn up my metaphors . . ." (John Bunyan)

Few concepts in the social sciences are more instantly recognizable than the "iron cage." Seemingly integral to the powerful denouement of *The Protestant Ethic and the Spirit of Capitalism*, the metaphor sums up, graphically and dramatically, the predicament of modern human beings trapped in a socioeconomic structure of their own making. Let us recall the context in which this striking image appears:

> The Puritan wanted to work in a calling; we are forced to do so. For when asceticism was carried out of monastic cells into everyday life, and began to dominate worldly morality, it did its part in building the tremendous cosmos of the modern economic order. This order is now bound to the technical and economic conditions of machine production which today determine the lives of all the individuals who are born into this mechanism, not only those directly concerned with economic acquisition, with irresistible force. Perhaps it will so determine them until the last ton of fossilized coal is burnt. In Baxter's view the care for external goods should only lie on the shoulders of the 'saint like a light cloak, which can be thrown aside at any moment'. But fate decreed that the cloak should become an iron cage. (Weber 1930 [1920]:181)

This passage, first published in English in 1930, established the "iron cage" as one of the key *topoi* of the social sciences, versatile enough to animate investigations ranging from scientific management (Andrew 1981) to the men's movement (Schwalbe 1996), or to invite literary pun (as in *The Ironist's Cage* [Roth 1995]) and oxymoron (as in *Hayek. The Iron Cage of Liberty* [Gamble 1996]). Asked to name its author, most social scientists will immediately reply "Max Weber." Yet the real author of the "iron cage" is not Weber, but one of his first translators, Talcott Parsons. What I propose to show in

this Appendix is that the metaphor Weber himself employed—
stahlhartes Gehäuse, or "shell as hard as steel"—is more complex,
more modern, and more sinister than Parsons' alternative.[1] I examine the status of Parsons's canonical translation; the putative sources
of its imagery (in Bunyan's *Pilgrim's Progress*); and the more complex idea that Weber himself sought to evoke with the "shell as hard
as steel": a reconstitution of the human subject under bureaucratic
capitalism in which "steel" becomes emblematic of modernity. Steel,
unlike the "element" iron, is a product of human fabrication. It is
both hard and potentially flexible. Further, whereas a cage confines
human agents, but leaves their powers otherwise intact, a "shell"
suggests that modern capitalism has created a new kind of being.
After examining objections to this interpretation, I argue that whatever the problems with Parsons's "iron cage" as a rendition of Weber's
own metaphor, it has become a "traveling idea," a fertile coinage, in
its own right, an intriguing example of how the translator's imagination can impose itself influentially on the text and its readers.

Two preliminary sections furnish the context for this argument.
The first reviews some general criticisms of Weber translations in
order to show the peculiarity of Parsons's "iron cage." The second
section examines the inconsistent reasons Parsons gave for *choos-
ing* the expression that has since become canonical, for here, too,
there are clues as to why his interpretation of Weber is problematic.

Weber and His Translators

Translators of Weber are frequently taxed for at least four kinds of
inadequacy, each of which has interpretive consequences for the
reception and understanding of his work. First, and most obviously,
they are charged with simple incompetence, rendering terms incor-
rectly, eliding them or omitting them altogether. Thus Guenther Roth
(1992) points out that Gerth and Mills's[2] translations of "Science as
a Vocation" and "Politics as a Vocation" are defective in at least two
respects, both of which have led to "great confusions." To begin
with, "Weber does not speak 'from' the standpoint of rejecting intel-
lectualism, as many young contemporaries did, but 'exactly in relation to' it. 'Science as a Vocation' is nothing but a defense of intel-
lectualism" (Roth 1992: 455). Equally, through the omission of an
all-important qualifying adjective, Gerth and Mills make Weber's
concluding remarks to "Politics as a Vocation" appear much more

apocalyptic than in fact they were. In the original German, Weber says that what "at present" or "for the time being" (*zunächst*) lies ahead "of us" (that is, German citizens) is "a polar night of icy darkness and hardness," an allusion to the Versailles Treaty and to the difficulties the fledgling Weimar Republic will strenuously have to overcome. This is not, then, Spenglerian cultural pessimism, but rather a bracing call for realism, sobriety, and stamina to face the specific demands of the day. The omission of the adjective (*zunächst*) appears to suggest the opposite: an impending catastrophe of civilization itself.[3] In a similar vein, Peter Ghosh (1994: 104) documents the "continuous stream of individual mistranslations, misprints and omissions of up to clause-length which can destroy the meaning of entire paragraphs" in Parsons's version of *The Protestant Ethic*.

These kinds of errors are largely attributable to simple and ubiquitous human failings: carelessness, negligence, rashness. A second criticism of Weber's translators concerns not simple mistakes, however, but something deeper and more sociologically problematic: an inability to understand, or at least convey, the conceptual matrix in which the original terms are located. Thus Gisela Hinkle (Hinkle 1986: 89) believes that an "insufficient awareness of [Weber's] neo-Kantian inclinations has repeatedly distorted the meaning of the text," an argument she supports by examining translations by Edward Shils, Henry Finch, and Talcott Parsons. A characteristic objection of hers is to the opening paragraph of the "Author's Introduction" to *The Protestant Ethic*[4] in which Parsons ignores the logical, propositional structure of the essay's "problematic" (*Fragestellung*), and recasts it into a formulation that is much more idiosyncratic and personalized in complexion. Similarly, Hinkle castigates Shils and Finch for a series of mistranslations that make it seem that Weber was far closer to modern empiricist or, alternatively, philosophical realist traditions than in fact he was. The fairness of these scholarly judgments is not our concern here, though let us note in passing that Weber's neo-Kantianism was never pristine, and that it coexisted with many other intellectual currents of thought. This complicates any reading of Weber, whose adaptations of other traditions and thinkers are both prodigious and astonishingly creative. Nonetheless, Hinkle's broader argument is fully warranted: a clash of philosophical perspectives between translators and authors can have major consequences for the latter, pulling a work into an interpretive orbit that disturbs the original constellation of themes, idioms, and emphases. A salient example occurs in *The Protestant Ethic* where Parsons's hostility to behaviorist psychology, and his determination to enlist Weber to the pantheon of thinkers similarly averse to it, leads him to downplay radically Weber's emphasis on psychological *Antriebe* (drives, impulses) (Ghosh 1994: 118).

A third, related deficiency in Weber translations is an underestimation of the literary qualities and philosophical allusions of the author's texts. This is yet another aspect of that "transformation of ideas, styles of thinking, modes of expression, indeed a whole context of mental imagery and assumptions" that Gisela Hinkle objected to previously, except that in this case it is a specific kind of thinking that is being transformed. The most famous example in *The Protestant Ethic* is Parsons's translation of "elective affinities" (*Wahlverwandtschaften*) as "correlations," a social scientific domestication that extinguishes the compressed imagery of eroticism, attraction, and alchemy that pervade the Goethian evocation (compare Kent 1983). Another instance occurs toward the end of *The Protestant Ethic* where Parsons substitutes "last stage" (of cultural development) for "last men" (*die "letzten Menschen"*), thereby obliterating the Nietzschean resonance of the original.

Finally, received translations are likely to prove defective as scholars become more conscious of the total configuration of Weber's language or train new perspectives onto it. Hence, commentators may highlight neglected, but "central" terms of Weber's *oeuvre*, offering a gloss on a German word but more often inviting Anglophone readers to familiarize themselves with the peculiarities of the German language itself, especially where no clear English equivalents are available. Random examples include *Lebensführung* ("a way of consciously conducting one's life"; Tribe, 2000: 210; Hennis 1988: 28 ff), *Sinnzusammenhang* ("configuration of meaning"; Albrow 1990: 214), *Arbeitsverfassung* ("organization of labor"; Scaff 1989: 40 ff), and *Gehäuse* (cage, shell, casing) itself. Equally, as Roth (1992: 457) acknowledges,

> general readability is the best that can be achieved in a translation, because it becomes outdated whenever new theoretical issues arise. Translators cannot anticipate which terms will become important in a few years. For each specific purpose new choices must often be made. Terms that were not standardized previously suddenly are in need of uniform rendering. An example is *Eigengesetzlichkeit*, literally "autonomy," but the noun gets adequate meaning only as part of a theory of social development and moder-

nity, indicating the emergence of separate value and institutional spheres. (I find that I must often change my own translation of Weber and others, and that includes texts I revised previously.)

Where does the "iron cage" stand in relation to the four perplexities I have just enumerated? It is not a simple textual error or omission because *stahlhartes Gehäuse* is a metaphor of great complexity allowing a range of possible interpretations. Neither can the "iron cage" be said to be a solecism induced by a cavalier and uninformed attitude to the sources. As we will see, Parsons claimed to be immersed in the Protestant texts Weber was describing. Equally, there is no lost philosophical allusion at stake here, or the *ex post facto* need to retranslate the term as a result of some major shift of intellectual horizon; on the contrary, most Weberian commentators appear happy enough with Parsons's rendition.[5] The chief problem with the "iron cage" is rather that it is hermeneutically superficial, possibly modeling itself on a false literary analogy, and failing to capture a disturbing nuance of Weber's argument. Yet Parsons's interpretation is not so easily "corrected." For the most intriguing peculiarity of the "iron cage" is that it now has a vibrant career of its own.

Parsons's Progress

Why did Parsons choose the "iron cage" as a rendition of *stahlhartes Gehäuse*? He offered at least two explanations for his preference. The first appears in a letter written to Benjamin Nelson on January 24, 1975, in which Parsons wrote: "I cannot remember clearly just how and why I decided when more than 35 years ago I was translating Weber's *Protestant Ethic* essay to introduce the phrase 'iron cage' . . . I think 'iron cage' was a case of rather free translation. I do not remember being aware at the time of the use of the phrase by John Bunyan. However, as you know, I was brought up deeply steeped in a puritan background, and whether or not I intentionally adopted the term from Bunyan seems to me probably secondary. The most likely explanation of my choice is that I thought it appropriate to the puritan background of Weber's own personal engagement in the Protestant Ethic problem" (Parsons 1975; and Swedberg 1998: 262-263, n. 44). However, just over four years later, Parsons's emphasis is somewhat different. Responding to a query of Edward Tiryakian, Parsons (1979: 35-36) remarked, "I am pretty sure that I did look up *Pilgrim's Progress* at the time I was working on the translation and that this influenced my choice of the phrase iron cage." Parsons went on to say that *The Protestant Ethic* was one of the easier Weber translations he attempted because "Weber chose to write particularly about 17ᵗʰ Century English Puritanism and the basic language was English. *Therefore, in a sense, all I had to do was to translate Weber's German back into English with which of course he was thoroughly familiar"* (my emphasis).

It transpires, then, that Parsons wondered whether "iron cage" may have come to him, subliminally or directly, as a result of his reading John Bunyan, the great Puritan preacher who was himself imprisoned, first, from November 1660 to March 1672, and then for a six-month period some time, no one is quite sure, between 1675 and 1677. *The Pilgrim's Progress* (1678) was the fruit of that first confinement.[6] In the allegory, the chief protagonist, Christian, has left his city and family, both doomed to hell fire, to make his way toward the Celestial City. On his journey, Christian suffers various self-inflicted setbacks before his final apotheosis, meeting a cast of characters who seek to deflect, destroy, or instruct him. The juncture in the story that concerns us is the moment Christian comes to the House of the Interpreter, who proceeds benignly to show him various personages. The man in the iron cage is one of them.

> Now, said Christian, let me go hence: Nay stay (said the Interpreter,) till I have shewed thee a little more, and after that, thou shalt go on thy way. So he took him by the hand again, and led him into a very dark Room, where there sat a Man in an Iron Cage.
>
> Now the Man, to look on, seemed very sad: he sat with his eyes looking down to the ground, his hands folded together; and he sighed as if he would break his heart. Then said Christian: What means this? At which the Interpreter bid him talk with the Man.
>
> *Chr.* Then Said Christian to the Man, What art thou?
>
> The Man answered, I am what I was not once.
>
> *Chr.* What wast thou once?
>
> *Man.* The Man said, I was once a fair and flourishing Professor [i.e., one who openly professes his religion], both in mine own eyes, and also in the eyes of others: I once was, as I thought, fair for the Celestial City, and had then even joy at the thoughts that I should get thither.
>
> *Chr.* Well, but what art thou now?
>
> *Man.* I am now a Man of Despair, and am shut up in it, as in this Iron Cage. I cannot get out; O now I cannot.
>
> *Chr.* But how camest thou in this condition?

Man. I left off to watch, and be sober; I laid the reins upon the neck of my lusts; I sinned against the light of the Word, and the goodness of God: I have grieved the Spirit, and he is gone; I tempted the Devil, and he is come to me; I have provoked God to anger, and he has left me; I have so hardened my heart, that I cannot repent . . .

Chr. Then said Christian, Is there no hope but you must be kept in this Iron Cage of Despair?

Man. No, none at all . . . God hath denied me repentance; his Word gives me no encouragement to believe; yea, himself hath shut me up in this Iron Cage: nor can all the men in the World let me out. O Eternity! Eternity! How shall I grapple with the misery that I must meet with in Eternity (Bunyan 1960 [1678]: 34-35).

I have quoted this passage at length to show that, in *The Pilgrim's Progress*, the iron cage is a metaphor of the deepest dejection. Man has turned away from God, and God has turned away from him. Man is now left to "grapple with the misery" that he will meet in the eternity of hell. In the critical edition of *The Pilgrim's Progress* from which I have been quoting, a footnote directs readers toward the multiple sources of the iron cage imagery. Specifically, Bunyan had in mind the example of John Child, an apostate of the Bedford congregation who, having joined the Church of England, later committed suicide in a fit of contrition. Bunyan was also alluding to one of the great engravings of Francis Quarles's *Emblemes* (1993 [1635]) that depicts a man in an iron cage, an angel in attendance, and an open cage above the man from which a bird has just flown and which represents his soul. In the original emblem (Book 5, number x, p. 280), Quarles inserts, just below the picture, the first clause of Psalm 142 "Bring my soul out of prison, that I may praise thy name" (the Psalm continues: "the righteous shall compass me about; for thou shalt deal bountifully with me"). Opposite the picture is a long quotation from Saint Anselm (1033-1109) that begins "My Soule is like a Bird; my Flesh, the Cage."

Weber's reference, in *The Protestant Ethic*, to the "shell as hard as steel" has a rather different target. This becomes clear when he speculates on those members of bourgeois civilization who, in the future, will come to live within this shell, and whether "entirely new prophets will arise, or [whether] there will be a great rebirth of old ideas and ideals, or, if neither, mechanized petrification, embellished with a sort of convulsive self-importance. For of the last men [Parsons has "last stage"] of this cultural development, it might well be truly said: 'Specialists without spirit, sensualists without heart; this nullity imagines that it has attained a level of civilization never before achieved" (Weber 1930: 132).

While Weber himself may have been in despair about some aspects of the modern condition, his summoning of Nietzsche's Last Man has precisely the opposite thrust: a ringing Zarathustrean indictment of a humanity that is "happy," sated, mediocre and philistine: "The earth has become small, and upon it hops the Last Man, who makes everything small. His race is as inexterminable as the flea; the Last Man lives longest." "I tell you," Zarathustra says a few lines earlier, "one must have chaos in one, to give birth to a dancing star. I tell you: you still have chaos in you" (Nietzsche 1961 [1883]: 46; translation modified). Chaos was no stranger to Weber, or to the Puritans who struggled heroically to contain it within their doctrines. That its eclipse was to be feared more than the inner conflict it provoked, was a typical Weberian sentiment. In contrast, the "specialists without spirit, sensualists without heart" are too vacuous to lament, believing they have "attained a level of civilization never before achieved." While their *Gehäuse* has not been freely chosen, it is willingly accepted, and is by no means a punishment. However, while Bunyan's Man must confront an eternity of misery and hopelessness, Weber's view of the future, dominated by the Last Man, is not quite so desperate, for the possibility arises that "entirely new prophets will arise, or there will be a great rebirth of old ideas and ideals." "Mechanized petrification" is avoidable. I conclude from this analysis that "cage" as a translation of *Gehäuse* is inappropriate because the despairing Man of Bunyan's creation, and the inane specialist of Weber's, are asymmetrical figures.[7] The former suffers and is being punished; the latter is a hedonist motivated by the quest for materialistic consumption and confident of his superiority. *Dum Coelum aspicio, Solum despicio* ("I aspire to heaven and despise the ground") reads the motto of Francis Quarles's *Emblemes*, on which Bunyan imaginatively drew. Weber's bourgeois philistine, in contrast, has his nose so close to the ground that he is incapable of aspiring to heaven or to any non-utilitarian value. Knowing Weber's familiarity with the English Puritan sources, Parsons believed that he had properly translated the German *stahlhartes Gehäuse* into an English idiom. Parsons's justification is ingenious, and the "iron cage" metaphor is remarkable in its own right (a point to which I will return presently). There are a number of reasons to believe, however, that the German original required more attention than Parsons gave to it.

From Iron to Steel

Stahlhartes Gehäuse is a difficult expression to translate, largely because of the many meanings that *Gehäuse* can assume, but it does not present the English translator with the intractable difficulties posed by words for which there are no strict English equivalents. Under those circumstances, translators are compelled to improvise, as they must with Heidegger's *Befindlichkeit*[8] or, even more so, with the noun *Vorleser*, the title of Bernhard Schlink's novel. Since English makes no clear distinction, in a single word, between a person who reads and a person who reads aloud to others, *Der Vorleser* was rendered simply as *The Reader.* But this was not Parsons's predicament; the English language offers a number of words that will adequately translate Weber's German phrase.

We might begin by noting that Weber wrote not of iron, but chose instead to invoke a compound adjective—*stahlhartes*—that directs the reader's attention to steel. Iron is a metal that is ancient (the earliest objects of smelted iron date back to around 3000 B.C.E.) and elemental.[9] Accordingly, the *"Iron Age"* denotes the third of an archaeological, archaic sequence (Stone, Bronze, and Iron), and the *"kingdom of iron,"* (and of iron and clay) is the last of the four kingdoms revealed by Daniel to Nebuchadnezzar.[10] Yet iron, and in particular the *"Age of Iron,"* is also associated with the industrial revolution and modernity.[11] Like steel, iron evokes hardness and unbending resolution: Bismarck was the "Iron Chancellor" (as Mrs Thatcher was the "Iron Lady"), the *Kaiserreich* the era of "Blood and Iron" (yet also of "Steel and Rye"). But steel has more complex and even more modern connotations[12] than its metallic counterpart. Steel, unlike iron, is an invention rather than an "element"; although pre-modern in origins, the breakthrough in steel came with its mass industrial production during the 1850s, a result of the pneumatic Bessemer process.[13] As such, steel is the product of *human fabrication*: steel is an alloy of iron. Increase its carbon content, and you increase its strength. Add other materials—manganese, silicon, tungsten—and steel becomes harder. Yet while steel can be made extremely hard, its hardness can vary along a continuum of "mild," "medium" and "high." This permits steel to be both rigid (enabling high-speed drills) *and* flexible (consider steel sheets and wire). Hence, as a metal that is associated in the European context with modernity, fabrication, ductility, and malleability, steel appears to have much more in common with rational bourgeois capitalism than the iron of which it is a refinement. Just as steel involves the transformation of iron by the mixing of carbon and other elements, so capitalism involves the transformation of labor power into commodities. It is thus appropriate that the father of scientific management, Frederick Winslow Taylor, began his working career (in 1878) in the Midvale Steel Company of Philadelphia; that he invented high-speed steel in 1898 while working for the Bethlehem Steel Works; and that his ideas for the rationalization of labor proceeded from his experience with metal; as Siegfried Giedion observed (1969 [1948]: 98), "[t]he stretching of human capacities and the stretching of the properties of steel derive from the same roots."[14]

If Weber had wanted to deploy the imagery of the "iron cage," he could have exercised that option in German with the expression *eiserner Käfig*.[15] His contemporaries might then have caught an allusion to John Bunyan, but are far more likely to have remembered a fable closer to home: the Brothers Grimm story of "Iron Hans"- the Wild Man who, dredged up from the bottom of a deep pool, is exhibited in an "iron cage" in the courtyard of a King's castle (Grimm and Grimm 1985 [1850]: 757-765). (The myth is the centerpiece of Robert Bly's [1990] theory of masculinity in *Iron John: A Book About Men.*)

Dead and Living Machines

Cage, as a translation of *Gehäuse,* raises other problems. *Gehäuse* is a noun that Weber repeatedly employs in his writings; its connotations include shell (or carapace), casing, housing, and dwelling. Conceivably, "cage" is also apt. Yet for it to be appropriate Weber would have had to mix a metaphor that begins with Baxter's contention that worldly goods should be like a cloak that can be thrown effortlessly aside. A cage, in contrast, is not something that is worn; it is something in which one is trapped.[16] Now, to the degree that "the technical and economic conditions of machine production" (Weber 1930 [1920, 1905]: 181) offer us no real escape from the world they permeate, the metaphor of confinement works—but only in part since iron bars can be filed down; cages can be opened; people can escape from them: images that contradict the notion of indefinite captivity. Further, the specter of people trapped within a cage implies that they are being punished, usually for an act *they* have committed or are believed to have committed;[17] and punishment itself is typically an experience associated with suffering and anguish (—we might consider the fate of the Münster Anabaptists, Jan van Leyden prominent among them, whose hideously disfigured remains were suspended in three iron cages from the tower of the Lamberti Church).[18] We have already seen why this state of lamentation does not characterize the Last Man.

Moreover, as David Chalcraft (1994) has argued in an article that exhaustively considers the linguistic options, the most convincing rendering of *Gehäuse* in *The Protestant Ethic* is "shell." Only this term captures the range of associations that Weber wishes to convey. In particular, "shell" suggests a living space both for the individual who must carry it around and a macro environment ("the universal world order of capitalism") within which individual experience is lived out. As Chalcraft (1994: 29-39) observes, "the steel shell of the capitalist order" conditions the priorities of modern society, and impresses these priorities on each of us as individuals. Our own shell, in which we live and breathe, is our shelter and constraint, yet it allows choices of various kinds, movements and directions which are our own. Chalcraft also remarks percipiently that the image of a shell symbolizes something that has not just been externally imposed (as in the iron cage metaphor), but that has become "part and parcel of [our] existence." That observation is worth developing.

For social scientists familiarized to the "iron cage," Weber's metaphor of the shell as hard as steel is likely to appear anticlimactic; it is certainly less arresting and sonorous than Parsons's creation. Yet, on closer inspection, it is more troubling. The habitation of a steel shell implies not only a new dwelling for modern human beings, but a transformed nature; Homo sapiens has become a *different* being, a degraded being. A cage deprives one of liberty, but leaves one otherwise unaltered, one's powers still intact even if incapable of full realization. A shell, on the other hand, hints at an organic reconstitution of the being concerned; a shell is *part* of the organism and cannot be dispensed with.[19] The steel that composes the shell is not that summoned up by Ernst Jünger in whose martial "storms of steel" ordinary men become heroes, and where "passive forces [are] melted down in the crucible of war," an "incomparable schooling of the heart" (Jünger 1929 [1920]: xii).[20] For Weber, on the contrary, the steel shell is the symbol *of* passivity, the transformation of the Puritan hero into a figure of mass mediocrity. True, we have not yet reached the terrifying dimension of Kafka's *Metamorphosis* in which the chief protagonist, Gregor Samsa, wakes to find himself transformed into a giant bug lying on his "hard, as it were armor plated back" (*panzerartig harten Rücken*), and whose first thoughts and worries are about his job and his timetable, rather than his fantastically changed state (Kafka 1971 [1915]: 89). But Weber's metaphor places *The Protestant Ethic* within a lineage that stretches past Kafka,[21] to embrace Hannah Arendt's concern that "watched from a sufficiently removed vantage point in the universe . . . modern motorization would appear like a process of biological mutation in which human bodies gradually begin to be covered by shells of steel";[22] and beyond her to those contemporary writers who speculate on cyborgs and the "posthuman" or "transhuman" condition (Fukuyama 1999; Hayles 1999; Ansell Pearson 1997; Gray 1995).

Nor is *The Protestant Ethic* the only place where Weber invokes the steel shell and reflects on the new being that modernity is creating. In one of his most powerful analyses of the "inescapability" of "rational" bureaucratic forms of organization, Weber (1994a [1917]:156-158) argued that "wherever the trained, specialist, modern official has once begun to rule, his power is absolutely unbreakable, because the entire organization of providing even the most basic needs in life then depends on his performance of his duties." The elimination of private capitalism, if that should come to pass, would not mean "that the steel shell of modern industrial work would break into pieces"[23] but in fact quite the reverse since then the state bureaucracy would rule alone, unimpeded by its private counterparts. "Is there," Weber asked rhetorically, "any appreciable *difference* between the lives of the workers and clerks in the Prussian state run mines and railways and those of people working in large private capitalist enterprises?" Indeed, Weber considered the former less free because there was no countervailing power to which they could appeal or with which they could align. Weber continued,

A lifeless machine is *congealed spirit*. It is *only* this fact that gives the machine the power to force men to serve it and thus to rule and determine their daily working lives, as in fact happens in factories. The same *congealed spirit* is, however, also embodied in that *living machine* which is represented by bureaucratic organization with its specialization of trained, technical work, its delimitation of areas of responsibility, its regulations and its graduated hierarchy of relations of obedience. Combined with the dead machine, it is in the process of manufacturing the *Gehäuse* of that future serfdom to which, perhaps, men may have to submit powerlessly, just like the slaves in the ancient state of Egypt, *if they consider that the ultimate and only value by which the conduct of their affairs is to be decided is good administration and provision for their needs by officials (that is 'good' in the purely technical sense of rational administration).* (Weber 1994a [1917]: 158)

One possible objection to the analysis I have offered here, and especially to my interpretation of the *stahlhartes Gehäuse* metaphor in *The Protestant Ethic*, is that it lends credence to a caricature of Weber as an opponent of modern capitalism and as an apostle of *Kulturpessimismus*. It is important that such a parody be avoided. Guenther Roth (1993) points out that *The Protestant Ethic* was intended, at least in part, as a wake-up call to Weber's German contemporaries, and especially to "otherworldly," naive *Kulturprotestanten*: it was meant to impress on them the inevitability of capitalism, the backward condition of Germany compared with Great Britain, and the need to employ the new industrial order to promote the interests of Imperial Germany's position as a world power.[24] "The Puritan wanted to work in a calling; we are forced to do so" is an affirmation of the modern world not an invitation to flee from it, a counsel of realism, not despair.[25] A blanket condemnation of capitalism or a prophecy of the decline of the West was never part of Weber's agenda. At the same time it is undeniable that Weber *was*, to put it mildly, wary, troubled, and disconsolate about the human prospect—in the Occident as a whole—and in that sense "pessimistic." The passages I have already quoted from *The Protestant Ethic* should make that plain enough, but if they do not there are many more to draw on. As Weber remarked, "How is it *at all possible* to salvage any remnants of 'individual' freedom of movement *in any sense*, given this all-powerful trend towards bureaucratization?... In view of the growing indispensability and hence increasing power of state officialdom . . . how can there be any guarantee that forces exist which can impose limits on the enormous, crushing power of this constantly growing stratum of society and control it effectively" (Weber 1994a [1917]:159; cf. Weber 1997a [1906): 109; Weber 1997b [1906]: 233). What Weber feared was not private capitalism, per se, but its rentier parasite, not individualism but "the accustomed *Gehäuse* of bureaucratic regimentation" (Weber 1994a [1917]: 268), not democracy but rule governed conformity, not administration in its place but the bureaucratic stultification of all sectors and spaces of life— made even worse by a protective welfare state orientation[26] that would, he thought, deprive the individual of responsibility, initiative, and the willingness to take risks.

Another possible objection to my discussion of the *stahlhartes Gehäuse* is that it misidentifies the primary object of Weber's concern. I have argued above that what exercised Weber most was the possibility that modern capitalism would produce, perhaps in abundance, the Last Men of Nietzsche's withering depiction. But is this too narrow? Was Weber more worried, instead, about the fate of the ordinary person, the ordinary worker, under capitalism?[27] I doubt it. For most of his adult life, Weber showed very little solicitude for the condition of the ordinary person, though he cared a great deal for the fate of humanity (*Menschentum*).[28] This is not a contradiction in (Weber's) terms. Weber typically spoke from the perspective of the *Bildungsbürgertum* (the educated elite of the middle class), a stratum that saw itself as the bearer of German culture and, with the officer corps and nobility, the custodian of German honor (Ay 1999). From this elevated standpoint, the ordinary people were little more than "masses" to be mobilized on behalf of the nation and, optimally, educated in economic, political and geopolitical realities.[29] Weber's chief concern was not with the average fate, if that means with the mundane and banal, but with a society's modes of *selecting* the best or the worst.[30] His priorities were above all "aristocratic," concerned with the conditions of excellence, by definition only achievable by the few. Was Weber, then, an insensitive man? His nervous breakdown, and his acute awareness of human tragedy and the existential dilemmas of life, show conclusively otherwise. But even those who admire Weber's work are constrained to admit that his code of honor and stringent standards promoted a disdainful attitude toward everyday life which, from another perspective, is rich precisely for the compromises it requires. It is telling that Weber's greatest, and frequently ventilated, anxiety is not about a lack of abundance or contentment but their *fulfillment*; and that it is not suffering that agitates him but the prospect, adapting an unlikely combination of Nietzschean and classical republican motifs, of a civilization that is "sated," "replete" and lacking in dignity and freedom.[31] As he observed in an essay written shortly after *The Protestant Ethic*,

What is not won for the individual now, or in the course of the next generations, in terms of the inalienable sphere of personality and liberty, as long as the economic and spiritual "revolution," the much reviled "anarchy" of production and the equally reviled "subjectivism" continue undiminished (and these things *alone* can take the individual out of the broad mass and throw him back on himself) will *perhaps* never be won, once the world is economically "sated" and intellectually "replete." So it appears as far as our feeble eyes are able to peer into the impenetrable mists of the future of the human race. (Weber 1995a [1906]: 110)[32]

Concluding Comments

"In this translation, I must admit, I have not been altogether faithful . . . "
(C. Wright Mills)[33]

What, then, are we to conclude about the "iron cage"? The first duty of the translator is to be faithful to the author and so "shell of steel" and not "iron cage" is the expression that an interest in precision requires us to adopt. Yet something important remains.

It is one of the great ironies of sociology that the man so often excoriated for the ungainliness and density of his own prose could produce a translation that is rich in stylistic pathos. Parsons's discreet infidelity to Weber inspired an expression that has proved remarkably productive and resonant. The "iron cage" would never have been quoted and adapted as much as it has been unless it had struck some deep vein of intelligibility and recognition. It is a great coinage in its own right, a triumph of the imagination, one of those "traveling ideas" (Said 1983: 226-247) that has steadily gathered a momentum of its own.[34] To the degree that many sociologists associate Weber with his ruminations on the "iron cage," and associate modern capitalism (or "technical rationality" or "modernity") with the image Parsons evoked, it is evident that author, translator, and object have become miraculously compounded. Keith Tribe (1988: 7) has written ruefully of the "agenda setting nature" of Parsons's reading of Weber. It appears that the agenda was even broader than that, encompassing the interpretation of modernity itself. This explains the tendency of scholars to suggest erroneously that Weber wrote about the "iron cage of bureaucracy,"[35] a usage that probably elides Parsons's "iron cage" with Robert Michels's "iron law of oligarchy" (Michels 1959 [1915]). And it also explains the curious fact that Parsons's "iron cage," an English rendering of German, has been adopted by German translators of English texts:[36] the Parsonian resonance in Zygmunt Bauman's *Der Mensch im Globalisierungskäfig* (the German version of Bauman 1998) is unmistakable.[37] Moreover if, as Walter Benjamin (1973 [1923]: 76) once remarked, the "task of the translator consists in finding that intended effect upon the language into which he is translating which produces in it the echo of the original," can we really say in good faith that an echo of the original is lacking in "the iron cage?" I think not: cages are stultifying, confining, and claustrophobic, and these are certainly among the ideas that Weber was trying to impress on his readers. Our translations can seek to make these echoes more, rather than less, audible by translating *stahlhartes Gehäuse* as "iron cage." But by so doing certain important misconceptions are introduced which mislead readers about Weber's fears for human life under capitalism. "Shell as hard as steel" avoids these misconceptions and better captures the subtleties of Weber's thought.

Notes

1. Weber wrote two versions of *The Protestant Ethic*, both of which, however, employ the *stahlhartes Gehäuse* metaphor. See Weber 1905: 108 and Weber 1920: 203-204. Parsons translated the 1920 version. For a survey of the major differences between the editions, see Lichtblau and Weiß' introduction to Weber 1993: vii-xxxv.

    The publishing success of Parsons's translation has confounded the initial gloomy expectations of Allen and Unwin; the company's governing director thought it unlikely that the book would sell as many as 2,500 copies (details in Roth 1999: 521).

2. Hans Gerth was the real translator. On the moral dynamics of the Gerth and Mills collaboration, particularly with respect to the *From Max Weber* project, see Oakes and Vidich 1999:15-56.

3. For two such ominous readings, see Ritzer 1993: 162, and Rinehart 1998: 19 who writes of the "'polar night of icy darkness and hardness' that is [Weber's view of] modern life."

4. More precisely, Weber's "Vorbemerkung" (Preliminary Remark) to the first volume of Weber 1920: 1-16 which includes a revised, expanded version of *The Protestant Ethic* (on pages 17-206).

5. The term "iron cage" is endorsed by Harry Zohn in his translation of Marianne Weber's biography of her husband (Marianne Weber, 1975 [1926]: 342, by Roth 1993: 87, and by Bell 1996 [1976]: 291, n. 11), among others too numerous to mention. It also appears prominently in the titles of books by Scaff (1989) and Mitzman (1970). However, when Mitzman translates the passage from which, purportedly, the "iron cage"metaphor is drawn, he departs from Parsons's interpretation. Mitzman quotes Weber as stating "But fate decreed that the cloak should become a housing hard as steel." For Mitzman (1970: 172) the "'housing hard as steel', of course, recalls the 'secure house' of his father's generation that Weber had publicly refused to enter in 1893. But Weber now recognized the ascetic mien of his mother as well as the bureaucratic spirit of his father as a threat to his autonomy." For some pertinent comments on Mitzman's usage, see Tiryakian 1981b pp. 28-30.

    Richard Matthews's translation in the W.G. Runciman anthology has "casing as hard as steel" (Runciman 1978:170). That phrasing is also preferred by Turner 1982. For a helpful discussion of some of the problems in rendering *Gehäuse*, see Lassman and Spiers (Weber 1994: 68, n. 57, 90, n. 11, 374).

6.   The language of confinement is also a prominent motif in the tracts of Martin Luther. See, for instance, his discussion of "the iron bars of ceremonies" (which Luther considered necessary for an ordered life) in "The Freedom of a Christian Man" (1520); and of "the prison of sin and death" in "Preface to the German Translation of the New Testament" (1522). A convenient collection of these documents can be found in Hillerbrand 1968: 3-29, 37-42; quotes on 28, 40.

7.   I thus take a very different view to Edward Tiryakian (1981b: 30) who remarks: "I suggest both that Weber was inspired by this passage and that he strongly identified not only with 'the Man' of despair but also with Christian."

8.   Heidegger 1962 [1927] §§ 29-30 = 172-182. For an illuminating discussion of the difficulties of this term, see Polt 1999: 64-68.

9.   Iron appears in Group VIII of the Periodic Table, and is distinguished by the atomic number 26, the atomic weight of 55.847, and the chemical symbol Fe.

10.   Daniel 2:1-49. The first three ages are of gold, silver, and bronze ("brass"). "And the fourth kingdom shall be strong as iron: forasmuch as iron breaketh in pieces and subdueth all things: and as iron that breaketh all these, shall it break in pieces and bruise" (2:40). The sequence of bronze and iron is touchingly reversed in Coetzee (1998 [1990]: 50. See also pp. 73, 75, 82, 124-126).

       For another ancient myth of ages in which iron figures prominently, see Hesiod's *Works and Days*, lines 106-201. Hesiod's degenerative succession of metallic "races" culminates in the miserable men of iron of which he himself is a member. "Not ever during the day will men cease from labor and grief; not even at night will they cease from being oppressed. . . . And Zeus will destroy this race of mortal people too, when they turn out to be grey-templed at birth," (The poem was composed in the early seventh century B.C.E.).

11.   For Weber's analysis of iron ("the most important factor in the development of capitalism") see Weber 1961 [1927, 1923]. 227, 275. I am grateful to Charles Camic for directing my attention to this source.

12.   Both iron and steel have strong masculine (and martial) overtones. Popular iconography is full of images that link iron and steel to forms of manhood; consider Iron John, John Henry (the "steel driving man,") Superman, The Man of Steel, etc. For more subtle connotations of iron, see Primo Levi's portrait of Sandro in Levi 1984 [1975]: 37-49.

13.   For a brief overview of the revolution in steel production unleashed by the Bessemer process, see Kanigel 1999 [1997]: 155-160). Writing for the New York *Evening Post*'s "Review of the Century, "(Jan. 12, 1901) Andrew Carnegie anointed the new era thus: "Farewell, then, Age of Iron; all hail, King Steel, and success to the republic, the future seat and center of his empire, where he is to sit enthroned and work his wonders upon the earth." To which Carnegie's biographer aptly adds, "This was a curiously belated *vive* from one who had been largely instrumental in enthroning steel as monarch some thirty years earlier . . ." (Wall 1989 [1970]: 307).

14.   See, especially, Taylor 1998 [1911]: 51-60.

       The totemic identification of steel with fortitude, efficiency and modernization is nowhere more evident than in the Communist experiments of the twentieth century. Lenin (1960 [1918]: 716-717) eagerly embraced Taylorism; Stalin means "man of steel." The subject is too complex to pursue here in any detail, but one of its more tragic manifestations was the Great Leap Forward (1958-1960): Mao's catastrophic attempt to outstrip Great Britain in steel production within a fifteen-year period. Exponentially increased steel production was one of his "two generals" (the other, far more disastrous, was the Lysenkoist campaign to accelerate grain production). On the backyard furnace campaign during the Great Leap, see Becker 1996: 63-64; cf. Chamberlin 1937.

15. As Nietzsche did in his scabrous comments on "the priests" in *The Will to Power*, section 397: "Morality is a menagerie; its presupposition is that iron bars can be more profitable than freedom, even for the prisoners; its other presupposition is that there exist animal-trainers who are not afraid of terrible means—who know how to handle red-hot iron. This frightful species which takes up the fight against the wild animal is called 'priest'....Man, imprisoned in an iron cage of errors became a caricature of man, sick, wretched, ill-disposed toward himself, full of hatred for the impulses of life...." (Nietzsche 1968b [1901]: 214).

16. See Marianne Weber's characterization of her husband, impatient about wasting time on his visit to New York: "Only when he was bored and wasted time needlessly—as on a streetcar ride of several hours through New York that was undertaken in the protective custody of a hospitable American colleague . . . —did the lion secretly rage in his cage, and then it was hard to restrain him from breaking out" (Marianne Weber 1975 [1926]: 281.

17. Of course, cages can also be occupied by people who are just doing a certain kind of job: for instance, postal workers in the late nineteenth century and later for whom the wood and wire lattice "cage" was a means of protection from thieves. For a play on "cage" as both protective and confining simultaneously, see James 1919 [1898]: 5-6, 17, 51-52, and passim.

18. A history of this incident can be found in Bax 1903: 282-331.

19. Again one recalls Marianne Weber (1975 [1926]: 232), this time describing Max Weber *senior's* last days: "It was not given to the aging man to break through the shell (*Gehäuse*) of his own nature."

20. Steel is a vital metaphor not only in *Storm of Steel* (*In Stahlgewittern*, 1920) but also in Jünger's *Battle as Inner Experience* (1922)—"we are at once the smith and the flashing steel" . . . "steel forms, whose eagle gaze seeks out the clouds above the whirling propellers, who are cramped into the apparatus of tanks, who venture Hell's journey through rolling minefields"—and *The Worker* (1932) where the coming "steel order" is ardently prophesied. See the study of Nevin 1996: 39-74, 114-140, and especially 65, 72, 126 from which the quotes in this footnote are taken.

    For a while, Jünger was a member of the *Stahlhelm* (the steel helmet was introduced to German infantry in 1916), the largest and most influential nationalist-conservative veterans' organization of the Weimar Republic. In 1934 it was renamed the *Nationalsozialistischer_Frontkämpferbund* and, proving itself to be insufficiently Nazi, was dissolved shortly thereafter. The image of steel, however, continued to find employment in the Third Reich: see Goebbels's evocation of "steely romanticism" (*stählernde Romantik*) as discussed in Herf 1984: 195-196, 220.

21. In aphorism 13 of *Reflections on Sin, Pain, Hope and the True Way*, Kafka wrote that "A cage went in search of a bird." In Kafka 1946: 237

22. Arendt 1958: 322. Though Arendt was a markedly anti-Weberian thinker along a number of axes, the conclusion to *The Human Condition* has some uncanny parallels with Parsons's translation of *The Protestant Ethic*'s finale. See especially Arendt (1958: 322): "The last stage of the laboring society, the society of jobholders, demands of its members a sheer automatic functioning . . . It is quite conceivable that the modern age—which began with such an unprecedented and promising outburst of human activity—may end in the deadliest, most sterile passivity history has ever known." For a sardonic interpretation of German intellectuals' perspective on the machine, see Bellow 1996 [1970]: 19.

23. I have modified Speirs' translation. Weber writes: "Etwa ein Zerbrechen des stählernen Gehäuses der modernen gewerblichen Arbeit? Nein!" (Weber 1988 [1917]: 221).

24. This final desideratum also comes across forcefully in the conclusion to Weber's 1896 pamphlet on the stock and commodity exchanges (*Die Börsenverkehr*) that he penned for the *Göttingen Worker's Library* (edited by Friedrich Naumann). See Weber 1924: 289-322, at 320-322. His argument is that so long as nations carry out a "ruthless and unavoidable" economic struggle, a strong German stock and commodity exchange is vital, though inescapably in tension with demands for "ethical culture" and "welfare institutions."

25. I am drawing on a letter from Guenther Roth to the author, March 6, 2000; cited with Roth's permission.

26. "Whether in the shape of American 'benevolent feudalism', the German 'welfare institutions', or the Russian factory constitution—everywhere the empty shell (*Gehäuse*) of the new serfdom stands ready; it will be occupied to the degree that the pace of technical-economic 'progress' slows down and the victory of 'income' over 'profit' together with the exhaustion of what remains of 'free' lands and the 'free' markets, renders the masses 'compliant'" (Weber 1997a [1906]: 108.

27. This is the view of Richard Swedberg who argues that the image of "the iron cage" (the designation Swedberg prefers) is "an attempt to capture the fate of the 'common man' in capitalism—in particular the suffering felt by the industrial worker in the inferno of the modern machine and all the ills that come from that . . . The image that to my mind best expresses Weber's idea of the iron cage . . . is one of the etchings of Max Klinger which portrays a skeleton smashing skulls, with the kind of iron contraption with which you produce gravel for roads," letter from Professor Swedberg to the author, January 23, 2000; cited with Swedberg's permission. The etching being referred to is no. 10 of Klinger's "Eve and the Future" cycle (Third Future). The image was composed in 1879.

28. Karl-Ludwig Ay (1999: 114) discerns some change in Weber's attitude towards the end of the Great War when he campaigned for universal and equal suffrage of the returning soldiers.

29. For an extended discussion of Weber's concept of "the masses," and especially their putative "irrationality," see Baehr 1998: 236-242.

30. Selection (*Auslese*) and its cognates (e.g. "struggle for existence") is a recurring theme of Weber's work carrying both Darwinesque and Nietzschean connotations. See Weber 1994: 2, 16, 84,134, 180, 225, 267, 283, 306. Also Weber 1978 [1922], pp. 38-40.

31. "The question which stirs us as we think beyond the grave of our own generation is not the *well-being* human beings will enjoy in the future but what kind of people they will *be*, and it is this same question which underlies all work in political economy. We do not want to breed well-being in people, but rather those characteristics which we think of as constituting the human greatness and nobility of our nature" (Weber 1994b [1895]: 15). Weber goes on to say that the quest for "social justice" is a lesser standard of value for political economy than "the quality of the human beings reared under [certain] economic and social conditions of existence" (emphasis omitted).

32. Weber is writing specifically about the Russian "revolution" of 1905-1906, but the context of this quote shows a broader concern about Western developments. He observes a little earlier: "It is absolutely ridiculous to attribute to the high capitalism which is today being imported into Russian and already exists in America—this "inevitable" economic development—any elective affinity with 'democracy' let alone 'liberty' (in *any* sense of the word). The question should be: how can these things exist at all for any length of time under the domination of capitalism?" Weber (1995a [1906]: 109). Also the concluding line of Weber (1995b [1906]: 233): " . . . the

future for 'sated' nations is bleak."
33. C. Wright Mills (1959: 29) on his selective "translation" of Parsons's *The Social System*.
34. One of its more recent manifestations is George Ritzer's distinction among the three major attitudes toward a "McDonaldized society" as a cage of iron, velvet and rubber. See Ritzer 1993: 160-163, and Ritzer 1998: 4, 77-78, 164.
35. For example, Maryanski and Turner 1992: 145, 167. See also Silberman 1993, and Wagner 1994: 64, 89-103.
36. And by the French translator of *The Protestant Ethic*. Thus Jaques Chavy (in Weber 1964: 246) follows Parsons in rendering *stahlhartes Gehäuse* as "une cage d'acier."
37. Volker Meja pointed this out to me.

Bibliography

Dates in square brackets in the main text denote original year of publication.

Abbott, Andrew 2000. *Department and Discipline. Chicago Sociology at One Hundred.* Chicago: University of Chicago Press.

Abbott, Andrew 2000. "Reflections on the Future of Sociology," *Contemporary Sociology* 29 (1): 296-300.

Abel, Theodore 1965. *Systematic Sociology in Germany. A Critical Analysis of Some Attempts to Establish Sociology as an Independent Science.* New York: Octagon.

Ackroyd, P.R. and Evans, C.F., eds. 1970. *The Cambridge History of the Bible,* Vol. 1. Cambridge: Cambridge University Press.

Adatto, Kiku and Cole, Stephen 1981. "The Functions of Classical Theory in Contemporary Sociological Research: The Case of Max Weber," *Knowledge and Society* 3: 137-62.

Albrow, Martin 1990. *Max Weber's Construction of Social Theory.* London: Macmillan.

Alexander, Jeffrey C. 1982a. *Theoretical Logic in Sociology,* Vol. 1. *Positivism, Presuppositions, and Current Controversies.* Berkeley: University of California Press.

Alexander, Jeffrey C. 1982b.*Theoretical Logic in Sociology,* Vol. 2. *The Antinomies of Classical Thought: Marx and Durkheim.* Berkeley: University of California Press.

Alexander, Jeffrey C. 1983a. *Theoretical Logic in Sociology,* Vol. 3. *The Classical Attempt at Theoretical Synthesis: Max Weber.* Berkeley: University of California Press.

Alexander, Jeffrey C. 1983b. *Theoretical Logic in Sociology,* Vol. 4. *The Modern Reconstruction of Classical Thought: Talcott Parsons.* Berkeley: University of California Press.

Alexander, Jeffrey C. 1987. *Twenty Lectures: Sociological Theory Since World War II.* New York: Columbia University Press.

Alexander, Jeffrey C. 1989. "Sociology and Discourse: On the Centrality of the Classics," in Jeffrey C. Alexander (ed.) *Structure and Meaning.* New York: Columbia University Press.

Alexander, Jeffrey C. 1991."Understanding Social Science: Giving Up the Positivist Ghost," *Perspectives: The Theory Section Newsletter* 14(1): 2-3.

Allen, Sandra, Sanders, Lee and Wallis, Jan, eds. 1974. *Conditions of Illusion.* Leeds: Feminist Books.

Alter, Robert (in discussion with William Phillips, Denis Donoghue, Steven Marcus, Lionel Abel, Catherine Stimpson, and David Thorburn) 1991. "The Revolt Against Tradition: Readers, Writers, and Critics," *Partisan Review* 58(2): 282-314.

Alter, Robert and Kermode, Frank, eds. 1987. *The Literary Guide to the Bible.* Cambridge, MA: Harvard University Press.

Althusser, Louis 1970. "Marx's Immense Theoretical Revolution," in Louis Althusser and Etienne Balibar (eds.) *Reading Capital* (translated by Ben Brewster), pp. 182-93. New York: Pantheon Books.

Althusser, Louis 1976. *Essays in Self-Criticism* (translated by Grahame Lock). London: New Left Press.

Anderson, Digby C. 1978. "Some Organizational Features in the Local Production of a Plausible Text," *Philosophy of the Social Sciences* 8: 113-35.

Anderson, G.W. 1970. "Canonical and Non-canonical," in P.R. Ackroyd and C.F. Evans (eds.), pp. 113-59.

Anderson, Perry 1976. *Considerations on Western Marxism.* London: New Left Review Editions.

Andrew, Ed. 1981. *Closing the Iron Cage. The Scientific Management of Work and Leisure.* Montreal: Black Rose Books.

Ansell Pearson, Keith. 1997. *Viroid Life. Perspectives on Nietzsche and the Transhuman Condition.* London and New York: Routledge.

Antoni, Carlo 1962. *From History to Sociology: The Transition in German Historical Thinking* (translated by Hayden V. White). London: Merlin Press.

Appignanesi, Lisa and Forrester, John 1992. *Freud's Women.* London: Weidenfeld and Nicolson.

Arendt, Hannah. 1958. *The Human Condition.* Chicago: University of Chicago Press.

Arendt, Hannah 1973. *On Revolution.* London: Penguin Books.

Arendt, Hannah 1978. *The Life of the Mind. One-Volume Edition.* New York: Harcourt Brace.

Arendt, Hannah 1993. "The Crisis in Education," in Arendt, *Between Past and Future. Eight Exercises in Political Thought,* pp. 173-196. New York: Penguin.

Aschheim, Steven E. 1992. *The Nietzsche Legacy in Germany, 1890-1990.* Berkeley: University of California Press.

Atkinson, John M. 1984. *Our Masters' Voices : The Language and Body Language of Politics.* London: Methuen.

Atkinson, Paul 1990. *The Ethnographic Imagination.* London: Routledge.

Austin, J.L. 1971. *How To Do Things With Words,* 2nd edn. Oxford: Oxford University Press.

Avineri, Shlomo 1972. *Hegel's Theory of the Modern State.* London: Cambridge University Press.

Ay, Karl-Ludwig 1999. "Max Weber: A German Intellectual and the Question of War Guilt after the Great War," in Sam Whimster (ed.), *Max Weber and the Culture of Anarchy,* pp. 110-128. Houndmills, Basingstoke: Macmillan.

Baehr, Peter 1993. "Beyond Bricolage," *Semiotic Review of Books* 4(2): 7-8.

Baehr, Peter 1998. *Caesar and the Fading of the Roman World: A Study in Republicanism and Caesarism.* New Brunswick, NJ: Transaction Publishers.

Baehr, Peter 2001. "Sentinels in a Pitch Black Night," *Society* March/April: 80-85.

Baehr, Peter and Wells, Gordon. C. 2002. "Editors' Introduction" to Max Weber, *The Protestant Ethic and the "Spirit" of Capitalism and Other Writings* pp. i-lxviii. New York: Penguin.

Baigent, Michael, Leigh, Richard and Lincoln, Henry. 1986. *The Messianic Legacy.* London: Jonathan Cape.

Baker, Paul J. and Rau, William C. 1990. "The Cultural Contradictions of Teaching Sociology," in Herbert J. Gans (ed.) *Sociology in America, pp.* 169-87. Newbury Park, CA: Sage.

Baker, Scott 1990. "Reflection, Doubt, and the Place of Rhetoric in Postmodern Social Theory," *Sociological Theory* 8(2): 232-45.

Barker, Paul 1979. "Preface," in Timothy Raison (ed.) pp. 7-8.

Barrett, Michelle 1980. *Women's Oppression Today: Problems in Marxist Feminist Analysis.* London: New Left Books.

Bauman, Zygmunt 1991. "A Sociological Theory of Postmodernity," *Thesis Eleven* (29): 33-46.

Bauman, Zygmunt 1998. *Globalization: The Human Consequences.* New York: Columbia University Press.

Baumgarten, E. 1964. *Max Weber. Werk und Person. Dokumente.* Tübingen: J.C.B. Mohr (Paul Siebeck).

Bax, E. Belfort. 1903. *Rise and Fall of the Anabaptists.* London and New York: Macmillan.

Becker, Howard S. and Rau, William C. 1992. "Sociology in the 1990s," *Society* 30 (1): 70-4.

Becker, Jasper. 1996. *Hungry Ghosts. China's Secret Famine.* London: John Murray.

Bell, Daniel. 1996. *The Cultural Contradictions of Capitalism.* (Twentieth Anniversary Edition, with a new Afterword.) New York: Basic Books.

Benjamin, Walter 1973. "The Task of the Translator," in Hannah Arendt (ed.), *Illuminations,* pp. 69-82 (translated by Harry Zohn.) Glasgow: Fontana/Collins.

Bellah, Robert N., Madsen, Richard, Sullivan, William M., Swidler, Ann and Tipton, Steven M. 1985. *Habits of the Heart: Individualism and Commitment in American Life.* New York: Harper & Row.

Bellamy, Richard 1992. *Liberalism and Modern Society.* University Park: Pennsylvania State University Press.

Bellow, Saul. 1970. *Mr. Sammler's Planet.* New York: Viking/Penguin.

Ben-David, Joseph 1975. "Innovations and their Recognition," HOPE 7 (4): 434-455.

Bendix, Reinhard 1971. "Two Theoretical Traditions," in Reinhard Bendix and Guenther Roth (eds.) *Scholarship and Partisanship: Essays on Max Weber,* pp. 383-98. Berkeley: University of California Press.

Berger, Brigitte (in discussion with William Phillips, Nathan Glazer, Catharine Stimpson, Elizabeth Dalton, Jean Elshtain, Ronald Radosh, Leonard

Bushkoff, and Mary Gordo) (1991) "The Idea of the University," *Partisan Review* 58(2): 315-49.

Berger, Peter L. 1992a. "Sociology: A Disinvitation?" *Society* 30(1): 12-18.

Berger, Peter L. 1992b. "Reflections on the Twenty-Fifth Anniversary of *The Social Construction of Reality.*" *Perspectives: The Theory Section Newsletter* 15(2): 14.

Berger, Peter L. and Luckmann, Thomas 1971. *The Social Construction of Reality.* Harmondsworth: Penguin.

Berman, Marshall 1988. *All That Is Solid Melts into Air: The Experience of Modernity.*" New York: Penguin.

Besnard, Philippe (1973) "Durkheim et les femmes ou le *Suicide* inachevé," *Revue française de sociologie* 14(1): 27-61.

Besnard, Philippe (ed.) 1983a. *The Sociological Domain: The Durkheimians and the Founding of French Sociology.* Cambridge: Cambridge University Press.

Besnard, Philippe 1983b. "The *Année sociologique* Team," in Philippe Besnard (ed. 1983a) pp. 11-39.

Bhaskar, Roy1975. *A Realist Theory of Science.* Leeds: Leeds Books.

Bhaskar, Roy 1989a. *The Possibility of Naturalism.* London: Harvester Wheatsheaf.

Bhaskar, R. 1989b. *Reclaiming Reality.* London: Verso.

Bloom, Allan 1987. *The Closing of the American Mind.* New York: Simon and Schuster.

Bloom, Harold and Rosenberg, David 1990. *The Book of J* (translated by David Rosenberg). New York: Vintage Books.

Blumenberg, Hans 1983. *The Legitimacy of the Modern Age* (translated by Robert M. Wallace). Cambridge, MA: MIT Press.

Bly, Robert. 1990. *Iron John. A Book About Men.* New York: Addison-Wesley.

Bologh, Roslyn W. 1987a. "Max Weber on Erotic Love: A Feminist Inquiry," in S. Whimster and S. Lash (eds.) pp. 242-58.

Bologh, Roslyn W. 1987b. "Marx, Weber, and Masculine Theorizing: A Feminist Analysis," in Norbert Wiley (ed.) *The Marx-Weber Debate, Key Issues in Sociological Theory*, pp. 145-68. Newbury Park, CA: Sage.

Bologh, Roslyn W. 1990. *Love or Greatness: Max Weber and Masculine Thinking-A Feminist Inquiry.* London: Unwin Hyman.

Bossman, David M. 1987. "Authority and Tradition in First Century Judaism and Christianity," *Biblical Theology Bulletin* 17(1): 3-9.

Bossy, John 1982. "Some Elementary Forms of Durkheim," *Past & Present* (95): 3-18.

Bottomore, Tom B. 1960. "The Ideas of the Founding Fathers," *European Journal of Sociology* 1(1): 33-49.

Bottomore, Tom B. 1981. "A Marxist Consideration of Durkheim," *Social Forces* 59(4): 902-17.

Bottomore, Tom B. 1993. "Sociology," in William Outhwaite and Tom Bottomore (eds.) *The Blackwell Dictionary of Twentieth-Century Social Thought*, pp. 632-7. Oxford: Blackwell.

Bottomore, Tom B. and Rubel, Maximillen (1961) "Introduction," in Karl Marx 1961. pp. 17-43.

Bouissac, Paul 1976. "The 'Golden Legend' of Semiotics," *Semiotica* 17(4): 371-84.

Bouissac, Paul 1990a. "'L'institution de la sémiotique: stratégies et tactiques," *Semiotica* 79(3): 217-33.

Bouissac, Paul 1990b. "Praxis and Semiosis: 'The Golden Legend' revisited," *Semiotica* 79(3): 289-306.

Bouissac, Paul 1990c. "The Lesson of Durkheim," *Semiotic Review of Books* 1(l): 1.

Bourdieu, Pierre 1988. *Homo Academicus* (translated by Peter Collier). Camridge: Polity Press.

Bovon, Francois 1988. "The Synoptic Gospels and the Noncanonical Acts of the Apostles," *Harvard Theological Review* 81(l): 19-36.

Branford, Victor 1904. "The Founders of Sociology," *American Journal of Sociology* 10(l): 94-125.

Brauns, Hans-Dieter (1981) "Die Rezeption der Psychoanalyse in der Soziologie," in Johannes Cremerius (ed.) *Die Rezeption der Psychoanalyse in der Soziologie, Psychologie und Theologie im deutschsprachigen Raum bis 1940*, pp. 31-133. Frankfurt-am-Main: Suhrkamp.

Bromwich, David 1993. *Politics by Other Means: Higher Education and Group Thinking*. New Haven, CT: Yale University Press.

Brown, Dennis 1990a. "Differences Within the Band," *Times Higher Education Supplement* 9(11): 17.

Brown, Dennis 1990b. *Intertextual Dynamics within the Literary Group—Joyce, Lewis, Pound and Eliot*. London: Macmillan.

Brown, Richard Harvey 1990a. "Rhetoric, Textuality, and the Postmodern Turn in Sociological Theory," *Sociological Theory* 8(2): 188-97.

Brown Richard Harvey 1990b. "Social Science and the Poetics of Public Truth," *Sociological Forum* 5(l): 55-74.

Bruce, F.F. 1970. *Tradition Old and New*. Exeter: Paternoster Press.

Bulmer, Martin 1984. *The Chicago School of Sociology: Institutionalization, Diversity, and the Rise of Sociological Research*. Chicago: University of Chicago Press.

Bulmer, Martin 1989. "A Review of *Jane Addams and the Men of the Chicago School, 1892-1918* by Mary Jo Deegan," *American Journal Of Sociology* 94(6): 1479-8.

Bunyan, John. 1960. *The Pilgrim's Progress From This World to That Which is to Come*, edited by James Blanton Wharey and Roger Sharrock. Oxford: Clarendon Press.

Burke, Peter 1990. *The French Historical Revolution. The Annales School, 1929-89*. Cambridge: Polity Press.

Butler, Judith 1992. "Contingent Foundations: Feminism and the Question of 'Postmodernism.'" in Judith Butler and Joan W. Scott, *Feminists Theorize the Political*, pp. 3-21. New York: Routledge

Cahnman, W.J. 1977. "Toennies in America," *History and Theory* 16: 147-67.

Calhoun, Craig J. and Land, Kenneth C. 1989. "Editors' Introduction," *Contemporary Sociology* 18(4): 475-77.

Calhoun, Craig 1996. "Whose Classics? Which Readings? Interpretation and Cultural Difference in the Canonization of Sociological Theory," in Stephen P. Turner (ed.), *Social Theory and Sociology. The Classics and Beyond*, pp. 70-96. Oxford: Blackwell.

Camic, Charles 1979. "The Utilitarians Revisited," *American Journal of Sociology* 85(3): 516-50.

Camic, Charles 1981. "On the Methodology of the History of Sociology: a Reply to Jones," *American Journal of Sociology* 86(5): 1139-44.

Camic, Charles 1982. "The Enlightenment and Its Environment: A Cautionary Tale," *Knowledge and Society* 4: 143-72.

Camic, Charles 1986. "The Matter of Habit," *American Journal of Sociology.* 91(5): 1039-87.

Camic, Charles 1987. "The Making of a Method: A Historical Reinterpretation of the Early Parsons," *American Sociological Review* 52(4): 421-39.

Camic, Charles 1989. "*Structure* after 50 Years: The Anatomy of a Charter," *American Journal of Sociology* 95(1): 38-107.

Camic, Charles 1992. "Reputation and Predecessor Selection—Parsons and the Institutionalists," *American Sociological Review* 57(4): 421-45.

Camic, Charles. 1997. (ed.) *Reclaiming the Sociological Classics: The State of the Scholarship*. Oxford: Blackwell.

Carver, Terrell 1975. "Editor's Preface," in Karl Marx, *Texts on Method* (translated and edited by Terrell Carver), pp. 3-45. Oxford: Basil Blackwell.

Carver, Terrell 1983. *Marx and Engels: The Intellectual Relationship*. Brighton: Harvester/Wheatsheaf.

Carver, Terrell 1998. *The Postmodern Marx*. Manchester: Manchester University Press.

Carver, Terrell [forthcoming]. "Imagery/Writing, Imagination/Politics: Reading Marx through the Eighteenth Brumaire," in Mark Cowling and James Martin (eds.), *Marx's Eighteenth Brumaire: (Post)Modern Interpretations* (London: Pluto Press).

Chafetz, Janet S. (1993) "Sociological Theory: A Case of Multiple Personality Disorder," *Perspectives: The Theory Section Newsletter* 6(1): 1-2.

Chalcraft, David. 1994. "Bringing the Text Back In: On Ways of Reading the Iron Cage Metaphor in the Two Editions of 'The Protestant Ethic,'" in Larry J. Ray and Michael Reed (eds.), *Organizing Modernity: New Weberian Perspectives on Work, Organization and Society*, pp. 16-45. London and New York: Routledge.

Chamberlin, William Henry. 1937. *Russia's Iron Age*. Boston: Little, Brown, and Company.

Chan, Hoi-Man 1993. "Some Metasociological Notes on the Sinicisation of Sociology," *International Sociology* 8 (1): 113-119.

Clark, Terry Nichols 1968a. "Emile Durkheim and the Institutionalization of Sociology in the French University System," *European Journal of Sociology* 9: 37-71.

Clark, Terry Nichols 1968b. "The Structure and Functions of a Research Institute: The Annéé sociologique," *European Journal of Sociology* 9(1): 72-91.

Clark, Terry Nichols 1973. *Prophets and Patrons: The French University and the Emergence of the Social Sciences*. Cambridge, MA: Harvard University Press.

Clark, Terry Nichols 1979. "Emile Durkheim Today," *Research in Sociology of Knowledge, Sciences and Art* 2: 123-53.

Coetzee, J.M. 1998. *Age of Iron. A Novel.* Harmondsworth: Penguin.

Coleman, James S. 1990-1. "The Sidney Hook Memorial Award Address: On the Self-Suppression of Academic Freedom," *Academic Questions* (Winter): 17-22.

Coleman, John A. 1987. "Conclusion: After Sainthood?" in John Stratton Hawley (ed.), *Saints and their Virtues*, pp. 205-25. Berkeley: University of California Press.

Collingwood, R.G. 1946. *The Idea of History.* Oxford: Clarendon Press.

Collini, Stefan (1978) "Sociology and Idealism in Britain 1880-1920," *European Journal of Sociology* 19(1): 3-50.

Collini, Stefan 1979. *Liberalism and Sociology: L.T. Hobhouse and Political Argument in England, 1880-1914.* Cambridge: Cambridge University

Collini, Stefan 1991. *Public Moralists.* Oxford: Clarendon Press.

Collins, Randall 1985. *Three Sociological Traditions.* New York: Oxford University Press.

Collins, Randall 1988. *Theoretical Sociology.* New York: Harcourt Brace.

Collins, Randall 1992. "On the Sociology of Intellectual Stagnation: The Late Twentieth Century in Perspective," *Theory, Culture & Society* 9(1): 73-96.

Collins, Randall 1997. "A Sociological Guilt Trip: Comment on Connell," *American Journal of Sociology* 102 (6): 1558-64.

Collins, Randall 1998. *The Sociology of Philosophies. A Global Theory of Intellectual Change.* Cambridge, MA: The Belknap Press of Harvard University Press.

Collins, Randall 1999. *Macrohistory. Essays in Sociology of the Long Run.* Stanford, CA: Stanford University Press.

Condren, Conal 1985. *The Status and Appraisal of Classic Texts.* Princeton, NJ: Princeton University Press.

Congar, Yves M.-J. 1967. *Tradition and Traditions: An Historical and Theological Essay.* New York: Macmillan.

Connell, R.W. 1997. "Why Is Classical Theory Classical?" *American Journal of Sociology* 102 (6): 1511-57.

Connell, R.W. 2000. "Sociology and World Market Society," *Contemporary Sociology* 29 (1): 291-296.

Conway, Sleelagh 1991. "Campus Critique Leaves Women on the Margins," *Globe and Mail*, 24 October: A21.

Conyers, James E. 1972. "Ibn Khaldun: The Father of Sociology?" *International Journal of Contemporary Sociology* 9(4): 173-81.

Coser, Lewis A. 1971. *Masters of Sociological Thought.* New York: Harcourt.

Coser, Lewis A. 1977. "Georg Simmel's Neglected Contributions to the Sociology of Women," *Signs* 2(4): 869-76.

Coser, Lewis A. 1981. "The Uses of Classical Sociological Theory," in Buford Rhea (ed.) pp. 170-82.

Crook, Stephen 1991. *Modernist Radicalism and its Aftermath.* London: Routledge.

Dahme, Heinz-Jürgen. 1986. "Frauen-und Geschlechterfragen bei Herbert Spencer und Georg Simmel," *Kölner Zeitschrift für Soziologie und Sozialpsychologie* 38(3): 490-509.

Dahme, Heinz-Jürgen and Köhnke, Klaus Christian 1985. "Einleitung," in Georg Simmel 1985, pp. 7-26.

Dai Kejing, 1993. "The Vicissitudes of Sociology in China," *International Sociology* 8 (1): 91-99.

Davis, Murray S. 1971 "That's Interesting!" *Philosophy of the Social Sciences* 1: 309-44.

Davis, Murray S. 1986. "That's Classic! The Phenomenology and Rhetoric of Successful Social Theories," *Philosophy of the Social Sciences* 16: 285-301.

Dawe, Alan 1978. "Theories of Social Action," in T. Bottomore and R. Nisbet (eds.) *A History of Sociology,* pp. 362-417. New York: Basic Books.

Deegan, Mary Jo 1988. *Jane Addams and the Men of the Chicago School, 1892-1918.* New Brunswick, NJ: Transaction Publishers.

Deegan, Mary Jo (ed.) 1991. *Women in Sociology: A Bio-Bibliographical Sourcebook.* New York: Greenwood Press.

Delaney, Carol 1986. "The Meaning of Paternity and the Virgin Birth Debate," *Man* 21(3): 494-513.

Delooz, Pierre 1983. "Towards a Sociological Study of Canonized Sainthood in the Catholic Church," in Stephen Wilson (ed.) *Saints and Their Cults,* pp. 189-216. Cambridge: Cambridge University Press.

Derrida, Jacques 1994. *Specters of Marx: The State of the Debt, the Work of Mourning, and the New International* (translated by Peggy Kamuf; introduction by Stephen Cullenberg and Bernd Magnus.) New York: Routledge.

Dhaouadi, Mahmoud 1990. "Ibn Khaldun: The Founding Father of Eastern Sociology," *International Sociology* 5(3): 319-35.

Dowd, James J. 1991. "Revising the Canon: Graduate Training in the Two Sociologies," *Teaching Sociology* 19(3): 308-21.

Durkheim, Emile 1938. *The Rules of Sociological Method,* 8th edn. (translated by Sarah A. Solovay and John H. Mueller; edited by George E.G. Catlin). New York: Free Press.

Durkheim, Emile 1959. *Socialism and Saint-Simon* (translated by Charlotte Sattler; edited by Alvin W. Gouldner). London: Routledge & Kegan Paul.

Durkheim, Emile 1964. *The Division of Labour in Society* (translated by George Simpson). New York: Free Press.

Durkheim, Emile 1970. *Suicide* (translated by John A. Spaulding and George Simpson; edited by George Simpson). London: Routledge & Kegan Paul.

Durkheim, Emile 1979. "Durkheim's Review of Georg Simmel's *Philosophie des Geldes*" (translated by Peter Baehr), *Social Research* 46(2): 321-8.

Durkheim, Emile 1982. *The Rules of Sociological Method and Selected Texts on Sociology and its Method* (translated by W.D. Halls; edited with an introduction by Steven Lukes). London: Macmillan Press.

Durkheim, Emile 1983. "Letter from Emile Durkheim to Céléstin Bouglé," in Philippe Besnard (ed.) pp. 40-1.

Eliot, T.S. 1945. "What is a Classic?" An address delivered before the Virgil Society on October 1944. London: Faber and Faber.

Erickson, V.L. 1989. "A Feminist Critique of the Sociology of Religion" (PhD thesis). City University of New York.

Fay, Brian 1987. *Critical Social Science.* Cambridge: Polity Press.

Finer, S.E. (ed.) 1979. *Five Constitutions.* Harmondsworth: Penguin Books.

Firestone, Shulamith 1971. *The Dialectic of Sex.* New York: Bantam Books.

Flanagan, Tom 2000. *First Nations? Second Thoughts.* Montreal and Kingston: McGill-Queens University Press.

Fogt, Helmut 1977. "Max Weber—Wirkung und Bedeutung, 1890-1993." Unpublished Master's thesis, Munich University, Faculty of Social Science.

Forbes, Joyce 1993. "The Inclusive University, Part 1: Educational Equity," *Canadian Association of University Teachers Bulletin: Status of Women Supplement*: 1-8.

Foucault, Michel 1969."Qu'est-ce qu'un auteur?" *Bulletin de la Société Française de Philosophie* 63(July): 73-104.

Foucault, Michel 1970. *The Order of Things.* London: Tavistock.

Foucault, Michel 1972. *The Archaeology of Knowledge* (translated by A.M. Sheridan Smith). London: Routledge.

Foucault, Michel 1984a. "What is an Author?" (translated by Josué V. Harari), in Paul Rabinow (ed.) *The Foucault Reader,* pp. 101-20. Harmondsworth: Penguin Books.

Foucault, Michel 1984b. "Polemics, Politics, and Problemizations: An Interview with Michel. Foucault" (translated by Lydia Davis), in Paul Rabinow (ed.) *The Foucault Reader*, pp. 381-90. Harmondsworth: Penguin Books.

Frank, Manfred 1992. "On Foucault's Concept of Discourse," in Timothy J. Armstrong (editor and translator), *Michel Foucault Philosopher*, pp. 99-116. New York: Routledge.

Freud, Sigmund 1986. "On the History of the Psychoanalytic Movement," in Sigmund Freud, *Historical and Expository Works on Psychoanalysis: History of the Psychoanalytic Movement, An Autobiographical Study, Outline of Psychoanalysis and Other Works* (translated by James Strachey; edited by Albert Dickson), pp. 63-128. Harmondsworth: Penguin Books.

Freund, Elizabeth 1987. *The Return of the Reader: Reader-Response Criticism.* London: Methuen.

Frisby, David 1981. *Sociological Impressionism: A Reassessment of Georg Simmel's Social Theory.* London: Heinemann.

Frisby, David 1984. *Georg Simmel.* Chichester: Ellis Horwood.

Frye, Northrop 1990. *Words with Power.* Toronto: Penguin Books.

Frye, Northrop, Baker, Sheridan and Perkins, George 1985. *The Harper Handbook to Literature.* New York: Harper and Row.

Fukuyama, Francis 1999. *The Great Disruption: Human Nature and the Reconstitution of Social Order.* New York: Free Press.

Fuller, Steve 2000. "A Very Qualified Success, Indeed: The Case of Anthony Giddens and British Sociology," *Canadian Journal of Sociology* 25 (4): 507-516.

Fulton, Keith L. 1993. "Audre Lorde: Sister Outsider," *Canadian Association of University Teachers Bulletin*, March: 11.

Furlong, Anne 2000. "Is it a Classic if No One Reads It? Relevance Theory and the Canon." Unpublished paper delivered to the Atlantic Provinces Linguistic Association Meeting, 4 November.

Gabriel, Ralph Henry 1956. *The Course of American Democratic Thought*, 2nd edn. New York: Ronald Press.

Gadamer, H.-G 1989. *Truth and Method*, 2nd edn. (revised translation by Joel Weinsheimer and Donald G. Marshall). London: Sheed and Ward.

Gallie, W.B. 1956. "Essentially Contested Concepts," *Proceedings: Aristotelian Society* 56: 167-98.

Gamble, Andrew. 1996. *Hayek. The Iron Cage of Liberty*. New York: Westview Press.

Gane, Mike 1983. "Durkheim: Woman as Outsider," *Economy and Society* 12(2): 227-70.

Gane, Mike 1988. *On Durkheim's Rules of Sociological Method*. London: Routledge.

Gane, Mike 1993. *Harmless Lovers? Gender, Theory and Personal Relationships*. London: Routledge.

Garfinkel, Harold 1967. *Studies in Ethnomethodology*. Englewood Cliffs, NJ: Prentice-Hall.

Gay, Peter 1988. *Freud: A Life for Our Time*. London: Papermac.

Geertz, Clifford 1988. *Works and Lives: The Anthropologist as Author*. Stanford, CA: Stanford University Press.

Ghosh, Peter. 1994. "Some Problems with Talcott Parsons' Translation of 'The Protestant Ethic,'" *Archives Européennes de Sociologie* 35: 104-123.

Giddens, Anthony 1971. *Capitalism and Modern Social Theory*. London: Cambridge University Press.

Giddens, Anthony 1976a. "Classical Social Theory and the Origins of Modern Sociology," *American Journal of Sociology* 81: 703-29.

Giddens, Anthony 1976b. *New Rules of Sociological Method*. London: Hutchinson.

Giddens, Anthony 1977. "Four Myths in the History of Social Thought," in Anthony Giddens, *Studies in Social and Political Theory*, pp. 208-34. London: Hutchinson.

Giddens, Anthony 1979. *Central Problems in Social Theory*. London: Giddens, Anthony 1987. "Weber and Durkheim: Coincidence and Divergence," in W.J. Mommsen and J. Osterhammel (eds.) *Max Weber and His Contemporaries*, pp. 182-9. London: Unwin Hyman.

Giedion, Siegfried. 1969. *Mechanization Takes Command. A Contribution to Anonymous History*. New York: W.W. Norton.

Gilcher-Holtey, Ingrid 1990. "Max Weber et les femmes," *Sociétés* (28): 65-73.

Goldthorpe, John H. 1979. "Introduction," in Timothy Raison (ed.), pp. 9-16.

Goodich, Michael 1983. "The Politics of Canonization in the Thirteenth Century: Lay and Mendicant Saints," in Stephen Wilson (ed.) *Saints and Their Cults*, pp. 169-87. Cambridge: Cambridge University Press.

Gorak, Jan 1991. *The Making of the Modern Canon*. London: Athlone.

Gordon, Daniel 1993. Review Essay on Michel Vovelle's *Ideologies and Mentalities* in *History and Theory* 32 (2): 196-213.

Gottdiener, M. 1990. "The Logocentrism of the Classics," *American Sociological Review* 55(3): 460-1.

Gouldner, Alvin W. 1959. "Introduction," in Emile Durkheim (1959), pp. v-xxvii.

Gouldner, Alvin W. 1970. *The Coming Crisis of Western Sociology*. London: Heinemann.

Gouldner, Alvin W. 1980. *The Two Marxisms: Contradictions and Anomalies in the Development of Theory*. London: Macmillan Press.

Granslow, Bettina 1993. "Chinese Sociology: Sinicisation and Globalisation," *International Sociology* 8 (1): 101-112.

Grant, R.M. 1970. "The New Testament Canon," in P.R. Ackroyd and C.F. Evans (eds.), pp.284-308.

Gray, Chris Hables, ed. 1995. *The Cyborg Handbook*. London and New York: Routledge.

Green, Martin 1974.*The von Richthofen Sisters*. London: Weidenfeld and Nicolson.

Greinacher, Norbert 1991. "On the Foundation of Apostles and Prophets (Eph. 2: 20)," *Theology Digest* 3 8(3): 241-3.

Griffiths, Sian 1993. "Classical Dilemma for English," *Times Higher Education Supplement* (1054),15 January: 20-1.

Grimm, Jacob Ludwig Carl, and Wilhelm Carl Grimm 1985. "Der Eisenhans," in *Kinder- und Hausmärchen, gesammelt durch die Brüder Grimm (Grimms Märchen)*, edited by Heinz Rölleke, pp. 757-765. Frankfurt am Main: Deutscher Klassiker Verlag.

Gubbay, Jon 1992. "Four Conferences on the Sociology Curriculum," unpublished paper presented at the Annual Conference of the British Sociological Association, University of Kent.

Gubbay, Jon and Caygill, Howard 1992. "Teaching Sociological Theory," unpublished manuscript, University of Glasgow, 17 January.

Guthrie, Donald 1987. "Canon of Scripture," in J.A. Komonchak, M. Collins, and D.A. Lane (eds.) *The New Dictionary of Theology*, pp. 189-90. Wilmington, DE: Michael Glazier.

Habermas, Jürgen 1971. *Knowledge and Human Interests* (translated by Jeremy J. Shapiro). Boston, MA: Beacon Press.

Habermas, Jürgen 1981. *The Theory of Communicative Action*, Vol. 1. *Reason and the Rationalization of Society* (translated by Thomas McCarthy). London: Heinemann.

Habermas, Jürgen 1987. *The Theory of Communicative Action*, Vol. 2. *Lifeworld and System: A Critique of Functionalist Reason* (translated by Thomas McCarthy). Cambridge: Polity Press.

Halbwachs, Maurice 1992. *On Collective Memory*, edited, translated and with an introduction by Lewis A. Coser. Chicago: University of Chicago Press.

Hale, Sylvia 1992. "Facticity and Dogma in Introductory Sociology Texts: The Need for Alternative Methods," in William K. Carroll et al. (eds.) *Fragile*

Truths: Twenty Five Years of Sociology and Anthropology in Canada.
Ottawa: Carleton University Press.

Hallberg, Robert von, ed. 1984. *Canons*. Chicago: University of Chicago Press.

Hamilton, Peter 1983. *Talcott Parsons*. London: Tavistock.

Hamilton, Richard F. 1996. *The Social Misconstruction of Reality. Validity and Verification in the Scholarly Community*. New Haven, CT: Yale University Press.

Harrington, Daniel J. 1978. "Canon of Scripture," in J.D. Douglas (ed.) *The New International Dictionary of the Christian Church*, pp. 156-9. Grand Rapids, MI: Zondervan.

Harvey, Sir Paul 1984. *The Oxford Companion to Classical Literature*. Oxford: Oxford University Press.

Hawthorn, Geoffrey 1976. *Enlightenment and Despair: A History of Social Theory*, 2nd edn. Cambridge: Cambridge University Press.

Hawthorn, Geoffrey 1979. "Characterizing the History of Sociology: Could They Know What They Were Doing?" *Sociology* 13(3): 475-82.

Hayles, N. Katherine. 1999. *How We Became Posthuman. Virtual Bodies in Cybernetics, Literature and Informatics*. Chicago and London: University of Chicago Press.

Hegel, Georg W.F. 1956. *The Philosophy of History* (translated by J. Sibree). New York: Dover Publications.

Heidegger, Martin. 1962. *Being and Time*. translated by John Macquarrie and Edward Robinson. New York: HarperSanFranciso.

Heilbron, Johan. 1995. *The Rise of Social Theory*. Cambridge: Polity Press.

Helprin, Mark 1988. "The Canon Under Siege," *New Criterion* 7(1): 33-40.

Hennis, Wilhelm 1983. "Max Weber's 'Central Question'" (translated. by K. Tribe), *Economy and Society* 12(2): 135-80.

Hennis, Wilhelm 1988. *Max Weber: Essays in Reconstruction* (translated by Keith Tribe). London: Allen & Unwin.

Henrich, Dieter 1987. "Karl Jaspers: Thinking with Max Weber in Mind," in W.J. Mommsen and J. Osterhammel (eds.) *Max Weber and his Contemporaries*, pp. 528-44. London: Unwin Hyman.

Herf, Jeffrey 1984. *Reactionary Modernism. Technology, Culture and Politics in Weimar and The Third Reich*. Cambridge: Cambridge University Press.

Hess, Elizabeth, Markson, Elizabeth and Stein, Peter 1988. *Introductory Sociology*, 3rd edn. New York: Macmillan.

Higginson, R.E. 1984. "Apostolic Succession," in Walter A. Elwell (ed.) *Evangelical Dictionary of Theology*, pp. 73-4. Grand Rapids, MI: Baker Book House.

Hillerbrand, Hans J. (ed) 1968. *The Protestant Reformation*. New York: Harper and Row.

Hinkle, Gisela J. 1986. "The Americanization of Max Weber," *Current Perspectives in Social Theory* 7: 87-104.

Hinkle, Roscoe C. 1994. *Developments in American Sociological Theory, 1915-1950*. Albany: SUNY Press.

Hirsche, E.D., Jr. 1989. "Who Needs The Great Works? A Debate between Jack Hitt, E.D. Hirsch, Jr., John Kaliski, Jon Pareles, Roger Shattuck, and Gayatri Chakravorty Spivak," *Harper's* 279(1672): 43-52.

Hitler, Adolf 1939. *Mein Kampf*. London: Hurst and Blackett.

Hobsbawm, Eric J. 1964. "Introduction," in Karl Marx, *Pre-capitalist Economic Formations* (translated by Jack Cohen), pp. 9-65. London: Lawrence & Wishart.

Hodges, Lucy 1993. "The Importance of Being Earnest," *Times Higher Education Supplement* (1054), 15 January: 20.

Hohendahl, Peter Uwe 1977. "Introduction to Reception Aesthetics," *New German Critique* 10 (Winter): 29-63.

Holub, Robert C. 1983. "Trends in Literary Theory: The American Reception of Reception Theory," *German Quarterly* 65(1): 80-96.

Holub, Robert C. 1984. *Reception Theory: A Critical Introduction*. London: Methuen.

Horowitz, Irving Louis 1992a "The Decomposition of Sociology." *Academic Questions* 5(2): 32-40.

Horowitz, Irving Louis 1992b. "Social Research and the Culture of Society," *Society* 30(1): 7-10.

Horowitz, Irving Louis 1994. *The Decomposition of Sociology*. New York: Oxford University Press.

How, Alan 1998. "That's Classic! A Gadamerian Defence of the Classic Text in Sociology," *Sociological Review* 46 (4): 828-848.

Hughes, H. Stuart 1974. *Consciousness and Society. The Reorientation of European Social Thought 1890-1930*. St Albans: Paladin.

Iser, Wolfgang 1974. *The Implied Reader*. Baltimore, MD: Johns Hopkins University Press.

Iser, Wolfgang 1978. *The Act of Reading: A Theory of Aesthetic Response*. Baltimore, MD: Johns Hopkins University Press.

Iser, Wolfgang 1979. "The Current Situation of Literary Theory: Key Concepts and the Imaginary," *New Literary History* 11 (1): 1-20.

Iser, Wolfgang 1980. "Interview," *Diacritics* 10(2): 57-74.

Iyer, Pico 1993. "The Empire Writes Back," *Time* 141(6): 68-73.

Jacoby, Russell 1994. *Dogmatic Wisdom. How the Culture Wars Divert Education and Distract America*. New York: Doubleday.

James, Henry1919. *In the Cage*. London: Martin and Secker.

Jameson, Fredric 1973. "The Vanishing Mediator: Narrative Structure in Max Weber." *New German Critique* 1 (Winter): 52-89.

Jauss, Hans Robert 1982. *Toward an Aesthetic of Reception*. Minneapolis: University of Minnesota Press.

Jaworski, Gary D. *Georg Simmel and the American Prospect*. 1997. Albany: SUNY Press.

Johnson, Barclay 1972. "Durkheim on Women," in Nona Glazer-Malbin and Helen Youngelson Waehrer (eds.) *Women in a Man-Made World*. Chicago: Rand McNally.

Johnson, Terry, Dandeker, Christopher and Ashworth, Clive 1984. *The Structure of Social Theory*. London: Macmillan.

Johnston Barry V. 1995. *Pitirim A. Sorokin. An Intellectual Biography*. Lawrence: University of Kansas Press.

Jones, Robert A. 1974. "Durkheim's Response to Spencer: An Essay Toward Historicism in the Historiography of Sociology," *Sociological Quarterly* 15(3): 341-58.

Jones, Robert A. 1977. "On Understanding a Sociological Classic," *American Journal of Sociology* 83(2): 279-319.

Jones, Robert A. 1981a "On Camic's Antipresentist Methodology," *American Journal of Sociology* 86(5): 1133-44.

Jones, Robert A. 1981b "On Quentin Skinner," *American Journal Of Sociology* 87(2): 453-67.

Jones, Robert A. 1983a "On Merton's 'History' and 'Systematics' of Sociological Theory," in L. Graham, W. Lepenies, and P. Weingart (eds.) *Functions and Uses of Disciplinary Histories*, pp. 121-42. Dordrecht: Reidel.

Jones, Robert A. 1983b "The New History of Sociology," *Annual Review of Sociology* 9: 447-69.

Jones, Robert A. 1984. "Demythologizing Durkheim: A Reply to Gerstein," *Knowledge and Society* 5: 63-83.

Jones, Robert A. 1985. "Second Thoughts on Privileged Access," *Sociological Theory* 3(1): 16-19.

Jones, Robert A. 1986a "Durkheim, Frazer, and Smith: The Role of Analogies and Exemplars in the Development of Durkheim's Sociology of Religion," *American Journal of Sociology* 92(3): 596-627.

Jones, Robert A. 1986b *Emile Durkheim*. Beverly Hills, CA: Sage.

Jones, Robert A. 1997. "The *Other* Durkheim: History and Theory in the Treatment of Classical Sociological Theory, " in C. Camic (ed.) 1997, pp. 142-172.

Jones, Robert A. 1999. *The Development of Durkheim's Social Realism*. Cambridge: Cambridge University Press.

Judt, Tony 1999. *The Burden of Responsibility. Blum, Camus, Aron and the French Twentieth Century.* Chicago: University of Chicago Press.

Junger, Ernst. 1929. *The Storm of Steel. From the Diary of a German Storm-Troop Officer on the Western Front.* London: Chatto and Windus. translated by Basil Creighton.

Kafka, Franz 1946. *The Basic Kafka*, edited by Erich Heller. New York: Pocket Books.

Kafka, Franz. 1971. "The Metamorphosis," in *Franz Kafka. The Complete Stories*, foreword by John Updike, pp. 89-139. (translated by Willa and Edwin Muir.) New York: Schocken Books.

Kalberg, Stephen 1997. "Contribution to 'Social Sciences: From Rationality to Subectivity,'" *Partisan Review* Spring 1997: 196-205.

Kandal, Terry R. 1988. *The Woman Question in Classical Sociological Theory.* Miami: Florida International University Press.

Kanigel, Robert. 1999 *The One Best Way. Frederick Winslow Taylor and the Enigma of Efficiency.* New York: Viking Penguin.

Karady, Victor 1981. "The Prehistory of Present-Day French Sociology (1917-1957)," in Charles C. Lemert (ed.) *French Sociology.* New York: Columbia University Press.

Karady, Victor 1983. "The Durkheimians in Academe. A Reconsideration," in Philippe Besnard (ed. 1983a) pp. 71-89.

Kasler, Dirk (1988) *Max Weber: An Introduction to his Life and Work.* Cambridge: Polity Press.

Kelsey, David H. 1975. *The Uses of Scripture in Recent Theology*. Philadelphia, PA: Fortress Press.

Kent, Stephen A. 1983. "Weber, Goethe, and the Nietzschean Allusion: Capturing the Source of the 'Iron Cage' Metaphor," *Sociological Analysis* 44 (4): 297-320.

Kermode, Frank 1975. *The Classic*. London: Faber and Faber.

Kermode, Frank 1985. *Forms of Attention*. Chicago: University of Chicago Press.

Kermode, Frank 1987. "The Canon," in Robert Alter and Frank Kermode (eds.) pp. 600-10.

Kettler, David, Meja, Volker and Stehr, Nico 1984. *Karl Mannheim*. Chichester: Ellis Horwood; London and New York: Tavistock.

Kettler, David and Meja, Volker 1993a. "Studying Mannheim: Projects, Negotiations, Settlements," Unpublished Paper, Presented at the International Institute of Sociology, Paris, 21-25 June.

Kettler, David and Meja, Volker 1993b. "Their 'Own Peculiar Way': Karl Mannheim and the Rise of Women," *International Sociology* 8(1): 5-55.

Kettler, David and Meja, Volker 1995. *Karl Mannheim and the Crisis of Liberalism. The Secret of These New Times*. New Brunswick, NJ: Transaction Publishers.

Kimball, Roger 1987. "The Academy Debates the Canon," *New Criterion* 6(1): 31-43.

Kimball, Roger 1990. *Tenured Radicals: How Politics has Corrupted our Higher Education*. New York: Harper and Row.

Kivisto, Peter and Swatos, William H., Jr 1988. *Max Weber: A Bio-Bibliography*. New York: Greenwood Press.

Klein, Jürgen 1985. "Trends in Modern German Literary Theory," *CLIO* 15(1): 31-45.

Knox, Bernard 1993. *The Oldest Dead White European Males and Other Reflections on the Classics*. New York: Norton.

Kraemer, David 1991. "The Formation of the Rabbinic Canon: Authority and Boundaries," *Journal of Biblical Literature* 110(4): 613-30.

Kuhn, Thomas 1962. *The Structure of Scientific Revolutions*. Chicago: University of Chicago Press.

Kuklick, Henrika 1980a. "Boundary Maintenance in American Sociology: Limitations to Academic 'Professionalization,'" *Journal of the History of the Behavioral Sciences* 16: 201-19.

Kuklick, Henrika 1980b. "Restructuring the Past: Toward an Appreciation of the Social Context of Social Science," *Sociological Quarterly* 21(1): 5-2 1.

Küng, Hans 1968. *The Church*. London: Burns and Oates.

Lang, Gladys Engel and Kurt Lang. 1988. "Recognition and Renown: The Survival of Artistic Reputation," *American Journal of Sociology* 94 (1): 79-109.

Lamont, Michèle 1987. "How to Become a Dominant French Philosopher: The Case of Jacques Derrida," *American Journal of Sociology* 95 (3): 584-622.

Lassman, Peter and Velody, Irving, eds. (with Herminio Martins) 1989. *Max Weber's "Science as a Vocation."* London: Unwin Hyman.

Leacock, E.B. 1972. "Introduction," in Frederick Engels, *The Origin of the Family, Private Property and the State*, pp. 7-67, London: Lawrence & Wishart.

Legge, James 1971. *Confucius. Confucian Analects, The Great Learning and the Doctrine of the Mean*. (Chinese text; translation and exegetical notes and dictionary of all characters by James Legge.) New York: Dover.

Lehmann, Jennifer M. 1990. "Durkheim's Response to Feminism: Prescriptions for Women," *Sociological Theory* 8(2): 163-87.

Lehmann, Jennifer M. 1991. "Durkheim's Women: His Theory of the Structures and Functions of Sexuality," *Current Perspectives in Social Theory* 11: 141-67.

Lehmann, Jennifer M. 1993. *Deconstructing Durkheim. A Post-Post Structuralist Critique*. London: Routledge.

Lemert, Charles 1993 (ed.). *Social Theory. The Multicultural and Classic Readings*. Boulder, CO: Westview Press.

Lemert, Charles 1994. "The Canonical Limits of Durkheim's First Classic," *Sociological Forum* 9 (1): 87-92.

Lemert, Charles 1997. *Postmodernism is Not what You Think* (Oxford: Blackwell).

Lengermann, Patricia Madoo and Niebrugge-Brantley, Jill 1992. "Contemporary Feminist Theory," in George Ritzer (ed.) *Sociological Theory*, 3rd edn. New York: McGraw-Hill.

Lenin, V.I. 1960. "The Immediate Tasks of the Soviet Government," in *Lenin: Selected Works, Vol. 2*, pp. 695-732 in. Moscow: Progress Publishers.

Lepenies, Wolfgang. 1981a. "Einleitung. Studien zur kognitiven, sozialen und historischen Identität der Soziologie," in W. Lepenies (ed.) Vol. 1, 1981b: i-xxxv.

Lepenies, Wolfgang, ed. 1981b. *Geschichte der Soziologie: Studien zur kognitiven, sozialen, und historischen Identität einer Disziplin*, Vols. 1-4. Frankfurt-am-Main: Suhrkamp.

Lepenies, W. 1988. *Between Literature and Science: The Rise of Sociology* (translated by R. J. Hollingdale). Cambridge: Cambridge University Press.

Lepsius, M. Rainer, ed. 1981. *Soziologie in Deutschland und Österreich 1918-1945*. Opladen: Westdeutscher Verlag.

Lepsius, M. Rainer 1987. "Sociology in the Interwar Period: Trends in Development and Criteria for Evaluation," in V. Meja, D. Misgeld, and N. Stehr (eds.) pp. 37-56.

Levi, Primo. 1984. *The Periodic Table* (translated by Raymond Rosenthal). New York: Schocken Books

Levine, Donald N. 1981. "Sociology's Quest for the Classics: The Case of Simmel," in Buford Rhea (ed.) pp. 60-80.

Levine, Donald N. 1985. *The Flight from Ambiguity*. Chicago: University of Chicago Press.

Levine, Donald N. 1991. "On the Proposal to Standardize Sociological Concepts," *Perspectives: The Theory Section Newsletter* 14(2): 6.

Levine, Donald N., Carter, Ellwood B. and Gorman, Eleanor Miller (1976a) "Simmel's Influence on American Sociology I," *American Journal of Sociology* 81(4): 813-41.

Levine, Donald N., Carter, Ellwood B. and Gorman, Eleanor Miller (1976b) "Simmel's Influence on American Sociology II," *American Journal of Sociology* 81(5): 111232.

Levine, Donald N. 1996. *Visions of the Sociological Tradition*. Chicago: University of Chicago Press.

Levine, Donald N. 1997. "Simmel Reappraised: Old Images, New Scholarship," in C. Camic (ed.) 1997.

Lichtblau, Klaus (1989-90) "Eros and Culture: Gender Theory in Simmel, Tonnies, and Weber," *Telos* 82 (Winter): 89-110.

Lipset, Seymour Martin 1994. "The State of American Sociology," *Sociological Forum* 9 (2): 199-219.

Link, Hannelore 1976. *Rezeptions-Forschung*. Stuttgart: W. Kohlhammer.

Long, Elizabeth 1993. "From the Chair," *Newsletter of the Sociology of Culture* 7(3, 4): 1-3.

Lukes, Steven 1973. *Emile Durkheim: His Life and Work*. Harmondsworth: Penguin Books.

Lukes, Steven (in discussion with Terry N. Clark et al.) 1979. "Emile Durkheim Today," *Research in Sociology of Knowledge, Sciences, and Art* 2: 123-53.

Lukes, Steven 1993. "Durkheim School," in William Outhwaite and Tom Bottomore (eds.) *The Blackwell Dictionary of Twentieth-Century Social Thought*, pp. 169-72. Oxford: Blackwell Reference.

McCloskey, H.J. 1971. *John Stuart Mill: A Critical Study*. London: Macmillian.

Macdonald, Timothy 1987. "Apostolicity," in J.A. Konionchak, M. Collins and D.A. Lane (eds.) *The New Dictionary of Theology*, pp. 52-4. Wilmington, DE: Michael Glazier.

Macfarlane David 1991. *The Danger Tree. Memory, War, and the Search for a Family's Past*. Toronto: Macfarlane Walter and Ross.

Macgregor, Karen 1993. "The shifting sands of race studies," *Times Higher Education Supplement* (1054) 15 January: 22.

Macintyre, Alasdair 1966. *A Short History of Ethics*. New York: Collier Books.

Macintyre, Alasdair 1988). *Whose Justice? Which Rationality?* London: Duckworth.

Macintyre, Alasdair 1990. *Three Rival Versions of Moral Enquiry*. Notre Dame, IN: University of Notre Dame Press.

McDonald, Lynn 1997. "Classical Social Theory with the Women Founders Included," in Charles Camic (ed.) 1997, pp. 112-141.

McDonald, Lynn 1998. *The Women Founders of the Social Sciences*. Montreal: Carleton University Press.

McKenzie, John L. 1965. *Dictionary of the Bible*. New York: Macmillan.

McLaughlin, Neil 1998a. "How to Become a Forgotten Intellectual: Intellectual Movements and the Rise and Fall of Erich Fromm," *Sociological Forum* 13 (2): 215-246.

McLaughlin, Neil 1998b. "Why Do Schools of Thought Fail? Neo-Freudianism as a Case Study in the Sociology of Knowledge," *Journal of the History of the Behavioral Sciences* 34 (2): 113-134.

McLaughlin Neil 1999. "Origin Myths in the Social Sciences: Fromm, the Frankfurt School and the Emergence of Critical Theory, *Canadian Journal of Sociology* 24 (1): 109-139.

McLellan, David 1975. *Marx*. Glasgow: Fontana/Collins.

Macrae, Donald G. 1961. *Ideology and Society*. London: Heinemann.

Macrae, Donald G. 1979. "Adam Ferguson," in Timothy Raison (ed.) pp. 26-35.

Machiavelli, Niccoló (1972) "Discourses on the First Decade of Titus Livius," in John Plamenatz (ed.) *Machiavelli: The Prince, Selections from The Discourses and Other Writings*, pp. 137-305. London: Fontana/Collins.

Magraw, Roger 1983. *France 1814-1915: The Bourgeois Century*. Oxford: Fontana Paperbacks.

Malos, Ellen, ed. 1980. *The Politics of Housework*. London: Allison and Busby.

Mandel, Ernest 1976. "Introduction," in Karl Marx, *Capital*, Vol.1, pp. 11-86. Harmondsworth: Penguin Books.

Megill, Allan. 1987. "The Reception of Foucault by Historians," *Journal of the History of Ideas* XLVIII (1): 117-141.

Mannheim, Karl 1936. *Ideology and Utopia: An Introduction to the Sociology of Knowledge* (translated by E. Shils and L. Wirth). London: Routledge.

Maryanski Alexandra and Jonathan H. Turner 1992. *The Social Cage. Human Nature and the Evolution of Society*. Stanford, CA: Stanford University Press.

Marx, Karl 1955. "Marx [in London] to Engels in Manchester, July 7, 1866," in Marx and Engels, *Selected Correspondence*, pp. 168-9. Moscow: Progress Publishers.

Marx, Karl 1961. *Selected Writings in Sociology and Social Philosophy* (edited by T.B. Bottomore and Maximilien Rubel; translated by T.B. Bottomore). Harmondsworth: Penguin Books.

Maus, Heinz 1962. *A Short History of Sociology*. London: Routledge & Kegan Paul [German edition 1956].

Mauss, Marcel 1983. "An Intellectual Self-Portrait," in Philippe Besnard (ed.) pp. 139-51.

Meek, Ronald L. 1967. "The Scottish Contribution to Marxist Sociology," in Ronald L. Meek (ed.) *Economics and Ideology and Other Essays*, pp. 34-50. London: Chapman and Hall.

Meinhof, Ulrike 1993. "Discourse," in William Outhwaite and Tom Bottomore (eds.) *The Blackwell Dictionary of Twentieth-Century Social Thought*, pp. 161-2. Oxford: Blackwell.

Meja, Volker, Misgeld, Dieter and Stehr, Nico, eds 1987. *Modern German Sociology*. New York: Columbia University Press.

Meja, Volker and Kettler, David 1990. "Mannheim's Mediated Receptions in America," unpublished paper presented at the 12th World Congress of Sociology, Madrid.

Merton, Robert K. 1968. *Social Theory and Social Structure*. New York: Free Press.

Merton, Robert K. 1972. "Insiders and Outsiders: A Chapter in the Sociology of Knowledge," *American Journal of Sociology* 78(1): 9-47.

Merton, Robert K. 1981."Forward: Remarks on Theoretical Pluralism," in Peter M. Blau and Robert K. Merton (eds.) *Continuities in Structural Inquiry*, pp. i-vii. Beverly Hills, CA: Sage.

Meštrovic, Stjepan G. 1991. *The Coming Fin De Siécle. An Application of Durkheim's Sociology to Modernity and Postmodernism*. London: Routledge.

Meštrovic, Stjepan G. 1992. *Durkheim and Postmodern Culture*. New York: Aldine de Gruyter.

Meyer, J.H. 1970. "The Charter: Conditions of Diffuse Socialization in Schools," in W. Richard Scott (ed.) *Social Processes and Social Structures*, pp. 564-78. New York: Holt, Rinehart & Winston.

Michels, Robert. 1959. *Political Parties. A Sociological Study of the Oligarchical Tendencies of Modern Democracy*. translated by Eden and Cedar Paul. New York: Dover Publications.

Mill, John Stuart (1961) "On Liberty," in Max Lerner (ed.) *Essential Works of John Stuart Mill*, pp. 249-360. New York: Bantam Books.

Miller, Jean Baker, ed. 1973. *Psychoanalysis and Women*. Baltimore, MD: Penguin Books.

Mills, C. Wright 1959. *The Sociological Imagination*. London: Oxford University Press.

Mitchell, Juliet 1971. *Woman's Estate*. Harmondsworth: Penguin Books.

Mitzman, Arthur 1970. *The Iron Cage: An Historical Interpretation of Max Weber*. New York: Alfred A. Knopf.

Mommsen, Wolfgang J.(1989a. "The Antinomial Structure of Max Weber's Political Thought," in W.J. Mommsen, *The Political and Social Theory of Max Weber: Collected Essays*, pp. 24-43. Cambridge: Polity.

Mommsen, Wolfgang J. 1989b. "Max Weber in Modern Social Thought," in W.J. Mommsen, *The Political and Social Theory of Max Weber: Collected Essays*, pp. 169-96. Cambridge: Polity.

Morioka, Kenneth K. and Steiner, Jesse F. 1959. "American Sociology in Japan," *American Journal of Sociology* 64(6): 606-9.

Morris, Meaghan 1990. "Banality in Cultural Studies," in Patricia Mellencamp (ed.), *Logics of Television. Essays in Cultural Criticism*, pp. 14-43. Bloomington and Indianopolis: Indiana University Press.

Mouzelis, Nicos 1991. *Back to Sociological Theory. The Construction of Social Orders*. New York: St. Martin's Press.

Mouzelis, Nicos 1997. "In Defence of the Sociological Canon: A Reply to David Parker," *Sociological Review* 45 (2): 244-253,

Mueller, G.H. 1982. "Socialism and Capitalism in the Work of Max Weber," *British Journal of Sociology* 33(2): 151-71.

Mullins, Nicholas C. 1973. *Theory and Theory Groups in Contemporary American Sociology*. New York: Harper & Row.

Mullins, Nicholas C. 1983. "Theories and Theory Groups Revisited," in Randall Collins (ed.) *Sociological Theory 1983*, pp. 319-37. San Francisco, CA: Jossey-Bass.

Muñoz, Braulio 1989. "Law-givers: From Plato to Freud and Beyond," *Theory, Culture Society* 6(3): 403-28.

Nandan, Yash (compiler) 1977. *The Durkheim School: A Systematic and Comprehensive Bibliography*. Westport, CT: Greenwood.

Naumann, Manfred 1976. "Literary Production and Reception," *New Literary History* 8(1): 107-26.

Neuenzeit, Paul 1975. "Canon of Scripture," in Karl Rahner (ed.) *Encyclopedia of Theology*, pp. 168-73. London: Burns and Oates.

Nevin, Thomas. 1996. *Ernst Jünger and Germany. Into the Abyss, 1914-1945.* Durham: Duke University Press.

Nicolaus, Martin 1973. "Foreword," in Karl Marx, *Grundrisse* (translated by Martin Nicolaus), pp. 7-63. Harmondsworth: Penguin Books.

Nietzsche, Friedrich 1954. "On Truth and Lie in the Extra-moral Sense," in Friedrich Nietzsche, *The Portable Nietzsche* (translated by Walter Kaufman), pp. 42-7. New York: Viking Press.

Nietzsche, Friedrich 1961. *Thus Spoke Zarathustra. A Book for Everyone and No One* (translated by R.J. Hollingdale). Harmondsworth: Penguin.

Nietzsche, Friedrich 1968a. *Twilight of the Idols and The Anti-Christ* (translated by R. J. Hollingdale). Harmondsworth. Penguin Books.

Nietzsche, Friedrich 1968b. *The Will to Power* (translated by Walter Kaufmann and R.J. Hollingdale). New York: Random House.

Nisbet, Robert A. 1966. *The Sociological Tradition*. London: Hememann.

Norris, Christopher 1992. *Deconstruction: Theory and Practice*. London: Routledge.

Novick, Peter 2001. *The Holocaust and Collective Memory* (American title: *The Holocaust in American Life*). London: Bloomsbury.

Nye, R. 1983. "Heredity, Pathology, and Psychoneurosis in Durkheim's Early Work," *Knowledge and Society* 4: 103-42.

Oakes, Guy 1984. "Translator's Introduction: The Problem of Women in Simmel's Theory of Culture," in Georg Simmel (1984) pp. 1-62.

Oakes, Guy, and Arthur J. Vidich 1999. *Collaboration, Reputation, and Ethics in American Academic Life: Hans H. Gerth and C. Wright Mills*. Urbana and Chicago: University of Illinois Press.

Oberschall, Anthony, ed. 1972. *The Establishment of Empirical Sociology: Studies in Continuity, Discontinuity, and Institutionalization.* New York: Harper & Row.

Olsen, Stein Haugom 1996. "The Concept of a Literary Canon," *Annals for Aesthetics* 36: 71-84.

Olsen, Stein Haugom 2001. "The Canon and Artistic Failure," *British Journal of Aesthetics* 41 (3): 261-278.

Overbye, Dennis 1990. "Einstein in Love," *Time*, 30 April: 108.

Overington, Michael A. 1977. "The Scientific Community as Audience: Toward a Rhetorical Analysis of Science," *Philosophy and Rhetoric* 10(3): 143-64.

Overington, Michael A. 1981. "A Rhetorical Appreciation of a Sociological Classic: Durkheim's Suicide," *Canadian Journal of Sociology* 6(4): 447-61.

Padover, Saul 1958. "The World of the Founding Fathers," *Social Research* 25(2): 191-214.

Pagels, Elaine 1979. *The Gnostic Gospels*. New York: Vintage Books, 1989.

Palonen, Kari 1999. "Max Weber as a Text," in Pertti Ahonen and Kari Palonen (eds.), *Dis-embalming Max Weber*, pp. 40-55. Jyväskylä: University of Jyväskylä Press.

Parker, David 1997. "Why Bother with Durkheim? Teaching Sociology in the 1990s," *Sociological Review* 45 (1): 122-146.

Parsons, Talcott 1951. *The Social System*. New York: The Free Press.

Parsons, Talcott 1963. "Introduction," in Max Weber, *The Sociology of Religion* (translated by Ephraim Fischoff). Boston, MA: Beacon Press.

Parsons, Talcott 1968. *The Structure of Social Action*, Vols. 1 and 2. New York: Free Press.

Parsons, Talcott 1975. Letter from Talcott Parsons to Benjamin Nelson, January 24, 1975. Harvard University Archives (HUG [FP] 42.8.8, Box 10).

Parsons, Talcott 1979. "Letter from Talcott Parsons to Edward Tiryakian, March 2, 1979," *Sociological Inquiry* 51 (1): 35-36.

Parsons, Talcott 1980. "The Circumstances of My Encounter with Max Weber," in (eds.) Robert K. Merton and Matilda White Riley, *Sociological Traditions from Generation to Generation*, pp. 37-43. Norwood, NJ: Ablex.

Parsons, Talcott 1981. "Revisiting the Classics throughout a Long Career," in B. Rhea (ed.) pp. 183-94.

Pateman, Carole 1988. *The Sexual Contract*. Stanford, CA: Stanford University Press.

Pearce, Frank 1989. *The Radical Durkheim*. London: Unwin Hyman.

Peel, J.D.Y. 1971. *Herbert Spencer*. New York: Basic Books.

Pellicani, Luciano. 1986-7. "Ortega's Theory of Social Action," *Telos* 19(4): 115-24.

Perrin, Robert G. 1976. "Herbert Spencer's Four Theories of Social Evolution," *American Journal of Sociology* 81(6): 339-59.

Peters, John Durham 1990. "Rhetoric's Revival, Positivism's Persistence: Social Science, Clear Communication, and the Public Space," *Sociological Theory* 8(2): 224-31.

Phelan, Thomas James 1989. "From the Attic of the American Journal of Sociology: Unusual Contributions to American Sociology, 1895-1935," *Sociological Forum* 4(1): 71-87.

Pickering, Mary 1997. "A New Look At Auguste Comte," in Charles Camic (ed.) 1997, pp. 11-44.

Pitkin, Hanna F. 1984. *Fortune is a Woman: Gender and Politics in the Thought of Niccoló Machiavelli*. Berkeley: University of California Press.

Platt, Jennifer 1985. "Weber's *Verstehen* and the History of Qualitative Research: The Missing Link," *British Journal of Sociology* 36 (3): 448-466.

Platt, Jennifer 1995. "The United States Reception of Durkheim's *The Rules of Sociological Method*," *Sociological Perspectives* 38 (1): 77-105.

Platt, Jennifer 1996. *A History of Sociological Research Methods in America 1920-1960*. Cambridge: Cambridge University Press.

Pocock, John G. A. 1972. *Politics, Language, and Time: Essays on Political Thought and History*. London: Methuen.

Polt, Richard. 1999. *Heidegger. An Introduction*. Ithaca, NY: Cornell University Press.

Pope, Whitney 1973. "Classic on Classic: Parsons' Interpretation of Durkheim," *American Sociological Review* 38(4): 399-415.

Popper, Karl R. 1961. *The Poverty of Historicism*. London: Routledge & Kegan Paul.

Porter, Marilyn 1993. "Call Yourself A Sociologist and You've Never Even Been Arrested?," Presidential Address of the Canadian Association of Sociology and Anthropology, Ottawa, June.

Prawer, S.S. 1976. *Karl Marx and World Literature*. Oxford: Oxford University Press.

Quarles, Francis 1993. *Emblemes and Hieroglyphikes of the Life of Man*. Hildesheim, Zürich and New York: Georg Olms Verlag.

Quinton, Anthony 1993. "Clash of Symbols," *Times Higher Education Supplement*, 30 April: 15-16.

Radcliffe, Timothy 1989. "Tradition and Creativity: The Paradigm of the New Testament," *New Blackfriars* 70(824): 57-66.

Raison, Timothy, ed. 1979. *The Founding Fathers of Social Science* (Revised Edition by Paul Barker). London: Scholar Press.

Ramp, William J. 2001. "Durkheim and the Unthought: Some Dilemmas of Modernity," *Canadian Journal of Sociology* 26 (1): 89-115.

Reed, Evelyn 1970. *Problems of Women's Liberation*. New York: Pathfinder Press.

Rhea, Buford, ed. 1981. *The Future of the Sociological Classics*. London: George Allen & Unwin.

Ricoeur, Paul 1981. *Hermeneutics and the Human Sciences* (edited and translated by John B. Thompson). Cambridge: Cambridge University Press.

Ricoeur, Paul 1981a. "The Hermeneutical Function of Distanciation," in Paul Ricoeur 1981 pp. 131-44.

Ricoeur, Paul 1981b. "What is a Text? Explanation and Understanding," in Paul Ricoeur 1981 pp. 145-64.

Riemer, Svend 1981. "Die Emigration der deutschen Soziologen nach den Vereinigten Staaten," in Wolf Lepenies (ed.) pp. 159-75.

Rinehart, Jane A. 1998. "It May Be a Polar Night of Icy Darkness, but Feminists are Building a Fire," in Mark Alfino, John S. Caputo, and Robin Wynyard (eds.), *McDonaldization Revisited. Critical Essays on Consumer Culture*, pp. 19-38. Wesport, CT: Praeger.

Riesman, David 1950. *The Lonely Crowd: A Study of the Changing American Character*. New Haven, CT: Yale University Press.

Ritzer, George 1993. *The McDonaldization of Society. An Investigation Into the Changing Character of Contemporary Social Life*. Thousand Oaks, London and New Delhi: Pine Forge Press.

Ritzer, George 1998. *The McDonaldization Thesis. Explorations and Extensions*. London: Sage.

Robertson, James Oliver 1980. *American Myth, American Reality*. New York: Hill and Wang.

Rorty, Richard 1979. *Philosophy and the Mirror of Nature*. Princeton, NJ: Princeton University Press.

Rorty, Richard 1989. *Contingency, Irony, and Solidarity*. Cambridge: Cambridge University Press.

Rosaldo, Renato 1989. *Culture and Truth*. Boston, MA: Beacon Press.

Roth, Guenther 1971. "'Value-Neutrality' in Germany and the United States," in Reinhard Bendix and Guenther Roth (eds.) *Scholarship and Partisanship: Essays on Max Weber*, pp. 34-54. Berkeley: University of California Press.

Roth, Guenther 1978. "Introduction," in Max Weber (1978a) pp. xxxiii-cx.

Roth, Guenther 1988. "Marianne Weber and her Circle," in Marianne Weber (1988) pp. xv-lxi.

Roth, Guenther 1989-90. "Durkheim and the Principles of 1789: The Issue of Gender Equality," *Telos* 82 (Winter): 71-88.

Roth, Guenther 1990. "Partisanship and Scholarship," in Bennet M. Berger, *Authors of Their Own Lives. Intellectual Autobiographies by Twenty American Sociologists*, pp. 383-409

Roth, Guenther 1992. "Interpreting and Translating Max Weber," *International Sociology* 7(4): 449-59.

Roth, Guenther 1993. "Weber the Would-Be Englishman: Anglophilia and Family History," in Hartmut Lehmann and Guenther Roth (eds.), *Weber's Protestant Ethic. Origins, Evidence, Contexts*, pp. 83-131. Cambridge: German Historical Institute (Washington, DC) and Cambridge University Press.

Roth, Guenther 1999. "Max Weber at Home and in Japan: On the Troubled Genesis and Successful Reception of His Work," *International Journal of Politics, Culture and Society* 12 (3): 515-525.

Roth, Michael S. 1995. *The Ironist's Cage. Memory, Trauma, and the Construction of History*. New York: Columbia University Press.

Rousseau, Jean-Jacques 1973. "The Social Contract or Principles of Political Right," in Jean-Jacques Rousseau, *The Social Contract and Discourses* (translated by G. D. H. Cole) pp. 163-278. London: J.M. Dent.

Rowbotham, Sheila 1973. *Woman's Consciousness, Man's World*. Harmondsworth: Penguin Books.

Runciman, W.G. (ed.) 1978. *Weber: Selections in Translation* (translated by Erich Matthews). Cambridge: Cambridge University Press.

Runciman, W.G. 1983. *A Treatise on Social Theory*, Vol. 1. *The Methodology of Social Theory*. Cambridge: Cambridge University Press.

Rüschemeyer, Dietrich 1981. "Die Nichtrezeption von Karl Mannheims Wissenssoziologie in der Amerikanischen Soziologie," in M. Rainer Lepsius (ed.) pp. 414-26.

Ryan, Alan 1993. "Invasion of the Mind Snatchers," *New York Review of Books*, 11 February: 13-15.

Said, Edward W. 1983. *The World, the Text and the Critic*. Cambridge, Mass.: Harvard University Press.

Said, Edward W. 1996. *Representations of the Intellectual*. New York: Vintage.

Salomon, Albert 1997. "Georg Simmel Reconsidered," edited with an introduction and notes by Gary D. Jaworski in Jaworski 1997, pp. 91-108.

Ste Croix, G.E.M. de 1981. *The Class Struggle in the Ancient Greek World from the Archaic Age to the Arab Conquests*. London: Duckworth.

Sanders, Claire 1993. "Come in Dr Kirk, British Sociology Needs You Now," *Times Higher Education Supplement* (1054) 15 January: 20.

Sayer, Derek 1991. *Capitalism and Modernity: An Excursus on Marx and Weber*. London: Routledge.

Scaff, Lawrence A. 1984 "Weber before Weberian Sociology," *British Journal of Sociology* 35(2): 190-2 15.

Scaff, Lawrence A. 1989. *Fleeing the Iron Cage: Culture, Politics, and Modernity in the Thought of Max Weber*. Berkeley: University of California Press.

Scaff, Lawrence A. 1998. "The 'Cool Objectivity of Sociation': Max Weber and Marianne Weber in America," *History of the Human Sciences* 11 (2): 61-82.

Schmitt, Carl 1985. *Political Theology* (translated by George Schwab). Cambridge, MA: MIT Press.

Schmitt, Carl 1987. "The Legal World Revolution," *Telos* 20(2): 73-89.

Schneider, Louis 1967. "Introduction," in Louis Schneider (ed.) *The Scottish Moralists*, pp. xi-lxxvii. Chicago: University of Chicago Press.

Scholes, Robert 1992. "Canonicity and Textuality," in Joseph Gibaldi (ed.) *Introduction to Scholarship in Modern Languages and Literatures*, 2nd edn., pp. 138-58. New York: Modern Language Association of America.

Schumpeter, Joseph A. 1967. History of Economic Analysis. London: George Allen and Unwin.

Schwalbe, Michael. 1996. *Unlocking the Iron Cage. The Men's Movement, Gender Politics, and American Culture*. New York and Oxford: Oxford University Press.

Schwentker, Wolfgang 1987. "Passion as a Mode of Life: Max Weber, the Otto Gross Circle and Eroticism,"in W.J. Mommsen and J. Osterhammel (eds.) *Max Weber and his Contemporaries*, pp. 483-98. London: Unwin Hyman.

Schwentker, Wolfgang 1998a. "Western Impact and Asian Values in Japan's Modernization: A Weberian Critique," in Ralph Schroeder (ed.), *Max Weber, Democracy and Modernization* pp. 166-181. London: Macmillan.

Schwentker, Wolfgang 1998b. *Max Weber in Japan. Eine Untersuchung zur Wirkungsgeschichte 1905-1995* (Tübingen: Mohr Siebeck).

Scruton, Roger 1993. "The Harrowed Tradition," *Partisan Review* 60(2): 208-20.

Seery, John E. 1999. "Castles in the Air. An Essay on Political Foundations," *Political Theory* 27 (4): 460-490.

Seidman, Steven 1983. "Beyond Presentism and Historicism: Understanding the History of Social Science," *Sociological Inquiry* 53(1): 79-84.

Seidman, Steven 1985. "The Historicist Controversy: A Critical Review with a Defense of a Revised Presentism," *Sociological Theory* 3(1): 13-16.

Seidman, Steven 1991. "The End of Sociological Theory: The Postmodern Hope," *Sociological Theory* 9(2): 131-46.

Shentalinsky, Vitaly 1995. *The KGB's Literary Archive*. With an Introduction by Robert Conquest. (translated, edited, and annotated by John Crowfoot). London: The Harvill Press.

Sherman, Lawrence W. 1974. "Uses of the Masters," *American Sociologist* 9(4): 176-81.

Shils, Edward 1982. "Tradition, Ecology, and Institution in the History of Sociology," in Edward Shils, *The Constitution of Society*, pp. 275-383. Chicago: University of Chicago Press.

Sica, Alan 1985. "Reasonable Science, Unreasonable Life: The Happy Fictions of Marx, Weber, and Social Theory," in Robert J. Antonio, and Ronald M. Glassman (eds.) *A Weber-Marx Dialogue*, pp. 68-88. Lawrence: University Press of Kansas.

Sica, Alan 1989. "Handbooks Past and Present," *Contemporary Sociology* 18(4): 504-8.

Silberman, Bernard S. 1993. *Cages of Reason: The Rise of the Rational State in France, Japan, the United States, and Great Britain*. Chicago and London: University of Chicago Press.

Sills, David L. and Merton, Robert K. (eds.) 1991. *The Macmillan Book of Social Science Quotations*. New York: Macmillan.

Simmel, Georg 1949. "The Sociology of Sociability" (translated by Everett C. Hughes), *American Journal of Sociology* 55 (3): 254-61.

Simmel, Georg (1984) *Georg Simmel On Women, Sexuality, and Love* (Edited and translated by Guy Oakes). New Haven, CT: Yale University Press.

Simmel, Georg 1985. *Schriften zur Philosophie und Soziologie der Geschlechter* (Edited by H.J. Dahme and K.C. Köhnke). Frankfurt-am-Main: Suhrkamp.

Simpson, George (ed.) 1969. *Auguste Comte: Sire of Sociology*. New York. Thomas Y. Crowell.

Skinner, Quentin 1969. "Meaning and Understanding in the History of Ideas," *History and Theory* 8(1): 3-53.

Skinner, Quentin 1970. "Conventions and the Understanding of Speech Acts," *Philosophy* 20: 118-38.

Skinner, Quentin 1972. "Motives, Intentions, and the Interpretation of Texts," *New Literary History* 3(2): 393-408.

Skinner, Quentin 1974. "Some Problems in the Analysis of Political Thought and Action," *Political Theory* 2(3): 277-303.

Skinner, Quentin 1978. *The Foundations of Modern Political Thought*, Vols. I, II. Cambridge: Cambridge University Press.

Smelser, Neil J. (ed.) 1988. *Handbook of Sociology*. Newbury Park, CA: Sage.

Smith, Canon Graham 1989. "This is the Word of the Lord," *Expository Times* 100(4) January: 137-9.

Smith, Dorothy E. 1987. *The Everyday World As Problematic*. Toronto: University of Toronto Press.

Smith, Dorothy E. 1990. *The Conceptual Practices of Power: A Feminist Sociology of Knowledge*. Toronto: University of Toronto Press.

Spencer, Herbert 1873. *The Study of Sociology*. New York: D. Appleton.

Spender, Dale 1982. *Women of Ideas and What Men Have Done to Them*. London: Routledge & Kegan Paul.

Sprondel, Walter M. 1981. "Erzwungene Diffusion. Die 'University in Exile' und Aspekte ihrer Wirkung," in Wolf Lepenies 1981b (ed.) pp. 176-201.

Stark, Werner 1967. "Max Weber and the Heterogeny of Purposes," *Social Research* 34: 249-64.

Steiner, Jesse Frederick 1936. "The Development and Present Status of Sociology in Japanese Universities," *American Journal of Sociology* 41(6): 707-22.

Stinchcombe, Arthur L. 1982. "Should Sociologists Forget their Mothers and Fathers?," *American Sociologist* 17(1): 2-11.

Stinchcombe, Arthur L. 2001. "Review and Two Markets for Sociology Books," *Contemporary Sociology* 30 (1): 6-8.

Stocking, G.W. 1968. "On the Limits of 'Presentism' and 'Historicism' in the Historiography of the Behavioral Sciences" in G.W. Stocking (ed.) *Race, Culture, and Evolution: Essays in the History of Anthropology*, pp. 1-12. New York: Free Press.

Stölting, Erhard 1990. "Institutionalization and Myth-Making: The Other History of Sociology in Germany," *Critical Sociology* 17(3): 111-30.

Strauss, Leo 1952. *Persecution and the Art of Writing*. Chicago: University of Chicago Press.

Strouse, Jean (ed.) 1974. *Women and Analysis*. New York: Viking.

Sun, Chung-Hsing 1993. "Aspects of 'Sinicisation' and 'Globalisation'," *International Sociology* 8 (1): 121-122.

Sutherland, John 1993. "My Missus," *London Review of Books*, 13 May: 23-4.

Sweedberg, Richard 1998. *Max Weber and the Idea of Economic Sociology*. Princeton, NJ: Princeton University Press.

Swingewood, Alan 1970. "Origins of Sociology: The Case of the Scottish Enlightenment," *British Journal of Sociology* 21(2): 164-80.

Sydie, Rosalind Ann 1987. *Natural Women, Cultured Men*. Milton Keynes: Open University Press.

Szacki, Jerzy 1973. "'Schools' in Sociology," *Social Science Information* 12: 173-82.

Taylor, Frederick Winslow 1998. *The Principles of Scientific Management*. New York: Dover.

Tenbruck, Friedrich H. 1980. "The Problem of Thematic Unity in the Works of Max Weber" (translated by Sam Whimster), *British Journal of Sociology* 31(3): 316--51.

Therborn, Göran 1976. *Science, Class and Society: On the Formation of Sociology and Historical Materialism*. London: Verso.

Thomas, Jem 1992. "Review of Karl Mannheim, *Ideology and Utopia*; Talcott Parsons, *The Social System*; and H.H. Gerth and C. Wright Mills (eds.) *From Max Weber*," *History of Human Sciences* 5(1): 114-18.

Thompson, Kenneth 1976. *Auguste Comte: The Foundation of Sociology*. London: Nelson.

Thorburn, David (in discussion with William Phillips, Robert Alter, Denis Donoghue, Steven Marcus, Lionel Abel and Catharine Stimpson) 1991. "The Revolt Against Tradition: Readers, Writers, and Critics," *Partisan Review* 58(2): 282-314.

Tiryakian, Edward 1979. "The Significance of Schools in the Development of Sociology," in William Snizek et al. (eds.) *Contemporary Issues in Theory and Research*, pp. 211-34. Westport, CT: Greenwood Press.

Tiryakian, Edward 1981a. "Sexual Anomie, Social Structure, Societal Change," *Social Forces* 59(4): 1025-53.

Tiryakian, Edward A. 1981b. "The Sociological Import of a Metaphor: Tracking the Source of Max Weber's 'Iron Cage'," *Sociological Inquiry* 51 (1): 27-33.

Tiryakian, Edward A. 1988. "Durkheim, Mathiez, and the French Revolution," *European Journal of Sociology* 29(2): 373-96.

Tribe, Keith 1988. "Translator's Introduction," to Wilhelm Hennis (1988) pp. 1-17.

Tribe, Keith 1989. "Introduction," in Keith Tribe (ed.) *Reading Weber*, pp. 1-14. London: Routledge.

Tribe, Keith. 2000. "Translator's Appendix," in Wilhelm Hennis, *Max Weber's Science of Man*, pp. 205-216. Newbury: Threshold Press

Turner, Jonathan H. 2000. "Herbert Spencer," in George Ritzer (ed.) *The Blackwell Companion to Major Social Theorists*, pp. 81-104.

Turner, Roy 1990. "Friends and Enemies of the Canon," *Queen's Quarterly* 97(2): 236-49.

Turner, Stephen P. 1982. "Bunyan's Cage and Weber's Casing", *Sociological Inquiry* 52 (1): 84-87.

Turner, Stephen P. 1983. "'Contextualism' and the Interpretation of the Classical Sociological Texts," *Knowledge and Society* 4: 273-91.

Turner, Stephen P. 1995. "Durkheim's *The Rules of Sociological Method*': Is It a Classic?" *Sociological Perspectives* 38 (1): 1-13.

Turner, Stephen P. (ed.) 1996. *Social Theory and Sociology. The Classics and Beyond*, pp. 70-96. Oxford: Blackwell.

Turner, Stephen P. and Factor, Regis A. 1984. *Max Weber and the Dispute over Reason and Value: A Study in Philosophy, Ethics, and Politics*. London: Routledge.

Turner, Stephen P. and Turner, Jonathan H. 1990. *The Impossible Science: An Institutional Analysis of American Sociology*. Newbury Park, CA: Sage.

Tysome, Tony 1993. "Positive Force or Change for Old Prejudice?" *Times Higher Education Supplement* (1054) 15 January: 22.

Van Vucht Tijssen, Lieteke 1988. "De plaats van de vrouw in de moderne cultuur. Marianne Weber contra Georg Simmel," *Sociale wetenschappen* 31(2): 83-101.

Van Vucht Tijssen, Lieteke (1991) "Women and Objective Culture: Georg Simmel and Marianne Weber," *Theory, Culture & Society* 8(3): 203-18.

Vromen, Suzanne 1987. "Georg Simmel and the Cultural Dilemma of Women," *History of European Ideas* 8 (4/5): 563-79.

Waal, Victor De 1983. "Apostolic Succession," in Alan Richardson and John Bowden (eds.) *The Westminister Dictionary of Christian Theology*, pp. 35-6. Philadelphia, PA: Westminister Press.

Wagner, Peter 1994. *A Sociology of Modernity. Liberty and Discipline*. London and New York: Routledge.

Wallace, Walter L. 1991a. "Standardizing Basic Sociological Concepts," *Perspectives: Theory Section Newsletter* 14(1): 1-2.

Wallace, Walter L. 1991b. "The Author Replies," *Perspectives: The Theory Section Newsletter* 14(2): 7-8.

Watanuki, Joji 1975. "The Social Sciences in Japan," *International Social Science Journal* 27(1): 185-9.

Weber, Marianne 1988/1975. *Max Weber: A Biography* (translated and edited by Harry Zohn). New Brunswick, NJ: Transaction Publishers.

Weber, Max 1905. "Die protestantische Ethik und der "Geist" des Kapitalismus, I. Das Problem," *Archiv für Sozialwissenschaft und Sozialpolitik* 20 (1): 1-54.

Weber, Max. 1905. "Die protestantische Ethik und der "Geist" des Kapitalismus, II. Die Berufsidee des asketischen Protestantismus,"*Archiv für Sozialwissenschaft und Sozialpolitik* 21 (1): 1-110.

Weber, Max 1920. *Gesammelte Aufsätze zur Religionssoziologie*, Vol.1. Tübingen: J.C.B. Mohr (Paul Siebeck).

Weber, Max 1924. *Gesammelte Aufsätze zur Soziologie und Sozialpolitik.* Tübingen: J.C.B. Mohr (Paul Siebeck).

Weber, Max 1930. *The Protestant Ethic and the Spirit of Capitalism* (translated by Talcott Parsons). London: Unwin University Books.

Weber, Max 1948. *From Max Weber: Essays in Sociology* (translated and Edited by H.H. Gerth and C. Wright Mills). London: Routledge & Kegan Paul.

Weber, Max 1948a. "Science as a Vocation," in Max Weber (1948) pp. 129-56.

Weber, Max 1948b. "The Protestant Sects and the Spirit of Capitalism," in Max Weber (1948) pp. 302-22.

Weber, Max 1948c. "Religious Rejections of the World and their Directions," in Max Weber 1948 pp. 323-59.

Weber, Max 1948d "Politics as a Vocation," in Max Weber (1948) pp. 77-128.

Weber, Max 1949. "'Objectivity' in Social Science and Social Policy," in *The Methodology of the Social Sciences* (translated and edited by Edward A. Shils and Henry A. Finch), pp. 49-112. New York: Free Press.

Weber, Max 1961. *General Economic History* (translated by Frank H. Knight). New York and London: Collier-Macmillan. .

Weber, Max 1964. *L'éthique Protestante et l'esprit du Capitalisme* (translated by Jacques Chavy). Paris: Librairie Plon.

Weber, Max 1977. *Critique of Stammler* (translated by Guy Oakes). New York: Free Press.

Weber, Max 1978a. *Economy and Society*, Vols. 1 and 2 (edited by Guenther Roth and Claus Wittich). Berkeley: University of California Press.

Weber, Max 1978b. "Parliament and Government in a Reconstructed Germany," in Max Weber (1978a), Vol. 2: 1381-469.

Weber, Max. 1988. "Parlament und Regierung im neugeordneten Deutschland. Zur politischen Kritik des Beamtentums und Parteiwesens," in Wolfgang J. Mommsen in collaboration with Gangolf Hübinger, *Max Weber. Zur Politik im Weltkrieg. Schriften und Reden 1914-1918. (Studienausgabe)*, pp. 202-302. Tübingen: J.C.B. Mohr (Paul Siebeck).

Weber, Max 1989. "Rußlands Übergang zum Scheinkonstitutionalismus," in Wolfgang J. Mommsen (ed.) in collaboration with Dittmar Dahlmann,

Max Weber zur Russischen Revolution von 1905: Schriften und Reden 1905-1912, pp. 281-684. Tübingen: J.C.B. Mohr (Paul Siebeck).

Weber, Max 1993. *Die protestantische Ethik und der "Geist" des Kapitalismus.* Edited by Klaus Lichtblau and Johannes Weiß. Bodenheim: Athenäum, Hain, Hanstein.

Weber, Max 1994. *Weber: Political Writings* (edited and translated by Peter Lassman and Ronald Speirs). Cambridge: Cambridge University Press.

Weber, Max 1994a. "Parliament and Government in Germany Under a New Political Order," pp. 130-271, in Weber 1994.

Weber, Max 1997a. "Bourgeois Democracy in Russia,"in *Max Weber: The Russian Revolutions* (translated and edited by Gordon C. Wells and Peter Baehr), pp. 41-147. Cambridge: Polity Press.

Weber, Max 1997b. "Russia's Transition to Pseudo-Constitutionalism," in *Max Weber: The Russian Revolutions* (translated and edited by Gordon C. Wells and Peter Baehr), pp. 148-240. Cambridge: Polity Press.

Weber, Max. 2002. *The Protestant Ethic and the "Spirit" of Capitalism and Other Writings.* Edited and translated by Peter Baehr and Gordon C. Wells. New York: Penguin.

Weinsheimer, Joel 1991. *Philosophical Hermeneutics and Literary Theory.* New Haven, CT: Yale University Press.

Weinstein Deena and Michael A. Weinstein 1993. *Postmodern(ized) Simmel.* New York: Routledge.

Weiss, Johannes 1981. *Das Werk Max Webers in der marxistischen Rezeption und Kritik.* Opladen: Westdeutscher.

Weisz, George 1983. "The Republican Ideology and the Social Sciences; the Durkheimians and the History of Social Economy at the Sorbonne," in Philippe Besnard (ed.) pp. 90-119.

Whimster, Sam and Lash, Scott, eds. 1987. *Max Weber, Rationality and Modernity.* London: Allen & Unwin.

Wiley, Norbert 1979. "The Rise and Fall of Dominating Theories in American Sociology," in William E. Snizek et al. (eds.) *Contemporary Issues in Theory and Research*, pp. 47-79. Westport, CT: Greenwood Press.

Wilkinson, Doris Y. 1991. "The American University and the Rhetoric of Neoconservatism," *Contemporary Sociology* 20(4): 550-3.

Williams, Gwyn A. 1979. "Antonio Gramsci," in Timothy Raison (ed.)1979, pp. 259-71.

Williams, Raymond 1976. *Keywords.* Glasgow: Fontana.

Wills, Garry 1993. "Hanging Out with Greeks," *New York Review of Books* 11(9): 36-9.

Winkmann, H. 1980. "Weber, Marianne," in Wilhelm Bernsdorf and Horst Knospe (eds.) *Internationales Soziologenlexikon*, pp.484-5. Stuttgart: Ferdinand Enke.

Wityak, Nancy L. and Wallace, Ruth A. 1981. "Durkheim's Non-Social Facts about Primitives and Women," *Sociological Inquiry* 51(1): 61-7.

Wolff, Kurt, H., ed. 1950. *The Sociology of Georg Simmel.* New York: Free Press.

Wolin, Sheldon S. 1960. *Politics and Vision.* Boston, MA: Little, Brown and Company.

Wolin, Sheldon S. 1969. "Political Theory as a Vocation," *American Political*

Wolin, Sheldon S. 1970. *Hobbes and the Epic Tradition of Political Theory*. Los Angeles, CA: William Andrews Clark Memorial Library.

Wolin, Sheldon S. 1981. "Max Weber: Legitimation, Method, and the Politics of Theory," *Political Theory* 9(3): 401-24.

Wolin, Sheldon S. 1985. "Postmodern Politics and the Absence of Myth," *Social Research* 52(2): 217-39.

Wolin, Sheldon S. 1990. "Democracy in the Discourse of Postmodernism," *Social Research* 57(1): 5-30.

Woodward, Kenneth L. 1990. *Making Saints*. New York: Simon and Schuster.

Zeitlin, Irving M. 1987. *Ideology and the Development of Sociological Theory*, 3rd edn. Englewood Cliffs, NJ: Prentice-Hall.

Index